CLUES
PG3328.Z6 N43 1983
NEW ESSAYS ON DOSTOYEVSK
CC CS
1 CUM 00 0075047 J

D1598593

New Essays on Dostoyevsky

This volume is respectfully dedicated to Professor Janko Lavrin, Professor of Slavonic Languages at the University of Nottingham, 1921–52, in recognition of his contribution to the study of Dostoyevsky

New Essays on Dostoyevsky

edited by
MALCOLM V. JONES
and
GARTH M. TERRY

Cambridge University Press

CAMBRIDGE
LONDON NEW YORK NEW ROCHELLE
MELBOURNE SYDNEY

Published by the Press Syndicate of the University of Cambridge
The Pitt Building, Trumpington Street, Cambridge CB2 1RP
32 East 57th Street, New York, NY 10022, USA
296 Beaconsfield Parade, Middle Park, Melbourne 3206, Australia

First published 1983

Printed in Great Britain by
New Western Printing Ltd, Bristol

Library of Congress catalogue card number: 82–14566

British Library cataloguing in publication data

New essays on Dostoyevsky.
1. Dostoevskii, F. M. – Criticism and interpretation
2. Laurin, Janko 3. Novelists, Russian – 19th century
I. Jones, Malcolm V. II. Terry, Garth M.
891.73′3 PG3328.Z6

ISBN 0 521 24890 6

N W P

Contents

Contributors

R. M. DAVISON, *Lecturer in the Department of Russian, University of Liverpool*

SERGEI HACKEL, *Reader in Russian Studies, University of Sussex*

MALCOLM V. JONES, *Professor of Slavonic Studies, University of Nottingham*

SIDNEY MONAS, *Professor of History, Slavic Languages and Comparative Literature, University of Texas at Austin*

DEREK OFFORD, *Lecturer in Russian, University of Bristol*

CHRISTOPHER R. PIKE, *Lecturer in the Department of Russian Studies, University of Keele*

F. F. SEELEY, *Professor of Russian and Comparative Literature, State University of New York at Binghamton*

STEWART R. SUTHERLAND, *Professor of the History and Philosophy of Religion, King's College, London*

VICTOR TERRAS, *Professor of Slavic Languages and Comparative Literature, Brown University, Providence, R. I.*

GARTH M. TERRY, *Librarian (Slavonic and East European Studies), University of Nottingham*

Editors' Preface

The impact of Dostoyevsky on the culture of the English-speaking peoples long ago reached noteworthy proportions, and his most important works have been translated into English many times. Similarly, the contribution of English-speaking critics and scholars to a better understanding of Dostoyevsky's art and its significance is also now considerable, and it seemed therefore appropriate that the centenary of his death in 1881 should be commemorated with a collection of essays by scholars currently working on Dostoyevsky.

Most of the contributors are from British universities and this, together with the concluding bibliographical survey, reflects the book's genesis. Like *New Essays on Tolstoy* (CUP, 1978), the impetus came from the activities of the Nineteenth Century Russian Literature Seminar – a group, meeting regularly in different British universities, which has in recent years held a number of fruitful seminars on Dostoyevsky and has close links with the International Dostoevsky Society. Five of the contributors have presented papers to the Seminar in the past and two others contributed to *New Essays on Tolstoy*. It is a pleasure to welcome contributions from two 'newcomers' – Sidney Monas and Victor Terras – who have already made substantial contributions to the study of Dostoyevsky in their own earlier publications. The present secretary of the group, W. J. Leatherbarrow, although he has not contributed to this volume, has met the centenary with a very welcome book of his own, *Fedor Dostoyevsky* (Boston, 1981).

Each of the essays, from its own particular viewpoint, constitutes a reassessment of some aspect of Dostoyevsky's legacy to the modern reader. It cannot, of course, be claimed that these essays even touch upon all that is of interest in the Russian novelist, but it is hoped that their range affords some impression of the breadth of Dostoyevsky's achievement and that the treatment of individual subjects is detailed and scholarly enough to make useful new contributions to the understanding of it. Although care has been taken to ensure that each essay is accessible to the general reader, it is hoped that recent trends in Dostoyevsky criticism will also become evident to the reader who is not already aware of them.

The system of transliteration employed here is that preferred by the *Slavonic and East European Review*, except that no semi-vowels are indicated in the spelling of proper names in the text. However, semi-vowels are retained in the spelling of proper names in the bibliography and in references in the notes.

The definitive edition of Dostoyevsky's works is *Polnoye sobraniye sochineniy v tridtsati tomakh*, published by the Academy of Sciences of the U.S.S.R. (Leningrad, 1972–). At the time of writing, publication had reached vol. 21, so references are given to earlier editions in the case of works not yet published here. In the notes, references to the Academy edition are preceded by the letters *PSS*. In order that references to Dostoyevsky's text shall be at the same time as useful and as brief as possible, they are given in the following form in the text of each essay, e.g. '(VIII, 339; III, vi)', where the numbers before the semicolon represent the volume of *PSS* (VIII) and the page number (339), and the numbers after the semicolon represent the internal divisions of the novel or story and may thus be used in conjunction with any edition, including reliable translations. Where only the first two numbers are given, the reference is often to something other than a work of fiction, e.g. notebooks, articles, editor's commentary. Numbers of the 'parts' into which Dostoyevsky divides *The Brothers Karamazov* are not given before 'book' and 'chapter' numbers, since they provide no additional information useful in looking up references.

Unless otherwise stated, translations from Dostoyevsky are by the authors or the editors. The titles of Russian works are given in English. In the case of other languages, practice varies according to the demands of the context.

We should like to express our thanks to all the contributors for their patience and cooperation, which have made the task of preparing this book all the more pleasant and rewarding. Our warmest thanks are also due to Mr Terence Moore and Mrs Veronica Ions of the Cambridge University Press, and to Miss Helen Jones for her assistance with the index.

MALCOLM V. JONES
GARTH M. TERRY

Introduction

MALCOLM V. JONES

I

On 31 January 1881, the day of Dostoyevsky's historic public funeral, one of those who helped to bear the coffin downstairs from the apartment at 5 Kuznechnyy pereulok, and followed it to its last resting place at the Aleksandr Nevsky monastery, was the Englishman E. J. Dillon.[1] At the time, Dillon was a student at St Petersburg University. Later he was to become Professor of Comparative Philology at the University of Kharkov and a close friend of Count Sergey Witte the Russian statesman. For years he wrote on Russian affairs for British periodicals and for *The Daily Telegraph*.[2] He was probably the first Englishman to have any glimmering of Dostoyevsky's true stature as a writer.

Now, a hundred years later, things have radically changed. The story of Dostoyevsky's reception in Britain, from its slow beginnings to the years of the 'Dostoyevsky cult' (1912–21) and on to the eve of the Second World War, has been told by Helen Muchnic in her well-known book.[3] It is a story, incidentally, in which Janko Lavrin, to whom this book is dedicated, played a significant and enduring role. Dostoyevsky has now been thoroughly assimilated into the Western literary tradition. Like Tolstoy, he long ago acquired the status of an English novelist by adoption. At the present time he is read and studied widely not only in Russian, by students of Russian, but also in English translation – in a language, that is, which he could not have read, let alone written – and appears on the syllabuses of English departments and Schools of European Studies in British universities. Such a study can be academically justified – the general reading public asks for no such justification – by the fact that translations, not the Russian originals, have exercised a powerful influence on important English writers. Something similar can be said about Dostoyevsky's status in France, Germany, the U.S.A.

and, more recently, Japan. Hesse, Kafka, Mann, Camus, Malraux, Faulkner, Lawrence, and others all read Dostoyevsky in their own native language. That is to leave out of account psychologists, sociologists, theologians, philosophers and others who have thought fit to devote time to and write at length on his works. The widespread respect which his artistic vision has commanded among specialists in non-fictional fields is quite remarkable and suggests not only that he anticipated modern developments in these fields to an astonishing degree, but also that his cast of mind is particularly congenial to that of twentieth-century man.

As the articles in this book testify by their references and allusions, the study of Dostoyevsky too has become very much an international affair. It is therefore appropriate that this volume, which, like the volume of essays on Tolstoy which preceded it, was originally conceived as a British contribution to the marking of a literary centenary, should include essays by distinguished American scholars as well.

The framework of this collection of essays follows the same pattern as that adopted in *New Essays on Tolstoy*.[4] Part I contains a series of articles on individual major works or, in the case of the first essay, on a series of minor works written during the period of Dostoyevsky's literary apprenticeship. Part II, on the other hand, consists of three essays on particular themes, with a concluding bibliographical essay and bibliography. More than was the case with *New Essays on Tolstoy*, the volume reflects the wide variety of approaches to the study of Dostoyevsky – and indeed imaginative literature in general – now current among literary scholars. The impact of M. M. Bakhtin, of Russian formalism, of studies influenced by linguistics and communication theory, of contemporary structuralisms as such, has become so widespread that it seemed proper that one essay should be devoted to this topic alone. Bakhtin's name and influence are, however, evident in most of the other essays, even though they generally do not share his or his successors' methodological assumptions. In general, the mode of presentation adopted in each essay makes it accessible to the reader unschooled in contemporary literary theory.

II

If Dostoyevsky gave much to European intellectual and cultural life, he also in his own time drew much inspiration from it. The first stage in Dostoyevsky's response to European literature was, not surprisingly, one of considerable dependence. As with many of his generation, he was an enthusiastic reader of his European predecessors and contemporaries both in the novel and in other genres, and his early attempts at translation and drafts for original works were clearly derivative. Into this last category come sketches for dramas entitled *Mariya Styuart* and *Boris Godunov*, both unfortunately lost to us. Still, it can hardly be doubted that Schiller's influence on the first would have been considerable, since Dostoyevsky was at the time infatuated with Schiller's work, and it is more than likely that it was Schiller as much as Pushkin who inspired the second title. In 1844, Dostoyevsky and his brother Mikhail conceived the idea of translating all Schiller's works, including, no doubt, the unfinished *Demetrius*. In fact, Dostoyevsky advised on his brother's translations of *Die Räuber*, *Don Carlos* and some well-known lyrics.[5] This stage, which consisted either of works based on European models, presumably with some new twist, or free translations of European originals, comes to a close with Dostoyevsky's translation of Balzac's *Eugénie Grandet*, his first publication, in 1844.[6]

The second stage may be taken to cover all his original pre-Siberian work and his early post-Siberian work. Here, Dostoyevsky had native Russian models as well – notably Pushkin, Lermontov and Gogol – and was attempting to respond to the demands of the Natural School, hence his concentration upon the little man and woman in the poor areas of St Petersburg and on the social and psychological problems bred by urban poverty. Balzac, Dickens, Sue, George Sand and Hoffmann are his European masters here; Gogol, Pushkin and the minor writers of the Natural School his chief Russian ones. As Victor Terras writes, some of his early characters seem to be 'revisions' of Gogolian characters, 'performed by addition of an individual, social and psychological dimension to Gogol's types' (p. 25). Whether we should think of Dostoyevsky's relationship to his models in terms of parody, of 'serious travesty' (to use the term which Terras coined in his book),[7] of 'correcting' Gogol or Hoffmann in terms of his own psychological insights and the demands of the Natural School (the view of Blagoy or, in Dostoyevsky's own time, of his colleague Strakhov), or of dialogue with the 'alien voice' (*chuzhoy golos*) of the model (Bakhtin), remains a matter of lively discussion which Terras takes up and develops in his article (p. 24).

Looking at it from another point of view, it is as if, in working out his own themes, Dostoyevsky is constantly distracted by the thought of how Hoffmann or George Sand, Pushkin, Balzac, Gogol or Dickens would treat his subject and, for whatever reasons, compulsively exploits, amends, reworks and transforms them. As I have said elsewhere in my analysis of *Netochka Nezvanova* and Sue's *Mathilde*, the relationship with the earlier text is rarely a case of transposition, but of transformation, and not a mechanical transformation, but a creative and variable one.[8] The idea of dialogue with an alien (and sometimes not so alien) voice or voices is an extremely appropriate and helpful one, not only because it bypasses the intractable methodological problems of tracing and establishing 'influences', but also because it is a very plausible way of describing what really happened in Dostoyevsky's mind during the creative process. It is clear that, in attempting to establish his own literary style, Dostoyevsky was at once exploiting the achievements of his predecessors and semi-consciously, at times even consciously, dominated by them. The relationship was highly complex and dynamic. N. M. Lary, in his book on Dostoyevsky and Dickens, reminds us of a feuilleton which Dostoyevsky published in 1861 called 'Petersburg visions in verse and prose':

> His starting point...was an article he had read in the papers about a retired petty official, a certain Soloviev, who had died in poverty and deprivation, leaving 169,022 roubles in silver among his papers. Dostoyevsky relates the facts about this miser, but even as he describes them literary analogies with Gogol and Molière suggest themselves: Soloviev was a 'new Pliushkin' or a 'new Harpagon', dying in terrible poverty, on top of heaps of gold...As Dostoyevsky starts to probe into his psychology, he turns into a 'colossal figure': a deliberate recluse, indifferent to the scenes of luxury in the city streets, content to enjoy his sense of power without needing to exert it. But now Dostoyevsky feels he is plagiarizing Pushkin's *Miserly Knight*, and so, must have got it wrong. He makes a fresh start...Even now, however, he suddenly switches from the name Soloviev to Akaky Akakievich [the hero of Gogol's *Overcoat*].[9]

This second period does not end with the return from Siberia but includes *The Village of Stepanchikovo* (1859) and his first long novel, *The Insulted and Injured* (1861). Here the voices of Gogol, Dickens, Schiller and even the Russian novelist Pisemsky form part of the textual dialogue.

III

But towards the middle of the 1860s a fundamental change took place in Dostoyevsky's literary work. Put very crudely, he started to write world classics. If he had died in 1863 it is doubtful whether the present-day Western reader would even have heard of him. Perhaps an odd short story, say 'White Nights', might have been included in an anthology of nineteenth-century Russian short stories. Perhaps his least typical work, *Notes from the House of the Dead*, so admired by Tolstoy and used by Janáček for his opera, would have taken an honourable place among Russian prison literature. The probable fate of *The Insulted and Injured* must remain uncertain. From 1864 onwards this prematurely aged man, actually still only forty-three, began to produce the great works for which he is now so widely known: *Notes from Underground*, *Crime and Punishment*, *The Idiot*, *The Devils*, *The Brothers Karamazov*.

How can we characterize this transformation and how do we account for it? As Victor Terras intimates, 'it seems likely that the young Dostoyevsky was secularly oriented and disinclined to undertake the incursions into the realm of metaphysics which characterize the mature writer' (p. 37). It is widely recognized that the major change is that from now on Dostoyevsky's novels are built around *ideas* with world-shattering implications: the usurping of legitimate power, both secular and divine; the taking of life in order to achieve some sort of 'good'; the confrontation of saintliness and a world of sin; social disintegration and anarchy; parricide, the death of the idea of God. There are still the little men of the earlier stories and novels, but they now occupy secondary places. There are still the slums of St Petersburg and provincial towns, but they now house would-be Napoleons, aspiring Rothschilds, young philosophers whose thought is subversive of the whole of traditional Christian and humanist teaching. And these are no longer dreamers or embarrassing eccentrics of the kind society can easily tolerate. The Underground Man just barely falls into this category. The heroes of the major novels either murder or connive in the taking of life. Such an accusation has even been levelled at Myshkin.

The ideas of the novels are presented in the context of what M. M. Bakhtin, in his extraordinarily influential book, called the Dostoyevskian 'polyphonic' novel.[10] As Christopher Pike points out (p. 199), there have been many objections to Bakhtin's thesis since the first edition appeared in 1929, the most recent from no less a figure than René Wellek,[11] but his basic analysis is so widely admired, not only by the French and Soviet structuralists who have themselves been profoundly influenced by it, but also by critics of a more traditional bent, that in an introductory survey of this kind we may simply reaffirm its principal point: that Dostoyevsky's novels are peopled by consciousnesses apparently independent of each other and apparently free of authorial domination. His is, or appears to be, a pluralist, polyphonic world as opposed to the traditional monologic novel dominated by the authorial point of view. The principle of polyphony is evident in Dostoyevsky's early works – though not always successfully executed[12] – but achieved its full potential only with the author's maturity. Bakhtin's other great critical perception, formulated when he revised his book for republication in 1963 after working on Rabelais,[13] was of Dostoyevsky's place in what he called the 'carnivalesque' tradition of literature. It is impossible to do justice to Bakhtin's thesis here. Let it suffice to say that it seems particularly appropriate to the great scandal scenes in Dostoyevsky with their overturning of conventional norms and expectations, the juxtaposition of opposites, the omnipresence of what Shklovsky called oxymoron in his work: the honest thief, the pure prostitute; plots based upon dramatic contrasts, for example 'the poor student plots to become Emperor', 'the son murders his father', 'the saint shares responsibility for the murder of the sinner'.

IV

What exactly triggered off this qualitative leap in Dostoyevsky's creative work is impossible to say. It may indeed have been the experience of looking into the eyes of death which effected a 'transformation of the soul', as Ivanov suggests (p. 37). Yet it is not difficult to account for the conditions which made the leap possible.

Firstly there are Dostoyevsky's own personal circumstances. Unlike Hugo or Sue, Dostoyevsky had no need to tax his imagination when writing of the experience of being condemned to death and being taken to the place of execution. It had actually happened to him in December 1849. He had no need to research into the life of the criminal or the convict. He was surrounded by the human barbarism of the prison in Omsk celebrated in his own novel of 1861. Nor did he need to turn to history to find examples of ambitious young intellectuals intent on plotting the overthrow of the state. He had mixed with such in the Petrashevsky circle. And his life on his return to St Petersburg in December 1859 was only slightly less dramatic. Beset by debts and creditors and importunate relatives, in chronic bad health in spite of his robust constitution, a victim of frequent and debilitating epileptic attacks and a gambling obsession – none of which he therefore needed to plagiarize from Romantic literature – his fortunes reached their lowest ebb in 1864 (the year of publication of *Notes from Underground*) with the death of his first wife from consumption, the death of his brother and business partner Mikhail, the death of his closest literary collaborator the brilliant and eccentric Apollon Grigoryev, and the inopportune closure by the government of his main source of income, the journal *Time* – a series of catastrophes eminently worthy of a novel by Sue. Nor did he have any need to borrow the type of the *femme fatale* from Sue or Balzac or Dickens or Byron, or any of the other myriad sources in world literature. In 1861 he had been approached by a young woman called Polina Suslova who had read and admired his works, was herself a budding writer, belonged to the new generation of socialists, atheists and nihilists which so horrified and yet fascinated Dostoyevsky, and had apparently fallen in love with him. The relationship developed until Dostoyevsky himself became passionately enamoured of Suslova, a relationship which eventually gave neither of them much satisfaction and which tormented them both for several years. Most commentators see echoes of Suslova in the predatory women of Dostoyevsky's mature novels.

In sum, Dostoyevsky had dramatically accumulated in his life the experiences so dear to the imagination of the Romantics, and these were not solitary fantasies: they were utterly concrete and real. It is perhaps not surprising that a man of his sensitivity and intelligence, steeped in the literature of his time, with a tendency to morbid introspection and self-analysis, yet with a lively interest in current affairs, and with an undoubted literary talent, should have succeeded in validating Romantic and sentimental themes on the plane of social and psychological realism.

V

It is clear that during this same period, and out of these experiences, the fundamental intuitions which underlie Dostoyevsky's literary work acquired a primacy which provided a firm foundation for a highly original and independent imaginative world...an imaginative world which, in Dostoyevsky's own view, approximated in its essentials to reality. Elsewhere I have formulated these primary intuitions in a more systematic way than it is possible to do here.[14]

The first intuition is well expressed in *The Idiot* by Ippolit, according to whom the world-order requires that creatures devour each other for the sake of some ultimate harmony which man cannot understand. Contemplating Holbein's picture of Christ in the tomb, he reflects:

> When one looks at that picture, Nature appears in the form of some huge, implacable and dumb beast, or to be more exact . . . in the form of some huge machine of the latest design, which has senselessly seized, cut to pieces and swallowed up, impassively and unfeelingly, that great and priceless being . . . The picture seems to give expression to the idea of a dark, insolent and senselessly eternal power, to which everything is subordinated and which suggests itself unconsciously. (VIII, 339; III, vi)

This is what is often called the reptilian or cannibalistic principle in Dostoyevsky's world, what Middleton Murry memorably called 'metaphysical obscenity'.[15] It is easy to see how such an intuition could have taken root in Dostoyevsky's mind during his years in Siberia.

The second intuition relates to a fundamental 'idealism' in Dostoyevsky. I am using the term not in any of the senses in which the history of philosophy uses it but in the highly personal sense in which Dostoyevsky could declare, in his *Diary of a Writer* in 1876: 'I seek sanctities. I love them, my heart thirsts for them, because I am so constituted that I cannot live without sanctities.'[16]

Elsewhere in his fiction he sets forth ideals of social harmony, beauty, harmony with Nature, emotional equilibrium and happiness, innocence and love, ideals for which, he says, men have sacrificed everything, prophets have been murdered or have died on the cross, without which nations cannot die and do not wish to live.[17] The ontological status of these ideals remains highly problematic, though some of Dostoyevsky's characters – Markel for instance – seem to think that if only we opened our eyes we should see that we already live in paradise (XIV, 262; VI, ii). For others it is a dream, but a compelling and haunting one which is an essential characteristic of man's humanity.

Undoubtedly, other formulations of Dostoyevsky's two basic intuitions are possible. I have suggested that the first has ontological primacy, because it seems to me that the evidence, both in the texts of the novels and in Dostoyevsky's personal life, supports this view. It is given greater force by the conclusion with which Sergei Hackel ends his essay on the religious dimension in Dostoyevsky:

> In the case of Zosima and Alyosha, who could have been, respectively, the proponent and the champion of belief, the unbelief is not so far to seek as might have been expected. And in the case of either, but especially Alyosha, the reader is ultimately confronted with what A. B. Gibson has succinctly termed 'the combination of the sincerest piety with the apparent absence of its object'. (p. 165)

The contrary hypothesis to mine – that the Christian view of the universe as the work of a loving Creator has ontological primacy in Dostoyevsky's world – is just tenable, although the bulk of evidence is against it. The view that the two primary intuitions are equally balanced in their claims to ontological primacy is a good deal more plausible but, I think, undermined to a large extent by the inadequacies of its champions in the novels.[18]

At all events, the crux of these two intuitions is (to use an expression borrowed from Karl Jaspers) that they involve an 'experience of reality in which the environment offers a *world of new meanings*'.[19] Dostoyevsky seems to have held that these intuitions – the basis of his 'fantastic realism' – represented not paranoid delusions but a profounder level of reality beneath surface phenomena, which may be caught by the artist's intuition and which expresses itself in the conscious ideas of an age as well as in semi-conscious and unconscious attitudes. His novels illustrate various states of heightened consciousness which throw these fundamental features of man's spiritual life into relief: the dream, the epileptic consciousness, seclusion from social intercourse, confrontation with the immediate prospect of death, the contemplation of great art. His anthropology in this respect accords with the expressivist tradition, as it has been called by Charles Taylor,[20] though Stewart Sutherland is undoubtedly right in his essay on 'Self and Freedom' to imply that, like the post-Kantian idealists, Dostoyevsky experienced problems in reconciling radical freedom with integral self-expression and that the Underground Man, for instance, here parts company with the Romantic tradition (p. 174).

While it is possible to give systematic accounts of reality which will accommodate these two intuitions, they may accord ill with experience or prove emotionally unacceptable to the individual. Dostoyevsky in his novels explores a wide variety of secondary intuitions whose function is to reconcile and account for these primary ones in more or less systematic ways. It is thus that he presents the conflict in modern times between Christianity and atheism, Orthodoxy and Catholicism or socialism.

Raskolnikov, as Derek Offord shows in his essay, attempts to suppress his idealism and intuitive sympathy and to justify indifference to social injustice by the argument that 'there must exist some "law of nature" which determines the "order of appearance of people, of all these categories and subdivisions"... This scientific explanation of lawbreaking in turn diminishes the status of any moral law from which human law might have derived some authority' (pp. 57–8).

Two further attempts to reconcile reformulations of these two primary intuitions are described by F. F. Seeley:

> The Grand Inquisitor rebels against Christ's teaching out of love and compassion for humanity; Ivan revolts against the order of the universe out of love and compassion for little children. It would seem that in the course of twelve months Ivan's revolt has broadened in scope while his sympathies have narrowed. The Grand Inquisitor proclaims the happiness of mankind as his objective; Ivan's clamour is for justice, without which his life will not be worth living. The Grand Inquisitor will devote his energies and his life to organizing society in peace and prosperity; Ivan returns his ticket to eternity and proposes to spend his life, or at least his youth, in the pursuit of personal satisfactions. (pp. 118–19)

The only extended attempt to give a Christian – albeit at points heretical – account is described and analysed in this volume by Sergei Hackel. It is, of course, that associated with the Elder Zosima in *The Brothers Karamazov*.

VI

It may well be significant that the emergence of the mature artist also coincides with Dostoyevsky's disillusionment with contemporary Europe. In his *Winter Notes on Summer Impressions*, he asked rhetorically:

> Why is it that the impression which Europe makes on us all, from the greatest to the least, is so overpowering, so magical and so irresistibly attractive?... Our whole way of life has been

> organized on European lines from our earliest years. Is it possible that none of us is capable of resisting this influence, this pressure, this irresistible attraction? (V, 51; II)

Of course European precursors did continue to play an important role in Dostoyevsky's fiction. He refers to works and authors by name, by allusion, by quotation and by stylistic echo. Motifs and episodes in his major works can be traced to European sources or to native Russian ones. Robin Feuer Miller, in a recent, very welcome book, has undertaken a detailed and successful analysis of Dostoyevsky's debt in *The Idiot* to the Gothic novel. [21]

The important new feature is that the centre of gravity has shifted to Dostoyevsky's own personal intuitions and experience, and those intuitions are incomparably profounder and that experience incomparably wider than in his earlier work. As he wrote in one of his later notebooks:

> In order to write a novel one must first of all acquire *one* or *several* strong impressions which the author's heart has actually experienced. *This is the task of the poet.* From this impression are developed a theme, a plan, a harmonious whole. *This is the task of the artist,* although artist and poet assist each other in both tasks (XVI, 10)

VII

Chapters 2 to 5 of the present volume explore some of the consequences of this transformation in Dostoyevsky's major novels. So, coincidentally, do chapters 6 and 7. In this Introduction it remains only to outline briefly how the 'poet' typically discharges his task and the 'artist' begins his work. For the sake of brevity and so as not to trespass on the territory allotted to other contributors and, most of all, because it exhibits in such an exemplary and concentrated form the essential features of Dostoyevsky's mature work, I have chosen a page or two from Dostoyevsky's notebooks for 1867 where he jotted down an initial sketch for a novel which was never to be written. He called it *The Emperor* (IX, 113–14).

The sketch is based upon the story of Ivan VI (1740–64), who was declared Emperor at the age of three months and deposed in the following year in favour of Elizabeth, the youngest daughter of Peter the Great. He was then imprisoned in the Schlüsselburg fortress for the rest of his life, and was killed by a guard in the reign of Catherine the Great, when an attempt was made to release him by an officer called Mirovich. Dostoyevsky's immediate sources for the sketch are well known. Chief among them are an article by Semyovsky in *Notes of the Fatherland* in 1866 and the publication of the draft for a novel on the subject by the Ukrainian novelist Kvitka-Osnovyanenko in 1863. A third possible source is Calderón's play *Life is a Dream* (*La vida es sueño*), published in Russian translation in 1861 and successfully staged at the Bolshoy Theatre in the 1866–7 season (IX, 485–90).

The idea is perhaps not yet sufficiently developed to exemplify Bakhtin's concept of Dostoyevskian polyphony, though it is easy to see how Dostoyevsky could have developed the dialogue between the captive Emperor contemplating the consequences of his release and the officer Mirovich with ambitions to be the power behind the throne.

However, two other insights by Bakhtin into the Dostoyevskian novel are extraordinarily apposite to this text. The first is the concept of the carnivalesque. In keeping with this tradition, the young Emperor is by birth and by right an all-powerful autocrat; in reality he is a helpless prisoner: the normal dominance hierarchy has been set on its head.

The second insight is that of the chronotope of the 'threshold'. Christopher Pike explains this concept in his essay (p. 198), and Sidney Monas makes use of it in his article on *The Idiot*. Bakhtin himself says:

> In literature the chronotope of the threshold is always metaphorical and symbolic, sometimes in an explicit but more often in implicit form. In Dostoyevsky, for example, the threshold and the related chronotopes of the staircase, the foyer and the corridor, and similarly their extensions in streets and squares, are the principal scenes of action in his works, places where there take place events of crisis, falls, resurrections, renewals, insights, decisions which determine man's life for ever. Time in this chronotope is in effect but a moment, as it were without duration, and falling outside the normal flow of biographical time. These decisive moments enter in Dostoyevsky into the great encompassing chronotopes of Mystery and Carnival time.[22]

As Pike says, 'this is undoubtedly one of Bakhtin's most exciting perceptions about Dostoyevsky'. Here, in *The Emperor*, the whole action focusses on such a moment of crisis and decision, insight, fall and resurrection – all of these things – the moment, which in fact never comes, of the Emperor's release to ascend his throne.

In the background looms the shadow of another chronotope which Bakhtin discovers in Romantic literature, which is not typical of Dostoyevsky in the concrete sense, but is undoubtedly to be found here – the chronotope of the 'castle'. It is characteristic of Dostoyevsky's imagination that whereas Tolstoy chooses for his historical setting the broad sweeps of rival armies cutting swathes across continents, and for his focus of human interest the life of an ordinary noble family, Dostoyevsky chooses for his the highly abnormal fate of a young man confined for his whole life to a prison cell, subjected to every possible kind of deprivation, cut off not only from family but from virtually all human contact, thrown in upon his own fantasies. Indeed the very first word of Dostoyevsky's sketch is *podpol'ye*, the 'underground'.

Dostoyevsky was very proud of being the creator of the concept of the underground. He is of course not merely referring to dungeons and cellars as dwelling places. He is talking primarily of a mentality, but a mentality which develops when the individual is closed in and cut off from social intercourse, either by choice or by external constraint, and turns to introspection and self-analysis.

One thinks immediately of the hero of *Notes from Underground*, and then of the two novels published on either side of the drafting of *The Emperor*. Raskolnikov, the hero of *Crime and Punishment*, spins his philosophy secluded in his coffin-like garret in St Petersburg, until he convinces himself that he must take a life in order to demonstrate that he is a superior individual destined, like Napoleon, to give a new word to the world. Myshkin, in *The Idiot*, returns to St Petersburg from Switzerland where he has been cut off from the turmoil of urban life in a sanatorium on the mountains. We meet him as he is returning from his leisured philosophizing on his 'magic mountain' to the stress and pressures of the Russian capital. What interests Dostoyevsky are the conditions which promote fevered introspection and what some would regard as paranoid projection of the extremes of good and evil, onto the self, society and the universe in general. It is here that the two primary intuitions discussed above play such an important role: the vision of an ineffable harmony and the vision of an order which requires subjection and destruction.

The Emperor is first confronted by these alternatives in his personal relations with Mirovich. Having sketched the nature and development of his hero, who in spite of his isolation seems to have preserved his simple ideals, Dostoyevsky proceeds to the point where the young officer, Mirovich, first meets the Emperor face to face. The opportunity for a genuine, equal relationship seems to present itself to the Emperor for the first time in his life, and his naive trust is confronted with a lie, a deception; his desire for equality is confronted by ideas of dominance and subjection.

Mirovich proceeds to educate the Emperor about his relationships with society in general. What this means is to confront him with the temptations of power, in his case, it is implied, limitless power. 'Everything is possible', 'all is yours,' he declares, showing him the world from aloft. No reader of the New Testament or, for that matter, of the 'Legend of the Grand Inquisitor', can fail to catch the echo of Jesus' temptations by the Devil in the wilderness. According to St Luke, 'the Devil took him up, and showed him all the kingdoms of the world in a moment of time, and said to him, "To you I will give all this authority and their glory; for it has been delivered unto me, and I will give it to whom I will."' In the 'Legend of the Grand Inquisitor' Dostoyevsky elaborates upon this theme, his implicit argument being that Western civilization has accepted the invitations of the Devil rejected by Christ, to rule men's imaginations by mystery, miracle and worldly authority, and to reduce them to order by means of seductive lies. The Emperor is appalled by the prospect of absolute power.

In Dostoyevsky's second run-through of his theme he elaborates several of these points: Mirovich introduces the Emperor to the idea of violent death, which horrifies him; he also attempts to justify the use of absolute political power by arguing that he may use it to do good. This had been one of the arguments advanced by Raskolnikov in *Crime and Punishment*, and it is interesting that as early as 1867 Dostoyevsky's notes remind us not so much of the utilitarian calculus of which Derek Offord writes, but of the scriptural basis for the 'Legend' of 1880.

Finally, the phrase 'shows him the world' has been subtly transformed in the second version into 'shows him God's world', elaborated in the note 'conveys to him the idea of God, of Christ'. The question of whether it is 'the world' or 'God's world' which the Emperor is looking at harks back to the two primary intuitions and raises in the context of Russian Orthodoxy the all-important question of whether the world is the creation of a benevolent God and should be accepted in humility with its freedom and its suffering, or whether it is a hostile environment which either must be conquered or will swallow men up.

Mirovich tries to seduce the Emperor with the beauty of the Commandant's daughter, actually engaged to him, but with secret ambitions to become Empress herself. Here, the theme of beauty with its many facets, which was to preoccupy Myshkin in Dostoyevsky's next novel, is lightly sketched in, and another character is introduced. A fourth character is the Commandant himself, who finally despatches the Emperor.

In Mirovich and the Emperor are adumbrated two heroes with typically Dostoyevskian problems. Mirovich is described as an 'enthusiast', an enthusiast, that is, of an idea which dominates and has taken possession of him – like Raskolnikov, Kirillov, Shatov or Ivan Karamazov. Exactly what constitutes this idea we cannot say, but it would appear to revolve around the conceptions he has been preaching to the Emperor. Mirovich, unlike Raskolnikov, does not aim to become an emperor. He apparently wishes to create an emperor and manipulate him according to the principles he has outlined. If Dostoyevsky had worked up his sketch into a novel, it is safe to assume that he would have elaborated Mirovich's psychology according to the dualistic pattern we discern in Dostoyevsky's other ideologue heroes.

The Emperor finally senses the deception around him, the ambition, hatred and jealousy beneath the surface beauty of the girl and the ideal of friendship he had projected onto Mirovich. He has understood and is revolted by the prospect of being the cause of violent death. His ideals are undermined by this understanding and when his moment comes he dies majestically and sadly. The moment of crisis, almost but not entirely without duration, has reached its climax. In *The Dream of a Ridiculous Man*, Dostoyevsky was to project this experience on a universal plane through the myth of the Fall.

This brief sketch therefore concentrates in a remarkable way the central concerns of Dostoyevsky's fictional world and it does so in a typically Dostoyevskian fashion. The work of the 'artist' – decisions about sequence of events, narrative point of view, the appropriate narrative style, the language of the characters and so on – has still to be accomplished, but the work of the 'poet' is done.

Thematically, *The Emperor* embodies an idea which at one and the same time has resonances in Dostoyevsky's personal experience, in current debate, in Russian history and culture and which echoes an archetypal theme which has received expression in the Western tradition too.

This is also true of each of Dostoyevsky's great works. Thus, the theme of the usurper or Promethean rebel which dominates *Crime and Punishment* is one which recalls Dostoyevsky's experience in the Petrashevsky circle and among political prisoners in Siberia; the debates of which Derek Offord writes; memories of Boris Godunov and the false Dmitrys, all the eighteenth-century Russian empresses, including Catherine the Great, not to mention the two Napoleons, both of whom sent armies onto Russian soil. Likewise, *The Idiot*, which is dominated by the idea of the saint or perfectly beautiful man thrust into a world of sin, echoing the Christian tradition and Christ himself, also takes up contemporary themes; this time in the context rather than in the person of the hero. The Russian type of the Holy Fool is of particular, though not exclusive, relevance, as Sidney Monas shows, in tracing Myshkin's ancestry. Interestingly, Dostoyevsky himself pointed to three European prototypes for his hero, in Don Quixote, Mr Pickwick and Hugo's Jean Valjean.

Or *The Devils*, as Roy Davison shows, built around a central character who has lost his sense of direction, depicts a society in the process of disintegration, whose moral and religious values together with other principles of social cohesion are being undermined. Anarchy threatens and that anarchy has an apocalyptic colouring, but its details are distinctly those of contemporary Russia and contemporary Russian debate. On the other hand, while virtually all countries have had their 'time of troubles', it is doubtful whether the threat of anarchy has such a hold over the collective imagination of any other European people as it has over the Russians. Dostoyevsky understood the threat of anarchy very well, not least because of his enforced stay in Siberia among the convicts, and he saw it as the ultimate fate of a Europe devoted to the principle of individualism.

Finally, *The Brothers Karamazov* has parricide as its central idea. With the allied theme of regicide (for the Tsar was traditionally regarded as the father of his people), this theme too is a haunting one in Russian history. As a young man Dostoyevsky had been trained as a military engineer in the very building where the Emperor Paul had been assassinated, it was suspected with the collusion of his son the future Alexander I. In Siberia, Dostoyevsky met a prisoner convicted of parricide (who later turned out to have been falsely accused); nor should it be forgotten that the Dostoyevsky family believed that Dostoyevsky's father had been murdered by his serfs, with whom he also, traditionally, stood in a paternal relationship. Also allied is the theme of deicide, or 'the death of God', as it is sometimes called in the history of modern thought. The attitudes of Ivan Karamazov and of Zosima to this problem are among those discussed in their essays by F. F. Seeley and Sergei Hackel respectively.

It is often said that the central philosophical problem of Dostoyevsky's oeuvre is that of freedom. *The Emperor* also makes this a central theme, psychologically, concretely (in the projected release from prison) and, to the extent to which it arises explicitly, philosophically. This question has been much discussed by commentators on Dostoyevsky, but rarely has it been discussed sympathetically by a philosopher from within 'the citadels of English-speaking philosophy' as it is here by Stewart Sutherland.

It is easy to appreciate the context in which Dostoyevsky chose a historical theme. The date was 1867. Tolstoy's *War and Peace* appeared from 1865 to 1869. Moreover, current interest in this and similar themes has been mentioned. It is not difficult to see why he abandoned it. The problem of finding a suitable narrative point of view may well have created difficulties; the psychology of a young man in his early twenties who had been almost entirely cut off from social intercourse for the whole of his life may have proved too great a challenge even for Dostoyevsky. But perhaps more important is the fact that he never showed any real inclination to delve into history for his subject matter and it is of interest to note that what survives of the sketch on the ideological plane resurfaces in the 'Legend of the Grand Inquisitor', which does not purport to be historical. On the plane of character portrayal, it seems possible that the Emperor played a role in the final conception of Myshkin. But that must remain speculative. The novel itself was never written.

Three more classic novels and a number of lesser works were however most certainly written. It is to Dostoyevsky's published oeuvre, in some of its most important aspects, that the remaining essays in this commemorative volume are devoted. It is to be hoped that each of them will make an original contribution to the study of Dostoyevsky in an area of perennial interest and in some cases of particular interest in the context of current debate.

Notes

1. E. J. Dillon, *Russia Today and Yesterday* (London, 1929), pp. 4 and 21.
2. *Dictionary of National Biography, 1931–1940* (London, 1949), pp. 227–8.
3. Helen Muchnic, *Dostoevsky's English Reputation (1881–1936)* (New York, 1969).
4. Malcolm Jones (ed.), *New Essays on Tolstoy* (Cambridge, 1978).

5. E. K. Kostka, *Schiller in Russian Literature* (Philadelphia, 1965), pp. 214–50.
6. Unfortunately, Dostoyevsky's translation of Balzac's *Eugénie Grandet* is not, it seems, to be included in the Academy Edition (*PSS*). An important recent analysis can be found in V. S. Nechayeva, *Ranniy Dostoyevsky, 1821–1849* (Moscow, 1979), pp. 95–129.
7. Victor Terras, *The Young Dostoevsky* (*1846–1849*) (The Hague/Paris, 1969), pp. 14–15.
8. M. V. Jones, 'An aspect of Romanticism in Dostoyevsky: *Netochka Nezvanova* and Eugène Sue's *Mathilde*', *Renaissance and Modern Studies*, 17 (1973), 38–61.
9. N. M. Lary, *Dostoyevsky and Dickens* (London, 1973), pp. 14–15.
10. M. M. Bakhtin, *Problemy poetiki Dostoyevskogo* (Moscow, 1963), translated by R. W. Rotsel as *Problems of Dostoevsky's Poetics* (Ann Arbor, 1973).
11. René Wellek, 'Bakhtin's view of Dostoevsky: "Polyphony" and "Carnivalesque"', *Dostoevsky Studies*, 1 (1980), 31–9.
12. Note Victor Terras's reservations on p. 35 of this volume.
13. M. M. Bakhtin, *Tvorchestvo Fransua Rable i narodnaya kul'tura Srednevekov'ya i Renessansa* (Moscow, 1965), translated by H. Iswolsky as *Rabelais and His World* (Cambridge, Mass., 1968).
14. In an article entitled 'Dostoyevsky and West European philosophy' to be published in a collection of papers delivered at the Fourth International Dostoevsky Symposium held in Bergamo in 1980.
15. J. Middleton Murry, *Fyodor Dostoevsky* (London, 1916), p. 36.
16. The volume of *PSS* containing the *Diary of a Writer* for 1876 has not yet appeared. This quotation is from the *Diary of a Writer* for February 1876, II, vi.
17. *The Dream of a Ridiculous Man* appeared as part of the *Diary of a Writer* for 1877, April, II. The volume of *PSS* containing it has not yet been published.
18. For a thorough treatment of Dostoyevsky's 'negative' and 'positive' philosophies, see Reinhard Lauth, *Die Philosophie Dostojewskis* (Munich, 1950).
19. Quoted in Graham Reed, *The Psychology of Anomalous Experience* (London, 1972), p. 154.
20. Charles Taylor, *Hegel* (Cambridge, 1975), pp. 13ff.
21. Robin Feuer Miller, *Dostoyevsky and 'The Idiot'* (Cambridge, Mass., 1981).
22. M. M. Bakhtin, *Voprosy literatury i estetiki* (Moscow, 1975), p. 397.

PART ONE

1

The young Dostoyevsky: an assessment in the light of recent scholarship

VICTOR TERRAS

A synthesis of recent scholarship dealing with the early Dostoyevsky (until 1849) will be attempted in this essay. Not nearly all of the books and articles which have appeared during the past ten or fifteen years will be explicitly referred to, nor will any of the works mentioned be given a comprehensive evaluation. Rather, an effort will be made to identify and outline certain important issues in the areas of Dostoyevsky's biography and its reflection in his fiction, his dialogue with Russian and foreign authors, his social and philosophical ideas, his style and his psychology (in that order). Some tentative assessments of recent discoveries, insights and interpretations will be offered.

I

The most important event in Dostoyevsky scholarship is of course the appearance of the thirty-volume Academy edition of his works. In addition to a reliable text and variants, its introductory essays and commentary provide valuable material on the genesis of each work, on the contemporary literary scene, and on public and critical reaction, as well as a wealth of historical and biographical background information.

Of almost equal importance is V. S. Nechayeva's *Ranniy Dostoyevsky: 1821–1849* (Moscow, 1979), a work based on an intimate knowledge of the period and a thorough familiarity with every detail of the writer's biography. Nechayeva's refutation of G. Fyodorov's attempt to cast doubt on the established tradition according to which Dostoyevsky's father was murdered by his serfs (though the official death certificate stated that he had died of natural causes)[1] is not only of interest to Dostoyevsky's biographer, but also has a bearing on psychological interpretations of Dostoyevsky's works. For example, when Dominique Arban suggests that the scene in Prokharchin's nightmare, where he sees himself attacked by an angry crowd, projects the writer's vision of his father's death, she takes for granted that there had been a murder and that Fyodor Mikhaylovich knew of it.[2] Fyodorov's article and Nechayeva's response have drawn attention to the fact, almost forgotten, that the manner of Dr Dostoyevsky's death, and hence its effect on his son, belongs to the realm of speculation, not certain knowledge. It also presents a case of *psikhologiya o dvukh kontsakh* (double-edged psychology), for even if Dr Dostoyevsky died of natural causes, his family may still have believed the rumours of his murder.

Soviet scholars, and this goes for Nechayeva too, emphasize the importance of concrete biographical and historical detail, concentrating on literary connections within Russian literature. This does not mean however that international connections are ignored. Thus, Nechayeva has an excellent chapter on Dostoyevsky's translation of *Eugénie Grandet.*

Nechayeva explains some apparent lacunas in 'Mr Prokharchin' by a residue in it of Dostoyevsky's lost story 'Povest′ ob unichtozhennykh kantselyariyakh' ('Tale of the Abolished Government Offices'), whose implied message had been that the world of these *kantselyarii* was crumbling (pp. 166–73). It stands to reason that the cuts made by the censor (Dostoyevsky refers to such cuts in his correspondence) affected precisely the socio-political aspect of the story. As a result of these cuts the hero's rebellion and 'Napoleonic' hubris seem not only grotesque, but also insufficiently motivated. Nechayeva's convincing arguments corroborate the view that the young Dostoyevsky was actually trying to introduce certain explosive social and political ideas into seemingly innocuous tales about little people.

In her discussion of *Netochka Nezvanova,* Nechayeva advances a plausible hypothesis according to which Prince Kh. had a prototype in Dostoyevsky's wealthy uncle A. A. Kumanin. This and other, similar observations (e.g. that the German fiddler B. is really Belinsky) are significant in that they counteract earlier suggestions concerning strong Western influences (of Sue, George Sand, Hoffmann, Dickens and Balzac) discernible in this work. As for Yefimov, by far the most interesting character in the novel, Nechayeva suggests that he is a 'realization' of Gogol's Chartkov ('The Portrait'), but with some autobiographical traits (pp. 177–82). I believe that Nechayeva has stretched the former point and downgraded the latter. I also agree with Joseph Frank, who not only accepts the notion, expressed earlier by Mochulsky and others, that Yefimov is a projection of Dostoyevsky's own self-doubts, but expands it by suggesting that Netochka too is a projection of the writer's personal preoccupations, specifically his 'Oedipal antagonism' and his guilt feelings after the death of his father.[3] Frank's hypothesis is supported by an episode in the journal version of *Netochka Nezvanova,* where the boy Larya loses both parents within a short period of time and develops a morbid notion that he had caused their death by his selfish and capricious behaviour.

Dominique Arban's book contains many intriguing intuitions regarding possible biographical sources of Dostoyevsky's early works. Regrettably their credibility is reduced by some suppositions that are simply too fanciful. For instance, Arban links to Dostoyevsky's father a passage in a feuilleton of 13 April 1847, where a cruel landowner says of his serfs that they are 'dogs who deserve a dog's life' (XVIII, 114) and suggests, furthermore, that Dmitry Karamazov's angry outcry in court, 'to a dog, a dog's death', is a reminiscence of the Dostoyevsky children's reaction to the news of their father's death (p. 320). The feuilleton in question is a collective effort by Pleshcheyev and Dostoyevsky, if Dostoyevsky was involved in its writing at all. Dmitry's outburst refers to Smerdyakov, not to his father. Moreover, the expression is a common and formulaic one. There is also a tendency in Arban's work to connect characters from Dostoyevsky's early stories with more famous characters of the great novels, without much specific evidence. Thus, Arban sees in 'Arkady's cruelty, of which he is not himself aware' ('A Faint Heart') a preview of Fyodor Pavlovich Karamazov's 'sentimental and cruel' character (p. 343) and suggests that Katerina's remorse for a crime she did not commit ('The Landlady') anticipates Dmitry Karamazov's willingness to bear his cross, though innocent (p. 333). This seems far-fetched. When Arban suggests that Golyadkin junior is a precursor of Stavrogin (specifically by virtue of being associated with the usurper Grishka Otrepyev) and other trespassers and usurpers of Dostoyevsky's great novels (p. 272), she follows Chizhevsky and other earlier scholars.

Arban's book, in spite of a number of particular instances in which one tends to disagree with her, must be commended as an imaginative effort to create, from oeuvre and what biographical material is available, a credible *Gestalt* of Fyodor Dostoyevsky as a young man and budding writer. A scholar engaged in such an effort will be inclined to reach out for possible links between biographical facts, however scanty, and details of the writer's fiction which would seem to fit these facts. For instance, Arban suggests that the heavy eroticism of Netochka's love affair with Princess Katya is a reminiscence of Dostoyevsky's own childhood crush on a peasant girl named Katya, attested by the writer's brother, Andrey Dostoyevsky (pp. 368–9): an attractive hypothesis, since Dostoyevsky's notes toward *Life of a Great Sinner* do indeed feature an episode of the youthful hero's love affair with a very young girl named Katya.[4] Arban's further conjecture that Katya eventually became the mistress of Dostoyevsky's father and that this love triangle served as a model of this theme in Dostoyevsky's novels, while intriguing, seems extravagant.

II

If there is one aspect of Dostoyevsky's art which appears clearest in his early work it is his tendency to engage other authors in a dialogue. In the 1920s Bem, Komarovich, Vinogradov, among others, identified numerous instances in which Pushkin, Gogol, Hoffmann and other authors were present in Dostoyevsky's texts, while Tynyanov and Bakhtin created a model which allowed one to get away from an unproductive pursuit of 'influences' and see quotations, reminiscences, echoes and allusions as integral elements of these texts. Tynyanov's observations on the theory of parody may be viewed as a preliminary stage of Bakhtin's theory of the 'alien voice' (*chuzhoy golos*), where parody is but one of its several forms. In recent years the 'alien voice' in the works of the young Dostoyevsky has been examined from some new angles. Soviet scholars, Blagoy and Nechayeva in particular, have adduced more evidence linking the early Dostoyevsky to the Russian literary scene of the 1840s and making it plausible that the basic tendency of his art was to give the idealist or metaphysical themes of Romantic literature, and of Gogol, a realistic social content.

Blagoy has sought to demonstrate an outright endorsement of 'Pushkinian realism' in several of the young Dostoyevsky's works.[5] He takes Devushkin's reading of 'The Stationmaster' to be Dostoyevsky's own (p. 469), interprets 'Mr Prokharchin' as a direct response to 'The Covetous Knight' (pp. 481–7) and develops a direct analogy between Arkady's epiphany at the conclusion of 'A Faint Heart' and Yevgeny's brief but poignant illumination in 'The Bronze Horseman' (pp. 472–3). W. J. Leatherbarrow has developed an interpretation of Dostoyevsky's early works which is rather close to Blagoy's.[6] He suggests that Pushkin was Dostoyevsky's example 'in his struggle to resist the influence of Gogol' and to overcome 'the caustic superficiality of Gogol's embittered view of his fellow man' (p. 378). It is a corollary of this view that the young Dostoyevsky's response to Gogol was primarily an antagonistic one.[7] Devushkin is then a straightforward correction of Gogol's Bashmachkin (Blagoy, pp. 466–7), and Dostoyevsky's Golyadkin and Prokharchin are likewise revisions of Gogolian characters, performed by addition of an individual, social and psychological dimension to Gogol's types. Blagoy is quite aware that by disregarding the ironic tensions pointed out by Vinogradov and Bakhtin he may be simplifying Dostoyevsky's art. His views find indirect support in some specific observations by Fanger[8] and Frank (p. 141), who see the young Dostoyevsky giving a more realistic content to the social relationships first depicted by Gogol. Dostoyevsky's advantage with regard to Pushkin is then that he has 'brought Pushkin's themes and characters up to date', as Leatherbarrow puts it (p. 371). Gyula Király has pointed out that the fantastic in Dostoyevsky is generated by the hero's consciousness, well within the bounds of psychological realism, which Király sees as an advance from both Gogol and Pushkin, as well as 'a return, on a higher level, to Hoffmann'.[9]

It has hardly been noted by these scholars, who all credit Dostoyevsky with having progressed beyond Gogol, that such gain was also a loss: a retreat from Gogol's metaphysics of Nonbeing and nostalgia for a metaphysics of Being to an empirical world of day-to-day living. Gogol's Hades of dead souls and phantasmagoric city of grotesque puppets is replaced by a very real Petersburg, populated by all-too-real titular councillors.

Belinsky was right when he greeted *Poor Folk* as the first social novel of Russian literature. The young Dostoyevsky's considerable power of psychological analysis was also duly appreciated. Even if one is inclined to agree with Frank's suggestion that Valerian Maykov's all-too-perceptive endorsement of Dostoyevsky's paradoxical psychology in *Poor Folk* was based on Dostoyevsky's own *explication de texte* (he and Maykov were friends), the young critic had reason enough to assume, as he did, that psychological subtlety was Dostoyevsky's forte and that it was here that he could and would surpass Gogol. It also seems likely that the young Dostoyevsky fancied himself as heir-apparent to Gogol's position in the world of Russian letters and saw a challenge and rivalry where contemporaries saw only Gogol's influence. The question whether Dostoyevsky ever met Gogol and whether or not certain details of that alleged encounter entered the text of *The Village of Stepanchikovo* continues to be debated.[10] So much seems certain, though: the young Dostoyevsky, like everybody else, underestimated the depth of Gogol's art. When he challenged Gogol, he came up with no more than a moderately spirited parody, at best, never touching the deeper strata of 'The Overcoat' or 'Memoirs of a Madman' and quite unaware of the 'shadows linking our state of existence to those other states and modes which we dimly apprehend in our rare moments of irrational perception' which other readers have sensed in them.[11]

Nevertheless, Apollon Grigoryev detected in the young Dostoyevsky's analyses of everyday reality moments where life's banality would turn to nightmare and madness. 'Alas! One cannot help recalling the idea of Gogol's "Portrait",' Grigoryev observed.[12] Apparently Grigoryev discovered in Dostoyevsky the very metaphysics of Nonbeing which Dostoyevsky had tried to replace with psychological realism. And quite correctly, he saw in these moments of 'nightmare or madness' a return to Gogol.

Among foreign writers whom the young Dostoyevsky engaged in a dialogue one finds Fourier, Hoffmann, and perhaps also George Sand, Balzac and Sue. Rudolf Neuhäuser has suggested that the young Dostoyevsky developed many of his characters in terms of Fourier's psychology, and specifically its scheme of perversion of natural human passion by an unnatural social order.[13] The plots which feature the undoing of Golyadkin, Prokharchin, Vasya Shumkov and Ordynov are cited as examples of this scheme (pp. 30–9). The story 'A Christmas Party and a Wedding' is a Fourierist piece not only by virtue of following this scheme, but also as an example of the oppression of the 'weaker sexes' (women and children), as well as in its whole pathos. It seems, though, that in general ('A Christmas Party and a Wedding' being an exception, not the rule) the young Dostoyevsky was too sophisticated a psychologist to confine himself to Fourier's scheme with any consistency. As Neuhäuser himself puts it, Dostoyevsky's *sujets* grew from his heroes (p. 22). Since Dostoyevsky's heroes are generally round characters, it is difficult to recognize his *sujets* as exercises in Fourierism. But then, the moral found at the conclusion of the journal version of 'An Honest Thief' (II, 426–7) is closer to Fourier than to the views of the mature Dostoyevsky: 'A man will die of a vice, as of a lethal poison, and therefore vice is an acquired, human thing, and not native to man – it comes and it goes: if this weren't so, Christ wouldn't have come to us, that is, if we were destined to remain sinful for ever and ever from original sin.' Frank recognizes Dostoyevsky's concern with the theme of moral freedom in this passage (p. 328). But the young Dostoyevsky sees it differently from the mature Dostoyevsky, who believed that Good and Evil are equally inherent in human nature.

Dostoyevsky belonged to the generation of Russian writers who were brought up on Romantic literature but who dealt with it critically as they began to write seriously themselves. The influence of Hoffmann thus acquires an active meaning as a dialogue with Romanticism. In 'White Nights' Dostoyevsky's encounter with Hoffmann is acknowledged as the Dreamer fantasizes about having become a member of the Serapion brotherhood. The fascination and charm of Romanticism *à la* Hoffmann are gratefully accepted and in fact duplicated, yet seemingly rejected in the end, because in conflict with the reality of life. So in the traditional interpretation, at least. Recently Gary Rosenshield has advanced good arguments (specifically the highly suggestive epigraph of the story) to prove that the voice of the implied author is dominant in 'White Nights', subordinating all other points of view, including those of the Dreamer and the narrator (the latter two are not identical, since the story is told in retrospect, fifteen years later).[14] Rosenshield contends that the contradiction between the alleged sterility of the hero's dreams and the palpable beauty which they generate is contrived by the implied author and is a major artistic asset. This means that the clash of a Hoffmannesque escape into a world of creative fantasy with the pragmatic and moral facts of life results in an ambiguity. Rosenshield's ingenious interpretation felicitously confirms what many readers have felt all along: that 'White Nights' is a genuine masterpiece. It also confirms the notion that Dostoyevsky used his foreign literary sources (Hoffmann, in this case) in antiphon, much as he used Gogol and Pushkin. Hoffmann is not the only foreign writer who plays such a role in the early Dostoyevsky. Pierre R. Hart has shown that 'A Little Hero' is written as it were in antiphon to a couple of themes from Schiller.[15] More recently, W. J. Leatherbarrow has suggested that in 'A Faint Heart', too, 'Schillerian idealism and Christian humanism – two vital stages in the young Dostoyevsky's intellectual development – are brought together and gently, but firmly discarded.'[16]

Belinsky immediately linked 'The Landlady' with Hoffmann.[17] It is possible that Dostoyevsky himself acknowledged this connection, much as he had acknowledged his connections with Pushkin and Gogol in earlier stories, or as he would acknowledge his debt to

Dickens in *The Insulted and Injured*. In one of Hoffmann's less well-known stories, *Erscheinungen*, the hero, a dreamer, meets a demonic old man, who at one point tries to kill him, and an angelically beautiful but demented peasant girl, Dorothee, who fancies herself to be Agafia, a Russian princess. Dorothee–Agafia is expecting the return of her betrothed, Alexei, who however seems to have drowned crossing a wide and deep river, while Dorothee and the old man reached the other shore safely. The visions which make up this tale, but especially those involving the girl and the old man, are as dream-like and disconnected as Ordynov's experiences in 'The Landlady', where the heroine's betrothed, Aleksey, was drowned in the Volga river by a demonic old man, Murin. The latter, at one point, also tries to kill Ordynov. Dostoyevsky at one time wrote to his brother that he had read 'all of Hoffmann' available in Russian, plus *Kater Murr* in German. *Erscheinungen* was one of the not too many stories that were available in Russian at the time in question.[18] The use of a name, Aleksey, and several details of plot and character found in a tale which many of Dostoyevsky's readers had read may well have been a signal on the author's part, directing attention to the circumstance that he was doing variations on a theme by Hoffmann.

Neuhäuser (p. 145) has drawn attention to a rather striking parallel between the text of a passage in 'The Landlady' (I, 279–80) and a celebrated highlight of German Romantic literature, Jean Paul's 'Oration of a Deceased Christ, Delivered from the Edifice of the Universe, on that there Is No God', from *Married Life, Death, and Wedding of F. St. Siebenkäs, Paupers' Advocate* (1796–7), a piece widely known since it was included in Mme de Staël's *De l'Allemagne*.[19] I suggest that the passage in 'The Landlady' is also quite Hoffmannesque, particularly in its hypostatization of a cosmic irony. Altogether then, what with its potpourri of Hoffmann (and perhaps Jean Paul), Gogol's arch-Romantic 'Terrible Vengeance', Marlinsky (surely Belinsky was right about his influence too) and an extra-heavy dose of Russian folklore, 'The Landlady' must be an attempt, successful or not, to realize the Romantic theme of the poet-dreamer's encounter with the Eternal Feminine held in captivity by the forces of Evil.

Some efforts have been made to attach a more specific allegoric meaning to 'The Landlady'. Following earlier attempts to find in the story's heroine the first seed of what is surely Dostoyevsky's greatest symbolic figure, Marya Timofeyevna of *The Possessed* (Vyacheslav Ivanov), and in its villain, Murin, an early version of the Grand Inquisitor (L. P. Grossman), Neuhäuser has developed an interpretation according to which Ordynov's 'idea' is utopian socialism and his work 'on the history of the Church' something along the lines of *De la célébration du dimanche* or *Das Wesen des Christentums* (pp. 182–3). Ordynov, symbolic of the Russian educated class, is struggling in vain to save Katerina, symbolic of the Russian people, from the clutches of superstition (Murin). Koshmarov's house, a den of thieves, is symbolic of Russia's corrupt social order (p. 138). Altogether, Neuhäuser, who distinguishes as many as six or seven different levels in the structure of the story, sees it as a social allegory (*gesellschaftspolitische Allegorie*, p. 182), apparently along Fourierist lines, on the deepest of these levels. It is my impression that 'The Landlady' is rather too flimsy to carry the whole weight of Neuhäuser's learned and ingenious construction. I agree with Frank, who accepts Neuhäuser's observations to the extent that 'Dostoyevsky meant *The Landlady* not only as a symbolic critique of Slavophilism but also of Orthodoxy' (p. 341), but rejects the notion that the story is a consistent allegory (p. 340).

Neuhäuser's observations, based on 'The Landlady' and other early works, suggest that the young Dostoyevsky was 'sceptical toward Christian ideology', replacing it by 'a faith in a social utopia' (p. 147). While this is probably correct – after all, Dostoyevsky's conservative critics, such as Konstantin Leontyev, saw precisely such a tendency even in his 'Discourse on Pushkin' – some of Neuhäuser's arguments in support of this thesis seem somewhat forced. Thus he suggests that the description of a parish church in 'The Landlady' (I, 267) is a detail which supports his thesis: 'In contrast to the light of the sun, the artificial light in the church suggests something artificial, false, a dead faith, frozen into a ritual' (p. 184). I do not find anything intrinsically negative in the text itself. Besides, it contains the first example of one of Dostoyevsky's favourite images, always used with a positive connotation: the slanting rays of the setting sun illuminating a deeply moving scene, such as the praying Sofya Ivanovna, mother of Ivan and Alyosha Karamazov.[20]

W. J. Leatherbarrow's recent interpretation of 'Mr Prokharchin' (see note 16) deserves careful attention. He sees in Ustinya Fyodorovna's lodgers a caricature of a Fourierist commune (Dostoyevsky himself briefly belonged to one), and in their putdown of Prokharchin's 'wilful individualism' a parody of socialist rhetoric. It appears, though, that Leatherbarrow is stretching his point when he suggests that 'in *Gospodin Prokharchin* Dostoyevsky resists impersonal, materialistic socialism with the Christian or Christian socialist ideals of personal love, mutual responsibility and human brotherhood' (p. 530).

In the same article, Leatherbarrow has drawn attention to some allusions to Prévost's *Manon Lescaut* in 'A Faint Heart', finding that the theme of both works is really the same: the futility of a 'faint heart's' attempts to master life and the impotence of idealism in the face of a cruel reality. Leatherbarrow attaches a symbolic meaning to Vasya's visit to Mme Leroux's millinery shop (that she is a namesake of the utopian socialist Pierre Leroux being no accident). 'All the great and the beautiful' (*vsyo prekrasnoye i velikoye*) that enthralls him there will prove to be irrelevant to life's crisis. Leatherbarrow's attractive interpretation has far-reaching implications, for it suggests that Dostoyevsky was no longer taking Fourierism seriously when he wrote the story.

Over the years, a good deal has been written on Dostoyevsky and George Sand.[21] Still there remains one interesting task: to establish to what extent the stylistic and psychological details of *Netochka Nezvanova*, a work clearly influenced by George Sand, even to the extent of choosing a female narrator for what was to be the young author's first full-length novel, bear specific imprints of George Sand's art. My own observations in *The Young Dostoyevsky* (*1846–1849*)*: A Critical Study*, pp. 88–90, are sketchy. What is needed is the kind of definitive study Malcolm V. Jones has done on the role played by Eugène Sue and his *Mathilde* in the genesis and text of *Netochka Nezvanova.*[22]

III

Dostoyevsky's political and philosophical positions after his Siberian exile were by no means constant, but they were generally clear. The philosophy of the young Dostoyevsky as reflected in his fiction is far from clear. Such difference cannot, I think, be accounted for solely by considering that censorship was more restrictive in the 1840s. Contemporary critics who only knew the early Dostoyevsky (and this goes for a right-wing Grigoryev as well as for a left-wing Dobrolyubov) saw in him mainly a champion of the 'insulted and injured' and the most talented representative of 'sentimental humanitarianism'. Only in the 1860s and 1870s did some critics begin to perceive the depths and ambiguities found even in the writer's early works. Dostoyevsky scholars of our own age have spent much critical acumen and scholarly ingenuity in finding meanings and messages concealed between the lines of Dostoyevsky's texts.

Gyula Király has suggested that in *Poor Folk*, *The Double* and other early works, a subtext of social criticism is present, masked by Devushkin's naivety, Golyadkin's madness and so forth. An attentive reader, Király suggests, will hear the author's ironic voice behind that of the hero or, in other words, will see the contrast between what really happens and what Devushkin thinks is happening.[23] In particular, Király points out the contrast between the facts of life in the Russia of Nicholas I, realistically presented by Dostoyevsky, a writer of the Natural School, and the conventional, still 'patriarchal' responses to social pressures on the part of his underdog heroes. Furthermore, Király sees a social allegory even in the duel between the two Golyadkins, each standing for a specific tendency in the development of Russian life. Altogether, Király sees the young Dostoyevsky as a genuine 'social novelist', who uses his heroes to perform a series of tests to determine the true nature of Russian social reality (p. 267).

Joseph Frank basically agrees with Király in suggesting that 'the Dostoyevsky of the 1840s is not that of the 1860s and 1870s, and his frame of reference in *The Double* is still purely social–psychological' (p. 311). But Frank also sees a problem, and this precisely in the ironic subtext of *The Double* (as well as *Poor Folk* and other works), because he senses here 'a puzzling ambiguity of tone because a character is shown simultaneously both as socially oppressed and yet as reprehensible and morally unsavory because he has surrendered too abjectly to the pressure of his environment' (p. 307). I believe that this ambiguity is, at least in *The Double*, motivated by the fact that the moral, rather than the social issue is the dominant: social underdog or not, Golyadkin gets what he deserves. Konrad Onasch suggested, twenty years ago, that the young Dostoyevsky's hero, like those of his great novels, puts to test various enlightened Western ideas, only to discover that they will let him down in a crisis. The judgement scene in the finale of *The Double* quite logically ends in Golyadkin's expulsion from Berendeyev's heaven and into the utter darkness of Dr Rutenspitz's hell.[24] It may not be too trivial to observe that *Rutenspitz* is an anagram of *Spitzruten*, 'rods', a symbol of the sinister aspect of the Western contribution to Petrine Russia.

Neuhäuser presents an interpretation which is close to Onasch's: Golyadkin is a homunculus bred in the retort of foreign, Romantic–Idealist masters.[25] His whole ambiance is marked as pagan and anti-Orthodox (Neuhäuser, *Das Frühwerk*, pp. 64–6). The judgement scene is a persiflage of the 'Christian myth' (*ibid.*, p. 146). Roger B.

Anderson has pushed this interpretation even further, suggesting that Golyadkin senior's principle of 'keeping one's own place' gradually becomes associated with Christ's acceptance of God's will, while Golyadkin junior, 'that willful and godless person', comes to represent the enemy of Christ, a mixture of Judas and Antichrist.[26]

While Dostoyevsky added the subtitle 'Peterburgskaya poema' in 1866, it is still likely that *The Double* was conceived by him, even in 1845, as an indictment not only of the existing social order, but also of the entire *Peterburgskaya Rossiya.* Golyadkin, very much a 'Petersburg type', therefore deserved the ironic treatment which Gogol had also given his own Petersburg types, specifically Golyadkin's prototypes Poprishchin and 'Major' Kovalyov. Another reason why Golyadkin senior as well as junior should be accorded such heartlessly ironic treatment may be found in Viktor Shklovsky's observation that *The Double* makes a travesty of the Romantic *Doppelgänger* theme: both Golyadkins are so trivial that the struggle between Good and Evil, featured by Romantic *Doppelgänger* plots, becomes irrelevant.[27] In a way, then, Dostoyevsky was exploding the very sentimental humanitarianism which Grigoryev said Dostoyevsky was promoting.

It appears that questions concerning the style and structure of Dostoyevsky's early works are inseparably linked with questions of his social philosophy and metaphysics (or absence of such). Questions as to whether Dostoyevsky was 'correcting' Gogol or endorsing him on a higher, or perhaps on a psychologically 'realized' level, whether he was challenging the existing social order, the drift of history or divine justice, and even whether he sentimentally identified with his heroes or kept them at an ironic distance, all these questions affect and are affected by our judgement of Dostoyevsky's art. The general pattern seems to be that direct extratextual evidence, produced by Nechayeva, Blagoy, the commentators of the Academy edition, Frank and others, supports a relatively simple interpretation of Dostoyevsky's early works, while interpretations suggesting the presence of very deep ironies, ambiguities or symbolism are based on textual analysis and circumstantial historical evidence.

I believe that even in *Poor Folk* the ironies are deeper than is suggested by Dostoyevsky's own pronouncements on the genesis and intent of that work. True, Dostoyevsky lets his hero produce 'a piercing vision of the contrasted lives of the rich and the poor (Frank, p. 145), but he also makes it rather clear that the poor are born losers rather than victims of social injustices. Devushkin's analysis of poverty (I, 68 and *passim*) leaves no doubt about that. True, Dostoyevsky lets Devushkin express his respect for the poor man who earns his bread in the sweat of his brow. But he also undercuts the argument by letting Devushkin choose an organ grinder as an example of such an honest toiler. The whole passage (I, 86) is clearly a 'dig' at Grigorovich's physiological sketch 'The Organ Grinders of St Petersburg' (1845). The scene at the kindly general's office, which Belinsky found so moving (Frank, p. 146), is undercut, at least in the original version, where we learn that His Excellency, 'himself not a wealthy man', does however 'own a house'. Devushkin says *domik*, 'little house', but this is irony (the author's, not Devushkin's, of course): it is a big house, 'two houses, in fact, and a couple of villages' (i.e., several hundred serfs, at least), yet can ill afford to give Devushkin a hundred roubles, because 'he is not supposed to live the way we do' (I, 450).

Surely many readers shed tears over Varenka's sad future as Mrs Bykov. Dostoyevsky himself explicitly approved such reading.[28] But the screw can be given another turn and the happily married Dunya of Pushkin's 'The Stationmaster' is there to give it a push. There is enough between, and even in, the lines of Varenka's last few letters to suggest to an unsentimental reader that she will be just fine.

IV

Discussions of Dostoyevsky's alleged polyphonic style tend to devote a great deal of attention to the writer's early works. Even Bakhtin devoted more space to them, proportionally speaking, than to the great novels. The extreme position of Bakhtin's theory, namely that Dostoyevsky's fiction is inherently dialogic, lacking a controlling narrative voice, is accepted by some scholars, rejected by others. The former, such as Bursov[29] or Schmid,[30] claim that Dostoyevsky created a new narrative style – Schmid actually says 'aesthetic canon' (p. 103) – and revolutionized the modern short story and novel. This, they say, was the reason why contemporaries were puzzled by the language of *Poor Folk* and *The Double*, and also why Belinsky warned Dostoyevsky against a 'diffuse narrative manner' (*rasplyvchataya manera rasskazchika*). If they are right, *The Double* is an early precursor of such twentieth-century works as Andrey Belyy's *Petersburg*.

Other scholars, such as Blagoy (p. 495) and Frank, insist that Dostoyevsky's works have a controlling voice like other nineteenth-century novels and short stories. However, Frank considers Bakhtin's conception 'useful' (p. 156), because it draws attention to the dialectic quality of Dostoyevsky's novelistic structure. V. A. Tunimanov, quite mindful of Bakhtin's and Vinogradov's observations, shows nevertheless that in 'Mr Prokharchin' the young Dostoyevsky mastered some of the difficulties that had stymied him in *The Double* and succeeded in creating a narrator who rather skilfully pulls the strings to which his characters are attached.[31] In this story, Dostoyevsky's narrator parodies the speech habits of several of his characters, including of course the hero, 'lays bare' his own devices by introducing the image of a puppeteer and his puppets, and creates other emblematic images, while retaining his own identity all along. Tunimanov leans toward a view according to which a controlling voice is present in 'Mr Prokharchin'. His observations, based on a close reading of the text without a theoretical preconception, seem to be not only ingenious but also correct.

Wolf Schmid has performed a meticulous analysis of the text of *The Double* which led him to the conclusion that the basic – and innovative – principle applied here is one that he calls 'interference of narrator's and character's text' (*Erzählertext und Personentext*).[32] Schmid suggests that it was precisely this phenomenon that caused Belinsky to say that 'the author relates the hero's adventures from his own standpoint, but entirely in the language and concepts of his hero'. He also suggests that it was this phenomenon that Vinogradov was referring to when he spoke of *skaz* in *The Double* and which Bakhtin defined as 'a dialogic orientation of the narrative toward the hero' (p. 103).

Schmid finds the same principle active in other early as well as later stories and asserts that it has an important aesthetic function which, due to its novelty, failed to connect with most contemporary readers. He sees the aesthetic function of textual interference in the creation of semantic polyvalence, an enigmatic quality, and a challenge to the reader (pp. 111–12). Schmid suggests, and Neuhäuser states explicitly (Neuhäuser, *Das Frühwerk*, p. 173), that textual interference implies a new approach to the problem of truth in art.

Neuhäuser, who seems to have no serious objections to Schmid's theory, nevertheless makes an important point which implicitly undermines it. He suggests that in *The Double* Dostoyevsky had tried but failed to do what he was to accomplish brilliantly in his late story 'The Gentle One', viz. expression of the deepest truth of his subject's consciousness (pp. 173–4). If Neuhäuser is right, the narrator's irony, elements of parody, Gogolian echoes and so forth in *The Double* are distractions which divert the reader's attention from the serious content of the story. Neuhäuser rightly draws attention to the fact that Dostoyevsky himself called *The Double* a failure, and this precisely on account of his not having found the correct form for his 'bright idea'. The very fact that the exact nature of this 'bright idea' has never been grasped by any reader suggests that the novel was not an artistic success.

W. J. Leatherbarrow's suggestion that the 'bright idea' of *The Double*, alluded to by Dostoyevsky in his *Diary of a Writer*, was that 'the human will in its search for total freedom of expression becomes a self-destructive impulse' is probably correct.[33] Golyadkin's morbid preoccupation with his own ego and his frantic efforts to find 'his own place' in the world lead to the disintegration of his personality. The theme is thus the same that we find later in *Notes from Underground*. But it emerges from *The Double* much less clearly, if at all.

Observations along similar lines have been made by other scholars. Roger B. Anderson connects Bakhtin's theory of the dialogic structure of Dostoyevsky's fiction, and of *The Double* in particular, with Otto Rank's psychological interpretation of the novel, which makes Golyadkin a symbol of modern man's repression of 'will' as a safeguard against social disruption.[34] Golyadkin is, according to Anderson, modern man, properly defined by conflicting voices (pp. 103–4).

There is no escaping the fact that a maximum of textual interference (or pure polyphony, without a controlling narrative voice) is found precisely in those works of Dostoyevsky which by almost general consensus are also his least successful: *The Double*, 'Mr Prokharchin', 'The Landlady' and, among later works, 'The Eternal Husband'. Hence it is not unreasonable to assume that the absence of a clear hierarchy of voices in the works in question is merely an artistic flaw, due to be sure to the author's efforts to give an authentic voice to his characters while also creating an active narrator, keenly interested in their fate. It would appear that Bakhtin's thesis regarding the polyphonic nature of Dostoyevsky's fiction, while based on many excellent insights into Dostoyevsky's art and of seminal importance for giving Dostoyevsky the reading he deserves, is fundamentally wrong in its theoretical postulates.[35]

V

The young Dostoyevsky was immediately recognized as a master psychologist. The critic Valerian Maykov suggested that, while Gogol's point of view was that of an observer of Russian society, Dostoyevsky's was that of the individual member of that society. The depth and accuracy of the young Dostoyevsky's psychological observations are not in doubt. *The Double*, in particular, has been the subject of as much serious psychological discussion as any work by Dostoyevsky. Some new and interesting observations have been made in recent years.

Katharine Strelsky has discussed 'A Faint Heart' from a psychoanalytic viewpoint and discovered in this story a theme, familiar in twentieth-century literature but rarely dealt with in the nineteenth century, namely that of 'intermediate homosexuality'.[36] Strelsky sees 'Vasya's unconscious guilt and horror of sex' as the latent cause of his escape into insanity (p. 149). Vasya's panic at the prospect of marriage is, so she assumes, '"displaced" (as psychology has it), into a wholly imaginary conviction of unforgivable failure toward his employer – clearly a father figure' (p. 153). Strelsky corroborates her interpretation by suggesting that Vasya is, like all of the young Dostoyevsky's protagonists, a projection of the writer's own sexual repressions and timidity (p. 149). She also points out that intermediate homosexuality occurs elsewhere in Dostoyevsky and makes the interesting observation that the passive party is in each case referred to by his/her first name only, while the active party has a normal name-and-patronymic (Vasya: Arkady Ivanovich, Aglaya: Nastasya Filippovna, Grushenka: Katerina Ivanovna). What with a quite carnal homosexual relationship in *Netochka Nezvanova*, Strelsky's interpretation does not seem implausible. It is an example of how a new awareness on the part of the reader may open up new meanings in a literary text.

Sonia Ketchian's interpretation of 'A Faint Heart'[37] complements Strelsky's. Ketchian suggests that a careful reading of the text reveals that this is a tragic tale of love and jealousy, where Arkady, moved by an unconscious resentment of Vasya's decision to leave him and marry Liza, implants the seeds of doubt, diffidence and eventual insanity in his friend's mind. She believes that Arkady's realization of his guilt is hinted at in the concluding passage of the story: 'It was as though he only now understood this anxiety and recognized what had caused his poor Vasya, who could not stand his own happiness, to go out of his mind' (II, 48). I think that Ketchian has overstated her point somewhat. A latent tension of the kind she perceives may in fact be found 'between the lines' of the text. Also, Ketchian's observations square with Strelsky's. But it still seems that the theme of homosexual love and jealousy is after all a side issue in this story, with the 'faint heart' motif (a recurrent one in the young Dostoyevsky) and the social theme of the terrible vulnerability of the poor dominant. I tend to agree with Blagoy, who suggests that Arkady's illumination (*prozreniye*) is of the same order as Yevgeny's in 'The Bronze Horseman'.

In summary, I believe that D. S. Mirsky's assessment of the early Dostoyevsky is still valid: 'For his own sake it is convenient to regard the young Dostoyevsky as a different writer from the author of his later novels: a lesser writer, no doubt, but not a minor one, a writer with a marked originality and an important place among his contemporaries.'[38] It seems likely that the young Dostoyevsky was secularly oriented and disinclined to undertake the incursions into the realm of metaphysics which characterize the mature writer. It is a matter of speculation when and how this change occurred. Vyacheslav Ivanov's conjecture is as good as any: 'It may be that during those moments when, at the place of execution, Dostoyevsky looked into the eyes of death, he underwent a sudden and decisive transformation of the soul.'[39]

Dostoyevsky's first effort to introduce the main character of his great novels, a young intellectual in search of God in a godless world, is a tentative one. Ordynov lacks the passion, vigour, and poignancy of a Kirillov or Ivan Karamazov. The rebels and usurpers of the young Dostoyevsky are, by and large, social rather than metaphysical rebels. Hence the young Dostoyevsky is not a tragic artist in the sense defined by Ivanov.

On the other hand, the young Dostoyevsky is quite the psychologist he will be in his great novels. He has that great command of language which signals the born master, as Arban has pointed out eloquently. He performs all kinds of stylistic experiments, some of which do not work out too well. But there is a great deal of brilliant writing to be found throughout the early stories. The young Dostoyevsky has some difficulty synchronizing different points of view (or 'voices'), something that will be the mature writer's great forte. But, as in the great novels, these voices are always alive.

Notes

1. G. Fyodorov, 'K biografii F. M. Dostoyevskogo', *Literaturnaya gazeta*, no. 25 (18 June 1975), 7.
2. Dominique Arban, *Les Années d'apprentissage de Fiodor Dostoievski* (Paris, 1968), pp. 312–13.
3. Joseph Frank, *Dostoevsky: The Seeds of Revolt 1821–1849* (Princeton, 1976), pp. 350–1.
4. F. M. Dostoyevsky, *Zapisnyye tetradi F. M. Dostoyevskogo*, ed. Ye. N. Konshina (Moscow/Leningrad, 1935), pp. 97–100, 102, 106.
5. D. D. Blagoy, 'Dostoyevsky i Pushkin', in his *Dusha v zavetnoy lire: Ocherki zhizni i tvorchestva Pushkina* (Moscow, 1977), pp. 453–525.
6. W. J. Leatherbarrow, 'Pushkin and the early Dostoyevsky', *Modern Language Review*, 74 (1979), 368–85.
7. See, e.g., G. V. Ivanov, 'O skrytoy polemike s Gogolem v rasskaze F. M. Dostoyevskogo "Gospodin Prokharchin" ', in I. G. Yampol'sky (ed.), *Russkaya literatura XIX–XX vekov* (Uchenyye zapiski Leningradskogo universiteta, no. 355, Seriya filologicheskikh nauk, Vypusk 71, Leningrad, 1971), pp. 179–80.
8. Donald Fanger, *Dostoevsky and Romantic Realism: A Study of Dostoevsky in Relation to Balzac, Dickens, and Gogol* (Cambridge, Mass., 1965), pp. 165–6.
9. D. Kiray (Gyula Király), 'Struktura romana Dostoyevskogo *Dvoynik*', *Studia Slavica Academiae Scientiarum Hungaricae*, 16 (1970), 293.
10. See V. Seduro, 'A vsyo-taki vstrecha Dostoyevskogo s Gogolem byla', *Novyy Zhurnal*, 117 (1974), 84–100, and N. V. Pervushin, 'Gogol' i Dostoyevsky: po povodu odnoy polemiki', *Novyy Zhurnal*, 121 (1975), 279–81.
11. Vladimir Nabokov, *Gogol* (Norfolk, Conn., 1944), p. 145.
12. Grigoryev's review of *Peterburgskiy sbornik*, *Finskiy vestnik*, 9 (1846), 30. Quoted in I, 491–2.
13. Rudolf Neuhäuser, *Das Frühwerk Dostoevskijs: Literarische Tradition und gesellschaftlicher Anspruch* (Heidelberg, 1979), pp. 136–47.
14. Gary Rosenshield, 'Point of view and imagination in Dostoevskij's "White Nights" ', *Slavic and East European Journal*, 21 (1977), 191–203.
15. Pierre R. Hart, 'Schillerean themes in Dostoevskij's "Malen'kij geroj" ', *Slavic and East European Journal*, 15 (1971), 305–15.
16. W. J. Leatherbarrow, 'Idealism and utopian socialism in Dostoyevsky's *Gospodin Prokharchin* and *Slaboye serdtse*', *Slavonic and East European Review*, 58 (1980), 524–40.
17. V. G. Belinsky, *Polnoye sobraniye sochineniy* (13 vols., Moscow, 1953–9), vol. 10, p. 351. For stylistic parallels, see Victor Terras, *The Young Dostoevsky (1846–1849): A Critical Study* (The Hague/Paris, 1969), pp. 90–1, 231–4.
18. See Norman W. Ingham, *E. T. A. Hoffmann's Reception in Russia* (Würzburg, 1974), p. 272.
19. Cf. Walter Rehm, *Jean Paul–Dostojewski: Eine Studie zur dichterischen Gestaltung des Unglaubens* (Göttingen, 1962).

20. See S. N. Durylin, 'Ob odnom simvole u Dostoyevskogo', in *Dostoyevsky* (Moscow, 1928), pp. 163–98.
21. Most recently: Sigurd Fasting, 'Dostoevsky and George Sand', *Russian Literature*, 4 (1976), 309–21.
22. Malcolm V. Jones, 'An aspect of Romanticism in Dostoyevsky: *Netochka Nezvanova* and Eugène Sue's *Mathilde*', *Renaissance and Modern Studies*, 17 (1973), 38–61.
23. D'yula Kiray (Gyula Király), *Khudozhestvennaya struktura rannikh romanov F. M. Dostoyevskogo (zhanr, metod, problema avtorskoy pozitsii): Avtoreferat dissertatsii na soiskaniye uchonoy stepeni kandidata filologicheskikh nauk* (Moscow, 1969), p. 9.
24. Konrad Onasch, *Dostojewski als Verführer* (Zürich, 1961), pp. 23–30.
25. Rudolf Neuhäuser, 'Re-reading *Poor Folk* and *The Double*', *Bulletin of the International Dostoevsky Society*, 6 (1976), 32.
26. Roger B. Anderson, 'Dostoevsky's hero in *The Double*: a reexamination of the divided self', *Symposium*, 26 (1972), 109.
27. Viktor Shklovsky, *Za i protiv: Zametki o Dostoyevskom* (Moscow, 1957), pp. 60–1.
28. See Dostoyevsky's letter to A. E. Vrangel, 23 March 1856, in F. M. Dostoyevsky, *Pis'ma*, ed. A. S. Dolinin (4 vols., Moscow/Leningrad, 1928–59), vol. 1, p. 175.
29. B. Bursov, 'Dostoyevsky i modernizm', *Zvezda*, no. 8 (1965), 181.
30. Wolf Schmid, *Der Textaufbau in den Erzählungen Dostoevskijs* (Munich, 1973).
31. V. A. Tunimanov, 'Nekotoryye osobennosti povestvovaniya v "Gospodine Prokharchine" F. M. Dostoyevskogo', in M. P. Alekseyev (chief ed.), *Poetika i stilistika russkoy literatury: Pamyati akademika V. V. Vinogradova* (Leningrad, 1971), pp. 203–12.
32. Wolf Schmid, 'Die Interferenz von Erzählertext und Personentext als Faktor ästhetischer Wirksamkeit in Dostoevskijs *Doppelgänger*', *Russian Literature*, no. 4 (1972), 100–13.
33. W. J. Leatherbarrow, 'The rag with ambition: the problem of self-will in Dostoyevsky's *Bednyye lyudi* and *Dvoynik*', *Modern Language Review*, 68 (1973), 617.
34. Otto Rank, *The Double: A Psychoanalytic Study* (Chapel Hill, 1971), pp. 27–32.
35. I am grateful to Professor René Wellek for having kindly allowed me to read his paper, 'Bakhtin's view of Dostoevsky: "Polyphony" and "Carnivalesque" ', delivered at the Fourth International Dostoevsky Symposium, 17–23 August 1980, and subsequently published in *Dostoevsky Studies*, 1 (1980), 31–9.
36. Katharine Strelsky, 'Dostoevsky's early tale *A Faint Heart*', *Russian Review*, 30 (1971), 146–53.
37. Sonia Ketchian, 'The theme of suggestion in Dostoevsky's *Slaboe serdce*', in J. T. Baer and Norman W. Ingham (eds.), *Mnemozina* (Munich, 1974), pp. 232–42. Ketchian finds other examples of the theme of suggestion in 'The Landlady' and in *The Double*. See her article 'The

psychological undertow in Dostoevsky's *Xozjajka*', *Die Welt der Slaven* 25 (1980), 280–92. Cf. also Arban, p. 343.

38. D. S. Mirsky, *A History of Russian Literature from Its Beginnings to 1900* (New York, 1958), p. 183.
39. Vyacheslav Ivanov, *Freedom and the Tragic Life: A Study in Dostoevsky* (New York, 1971), pp. 34–5. Leatherbarrow's arguments to the contrary (see his article 'Idealism and utopian socialism', note 16 above) are by no means trivial, but neither are they entirely convincing.

2

The causes of crime and the meaning of law: *Crime and Punishment* and contemporary radical thought

DEREK OFFORD

I

It is one of the qualities of the greatest writers of imaginative literature that they succeed in capturing in their works both what is of lasting, universal significance and what is of most pressing concern in their own age and for their own nation. They deepen our knowledge both of man's experience in general and of his condition in a given society in particular. Thus Turgenev, in *Fathers and Children*, the novel generally acclaimed as his masterpiece, recorded in the most topical terms a conflict between generations and classes which has a relevance far beyond the Russia of the 1860s. Similar praise may be accorded to Dostoyevsky. His works have a profound bearing on some of the philosophical doctrines and political systems of the twentieth-century world and on the psychological condition of the individual in modern urban societies. They also throw light on problems such as crime, so central in Dostoyevsky's major fiction, which have come increasingly to disturb those societies. There is much in his works, for example, that is portentous for a world in which antisocial behaviour often constitutes a pastime for the reasonably well-to-do rather than a matter of economic necessity for the destitute, and in which, perhaps even more importantly, indiscriminate violence is often accepted as a legitimate means to a supposedly worthy end. And yet the insights into these problems with which Dostoyevsky can furnish us are the product of his participation in a debate about issues of great local and contemporary importance at the time when his novels were written. It is the relationship of *Crime and Punishment* to this debate that this article is intended primarily to discuss.

II

Dostoyevsky, when he came to write *Crime and Punishment* in 1865, had already made an extensive contribution, both in publicism and in imaginative literature, to the vigorous intellectual life of those years following the Crimean War and the death of Nicholas I when a more liberal regime flowered briefly in Russia and when the old order began to undergo irreversible change. In particular the hostility towards the radical camp which found expression in Dostoyevsky's writing in the early sixties was to become one of the prime creative influences in his major fiction.[1]

The radical camp, of course, contained individuals with divergent opinions. Moreover, the Western thinkers from whom the Russian radicals derived their convictions were themselves numerous and of varied complexion, ranging from the English utilitarian Jeremy Bentham, the early Welsh socialist Robert Owen, French utopian socialists such as Fourier, Cabet and Considérant, and the positivist Comte, to German philosophers and thinkers such as Feuerbach and L. Büchner, the contemporary English historian Buckle, scientists such as Darwin and popularizers of scientific thought, such as G. H. Lewes. But it is probably not grossly inaccurate to suggest that what was of most interest in Western thought to the Russian radicals of the sixties, and what constituted for Dostoyevsky a core against which his creative energies should be directed, might be reduced to a fairly limited number of propositions which were given wide currency in the journal *Contemporary* and in the voluminous, wordy and extremely influential writings of Chernyshevsky in particular.

These propositions may be summarized as follows: firstly, that 'no dualism is to be seen in man',[2] that is to say man does not possess a spiritual dimension which is qualitatively different from his physical being; secondly, that man is governed by self-interest; thirdly, that he is at the same time a rational creature; fourthly, that he may therefore be made to see where his best interest lies and to act accordingly; fifthly, that since man is amenable to rational persuasion and since his best interest lies in cooperation with his fellows, one might realistically hope to construct in theory and then in practice a perfectly ordered society; sixthly, that the good is that which is useful, and the useful, for the radical 'men of the sixties', was in turn that which promoted the dissemination and acceptance of the preceding propositions; and finally, that a scientific method of enquiry, and only that method of enquiry (with the help of which all the preceding propositions were supposedly formulated), could be applied successfully and profitably to the examination of human conduct, society and government.

Dostoyevsky disagrees profoundly with every one of these propositions. In his first major novel, *Crime and Punishment*, he makes explicit or oblique references, which are caustic in their context, to thinkers who defend them,[3] and vigorously disputes the propositions themselves. He implies, for example, that it is resurrection of the spiritual side of Raskolnikov's being which offers him his only hope of salvation after he has taken other lives. Furthermore, it is love of others, as preached and practised by Sonya, rather than love of self, which makes possible such regeneration. Raskolnikov is not capable of consistently rational conduct. His behaviour is frequently self-destructive. And Razumikhin inveighs bitterly against the socialist utopia (VI, 197; III, v). But in particular Dostoyevsky sets out to test in his novel the strength and acceptability of the last two propositions of the radicals, which concern the equation of the good with the useful and the omnicompetence of the scientific method of enquiry.[4] And it is through his examination of the subjects of the causes of crime and the nature and status of law that Dostoyevsky explores the implications of these two propositions and concentrates his argument against those who defend them.

III

There are no doubt several reasons for Dostoyevsky's choice of the subjects of crime and the law as his ground on which to do battle with the radicals.

Firstly, legal questions very much preoccupied educated people in Russia in the early 1860s and the novelist of the time, with his interest in contemporary reality, was entitled to devote attention to them. Overhaul of the judicial system was one aspect of the great reforms planned and carried out in Russia in the late 1850s and early 60s. An ukase of 1864 finally provided for the establishment of new courts on the Western model. Numerous foreign books on jurisprudence were translated, published and reviewed in this period and the journals devoted much attention to legal questions. Dostoyevsky's own journal *Epoch*, for example, carried lengthy articles on legal procedure, punishments, criminal law and lawyers, as well as the memoirs of an investigator, in the course of 1864–5.[5] In 1865 Dostoyevsky himself was contemplating an article on the courts, some notes for which are preserved in one of his notebooks.[6] Thus references to changes in the law and its administration, the proliferation of the legal profession, litigation, the increase in crime – there are allusions to forgery, seduction, and poisoning, as well as description of Raskolnikov's murders, in *Crime and Punishment* – help on one level to provide a broad social backcloth for the novel's main action.

Secondly, on a deeper level, the mentality of the criminal was a subject that already absorbed Dostoyevsky, the novelist of profound psychological insight. He had intimate knowledge of the criminal, gained in his years in prison among hardened convicts and recorded in *Notes from the House of the Dead*. In the journal *Time*, which he had edited from 1861 to 1863, there had appeared transcripts of famous trials of the century, and Dostoyevsky himself had written a preface to the first transcript (XIX, 89–90), dealing with the trial of the French professional criminal Lacenaire, a murderer who exhibits striking similarities to Raskolnikov (both Lacenaire and Raskolnikov are educated but impoverished young men driven obsessively to dominate; both are influenced by Napoleon, atheistic, antisocial and vengeful; and both publish speculative articles, Raskolnikov on crime and Lacenaire on the penal system).[7] It may also be that the great fictional possibilities of the subject of crime and its detection were underlined for Dostoyevsky by the novels of Dickens, in so many of which crime, including murder, is a central feature.

Thirdly, on the polemical level, the question of crime was one which also preoccupied the socialists with whom Dostoyevsky was taking issue. Like their Western European mentors, the Russian radicals of the 1860s expressed deterministic views on the causes of crime which seemed to Dostoyevsky as oversimplified as their views on the nature of man and his society. Robert Owen – whom Chernyshevsky's hero, Lopukhov, describes as a 'holy old man' and whose portrait hangs in Lopukhov's room – had taught the Russian radicals that crime was a natural product of the irrational organization of the British society of his day.[8] The 'poor and uneducated profligate among the working classes,' he wrote in his *New View of Society*, 'are now trained to commit crimes'; but with man's natural progression from a 'state of ignorance to intelligence', and the consequent implementation of 'rational plans for the education and general formation' of a society's members, crime would be eradicated. 'Withdraw these circumstances which tend to create crime in the human character,' he wrote with the ingenuous benevolence of the early socialists, 'and crime will not be created', for the 'worst formed disposition, short of incurable insanity,' would not long resist a 'firm, determined, well-directed, persevering kindness.'[9] Similarly, Büchner, who in the late fifties and early sixties exercised an influence on the Russian radical intelligentsia out of all proportion to his importance in the history of European thought, argued in *Kraft und Stoff* – a work much admired, incidentally, by Bazarov – that the 'chief causes of crime' were 'deficiency of intellect, poverty and want of education'.[10] In the Russia of the 1860s, where it became customary to explain a man's behaviour deterministically, as a product of his environment, views such as these were commonplace. Chernyshevsky, for example, in his major profession of faith, the article on the 'anthropological principle in philosophy' asserted:

> After the need to breathe...man's most pressing need is to eat and drink. Very often, very many people lack the wherewithal for the proper satisfaction of this need, and this lack is the source of the greatest number of all bad actions, of almost all situations and institutions which are constant causes of bad actions. If one were to remove this cause of evil alone, at least nine tenths of all that is bad would quickly disappear from human society: the number of crimes would decrease ten times.[11]

Likewise Dobrolyubov stated, in the tortuous style characteristic of the radical publicism of the time, that 'any crime is not a consequence of man's nature, but a consequence of the abnormal relationship to society in which he is placed'.[12]

Dostoyevsky's antagonism to such views is a major source of tension in *Crime and Punishment*.

IV

Now it is one of the qualities of Dostoyevsky as a novelist that he seems rarely to come down decisively in his works of art on the side of those views which it is clear from his publicistic works that he wished to promote. His vision as an artist is too complex to permit him to be one-sided or tendentious. It is arguable, for example, that he failed adequately to rebut the arguments of Ivan Karamazov against acceptance of God's world, although he himself evidently needed to disbelieve them. And by emphasizing the loathsomeness of the pawnbroker Alyona and the exploitative Luzhin he sets up persuasive arguments in *Crime and Punishment* in favour of the crime whose moral inadmissibility he undoubtedly hoped eventually to demonstrate.

Similarly he does not simply reject out of hand the radicals' thesis that poverty was a possible cause of crime (or at least a cause of the derangement which might induce it). On the contrary, he points out on the very first page of the novel that Raskolnikov was 'crushed by poverty' (VI, 5; I, i); for the second day running, we read shortly afterwards, he had eaten virtually nothing (VI, 6; I, i), and clearly his debility and illness are related. The oppressive and stinking milieu, moreover, 'jarred the young man's nerves which were already disturbed without that' (VI, 6; I, i). And when Raskolnikov does refresh himself after his first visit to Alyona's, his thoughts clear and all that has been passing through his mind suddenly seems nonsense, the result of physical disorder (VI, 10–11; I, i). Furthermore, the view that crime and social conditions are related is openly advanced in those chapters of the novel in which characters, with the murder of Alyona and Lizaveta in mind, debate the causes of crime. Luzhin, trying to restore his rapidly dwindling credit when he visits Raskolnikov in part II, delivers himself of a disquisition on the growth of crime in Russia, a phenomenon which Zosimov attributes to the fact that there have been 'many economic changes' (VI, 118; II, v). Later, during Raskolnikov's first visit to Porfiry, Razumikhin refers to a heated debate that had taken place the night before, in which someone had expressed the view of the 'socialists' that 'crime is a protest against the abnormality of the social order – and only that, and nothing more, and no other causes are admitted'. According to this view 'all crimes' would disappear once society was organized 'normally' (VI, 196; III, v). It is a view which even Porfiry appears to endorse: '"environment" means a lot in crime,' he affirms. And he seems prepared to carry it to the extreme, since when Razumikhin asks him whether 'environment' could be said to explain the seduction of a ten-year-old girl by a forty-year-old man, he replies 'with surprising gravity': 'Well, in a strict sense it very probably is environment, even a crime committed against a little girl may very well be explained by "environment"' (VI, 197; III, v). Lebezyatnikov argues with even more conviction in favour of such social determinism. He believes that everything depends on man's 'surroundings' and 'environment'. 'All on the environment,' he says in his broken Russian, 'and man himself is nothing' (VI, 283; V, i). In the society of the future, therefore, when all is rationally arranged in the interests of equality, there will not even be any fights (VI, 281–2; V, i).

However, we are not expected to accept the deterministic view of man's behaviour and of the incidence of crime uncritically. We are put on our guard against it by the fact that its advocates are, in Dostoyevsky's terms, unreliable. Zosimov, for example, merely voices the commonplaces fashionable among the younger generation. As a doctor he is the novel's main practitioner of the exact sciences which that generation exalted. He is the target of the invective of Razumikhin – the physically and spiritually healthy foil to the sickly Raskolnikov – against the 'dumb progressives' who understand nothing and show disrespect for man because they take too narrow a view of him (VI, 104; II, iv). And in practice Zosimov's judgement is repeatedly at fault: for instance he mistakenly assumes the murderer to be an experienced criminal (VI, 117; II, v); he wrongly predicts that the arrival of Raskolnikov's mother and sister will have a beneficial effect on Raskolnikov (VI, 159; III, i); and he fails to see in what way Luzhin is a bad suitor for Dunya (VI, 163; III, ii). As for Lebezyatnikov, he is discredited morally – he beats Katerina Marmeladova (VI, 14; I, ii) – and intellectually – he is the main apostle of Western rationalism in the novel but has great difficulty in talking coherently in his native language (VI, 307; V, iii). And Porfiry, although he is by no means an object of Dostoyevsky's criticism, does have a notorious capacity to mislead others for his own ends (VI, 197–8; III, v). On the other hand Razumikhin, the most vehement opponent of the view that 'crime is a protest against the abnormality of the social order', and 'nothing more' (VI, 196; III, v), is the champion of values close to Dostoyevsky's own. Indeed in a sense he is the 'positive hero' of the novel, Dostoyevsky's fictional response to the hero of Chernyshevsky's *What is to be Done?* Rakhmetov, with whom Dostoyevsky even confuses him at one point in a rough draft for one of the scenes of *Crime and Punishment*.[13] Like Rakhmetov, Razumikhin is physically strong, resourceful, independent, strong-willed and solicitous for his friends. He too is capable of feats of great endurance: Rakhmetov lies on a bed of nails to strengthen his will;[14] Razumikhin has gone through a whole winter without heating his room (VI, 44; I, iv).

More importantly, besides casting doubt on the reliability of those who uphold the deterministic explanation of crime or appear to do so, Dostoyevsky underlines the limitations of the explanation itself by demonstrating – as was habitual with him – that the problem could be approached from the opposite angle. The radicals' hatred of existing society and their overriding desire to bring about its material transformation lead them to attribute even individual acts of wrongdoing to unsatisfactory social conditions.[15] Dostoyevsky, on the other hand, being concerned above all with the spiritual condition of the individual, seeks to direct the attention of those who would examine the incidence of crime in a given society not so much to any aspects of the material environment as to those psychological factors which allow the individual to commit crime or fail to prevent him from doing so. Thus in *Crime and Punishment* he is perhaps less interested in motives for murder, such as the desire of the impoverished Raskolnikov to 'get rich quick' (VI, 27; I, iii), than in the modern attitudes which appear to make it irrational for him not to kill, given the weakening or absence of conscience. In particular he has in mind the utilitarian morality of the radicals who, in the course of their endeavours to redefine concepts and transform values associated with the established order, described the good as that which was useful and the greatest good as that which was useful to the greatest number, and commended the moral doctrine which they designated 'rational egoism'.

As critics have frequently pointed out, Dostoyevsky emphasizes the prevalence of the utilitarian morality of the radicals and makes clear its bearing on the murder which Raskolnikov commits.[16] In the letter to his prospective publisher Katkov, which he drafted in September 1865 when *Crime and Punishment* was taking shape in his mind, Dostoyevsky associated his hero's crime with current theories: the action was to take place in that year and the hero, who was to be a 'man of the new generation', had been carried away by certain badly thought out ideas which were 'in the air'.[17] Moreover, in order to emphasize that conversations about the possibility of killing in the interests of public utility were commonplace among the young generation, Dostoyevsky has Raskolnikov overhear a student advancing '*exactly the same ideas*' as those he himself is pondering (VI, 55; I, vi). (It is significant too that these ideas are put forward by a student, for it was in the higher educational institutions that the radicals found their most enthusiastic support.) Again, Porfiry emphasizes that the murder of the pawnbroker is a 'modern' crime and that the murderer killed 'in accordance with theory' (VI, 348; VI, ii).

But how precisely does the ascendancy of the new morality account for the commission of crimes which the proponents of that morality would attribute to social deprivation? The morality of the radicals, Dostoyevsky seems to argue, may produce such destructive results in three ways. Firstly, the adoption of utility as the criterion by which to judge the value of actions makes for a blurring of distinctions between acts which are absolutely right and acts which are absolutely wrong, that is right or wrong, moral or immoral, in all circumstances. Judgement of the quality of an action becomes dependent on extrinsic factors such as the value of its probable consequences. Seen from this point of view, acts which have traditionally appeared to be immoral are no longer necessarily held to be so. Lebezyatnikov exhibits this relativistic attitude when he says that what in the present society is 'stupid' may in the rationally ordered society of the future be 'intelligent' (VI, 283; V, i). But more importantly Raskolnikov himself applies it to crime. The murder, when its advantages have been calculated and the sum of its disadvantages subtracted, seems a useful act and is therefore '"not a crime"' (VI, 59; I, vi).

Secondly, by asserting the pre-eminence of the greatest number, utilitarianism tends to reduce individual human beings to mere ciphers who have value not so much in themselves as in relation to the larger groups to which they belong. It was not difficult to decide, Chernyshevsky wrote, on whose side 'theoretical justice' lay: the interests of mankind in general stood higher than the advantage of an individual nation, the general interest of a whole nation stood higher than the advantage of a single class, and the interest of a numerous class stood higher than that of a numerically inconsiderable group. This 'theoretical justice' had about it an inflexible quality which precluded appeal by the minorities or individuals who might be the victims of its implementation; it represented merely an 'application of geometrical axioms' such as the '"whole is greater than part of it"'.[18] Likewise for Dostoyevsky's student in part I of *Crime and Punishment* 'justice' (VI, 55; I, vi) consists in the promotion of the interests of the many at the expense of the pawnbroker and may be expressed simply and indisputably in the form of an equation: 'What do you think, wouldn't one tiny little crime be cancelled out by thousands of good deeds? For one life – thousands of lives, saved from rotting and decay. One death and a hundred lives in exchange – why it's arithmetic, isn't it?' (VI, 54; I, vi).[19]

Thirdly, by their doctrine of 'rational egoism' – in which the Russian utilitarianism of the 1860s chiefly found expression – the radicals tended to vindicate *egoistic* actions if the consequences of those actions could be claimed to have general utility. In this doctrine – which appears oddly incompatible with the socialist convictions it was supposed to bolster – the radicals contrived to accommodate both the proposition that man was governed by self-interest and belief in the feasibility of a utopia based on cooperation, by maintaining that man, when properly enlightened, would derive his selfish pleasure from performing acts of general utility. Raskolnikov clearly finds justification for his crime in the doctrine's identification of pursuit of personal profit, on the one hand, and promotion of general wellbeing, on the other (even though later, when he hears Luzhin parrot the doctrine (VI, 116; II, v), he is repelled by this potentiality in it (VI, 118; II, v)). For Raskolnikov seems to believe, as it was Dostoyevsky's intention that he should, that the murder of the pawnbroker and the theft of her money would benefit both himself and others: it would alleviate his own poverty but would also liberate his exploited sister from Luzhin and rid society of a louse.

Thus the radicals, far from providing a correct explanation of the incidence of crime in society, are putting forward moral views which are themselves responsible for crime's growth. The establishment of their doctrines, whose apparently incontestable veracity seemed to Chernyshevsky to preclude any 'unsteadiness in convictions',[20] has in the view of Dostoyevsky and those who were likeminded had the opposite effect: it has actually produced a discernible 'unsteadiness in the moral order'.[21] And far from tending to hasten the advent of a utopia in which acts hitherto considered criminal cease to be perpetrated, these doctrines encourage the development of an anarchic society in which such acts merely cease to be considered criminal and therefore may proliferate.

V

From the early stages of *Crime and Punishment* Dostoyevsky puts forward implicit arguments against the acceptability and even against the practicability of the utilitarian rationalization of crime. In the first place Raskolnikov himself tends to criticize rationalistic thinking when those he loves are the victims of its application. He is infuriated, for example, at the prospect of statisticians treating his sister as merely a number in a table indicating the percentage of the population which turns to prostitution each year (VI, 43; I, iv). In the second place, there are strong indications that human behaviour is not so exclusively rational as the utilitarians believe: Raskolnikov's crime is logically planned – he even measures the distance ('exactly 730' paces (VI, 7; I, i)) between his lodging and the pawnbroker's – and yet over its actual commission his reason has very little control. (Indeed he is forced to commit another murder, the need for which he had planned to obviate by ensuring that Lizaveta would not be at home.) Moreover, the deliberate artistic confusion of the first part of the novel, with its disjointed time sequence and sometimes fractured style, serves to point up the disorientation of the character to whom issues seem in theory to be so clearcut. But although these factors serve from the beginning to undermine the value of the morality Raskolnikov has adopted, in fact the search for a sound explanation of his crime leads deeper into error. For the theories which Dostoyevsky has Raskolnikov express in part III of the novel, concerning the right of certain individuals to 'cross over' normal moral boundaries and to commit acts generally deemed criminal, represent an examination of some of the further implications of the new outlook. Whereas the first apparent explanation of the murder raises the question of how an act should be judged and affirms that its utility should be calculated, the second explanation raises the question as to who should make that judgement and calculation.

Commentators have drawn attention to the relationship between, on the one hand, the ideas Raskolnikov expresses in part III of the novel, and, on the other, those advanced in a book by Napoleon III and in the works of certain Russian radicals who wrote for the journal *Russian Word* and were by 1865 conducting an acrimonious polemic with the epigones of Chernyshevsky on *Contemporary*.[22] It has also been noted that the use of the word *raskol*, chosen by Dostoyevsky to denote the schism in the radical intelligentsia in the title of an article published in 1864 in his journal *Epoch*[23] (which on more than one occasion mentioned the disagreements among the radicals with evident satisfaction),[24] would seem to anticipate the name, Raskolnikov, chosen by him for the hero of the novel he began to write in the following year.[25] And, of course, Lebezyatnikov refers obliquely to this schism in the novel itself (VI, 283; V, i). But since a few very striking similarities between the views expressed in *Russian Word* and those of Raskolnikov have not been fully brought out, it is worth briefly glancing again at this polemic and at the writings of Pisarev in particular.

In many respects Pisarev's views coincide with Chernyshevsky's. Pisarev preaches a materialistic doctrine similar to Chernyshevsky's; he believes that man is governed by self-interest; he repeatedly upholds the view that it is profitable for the individual to behave in socially useful ways; and he writes an extended encomium to the new men who practise this doctrine and whom Chernyshevsky had portrayed in his novel *What is to be Done?*[26] But Pisarev's rebellion is altogether more iconoclastic than Chernyshevsky's.

Whereas Chernyshevsky, writing in 1855 as the old order was just beginning to weaken, had given the cautious title *Aesthetic Relations of Art to Reality* to the dissertation in which he called in question the old belief that the beautiful was superior to everyday reality,[27] Pisarev, writing in 1865, when the attack on the old order was well advanced, undertook nothing less than a 'destruction' (*razrusheniye*) of aesthetics.[28] Old barriers were to be torn down unceremoniously. Literature, Pisarev wrote in 1861, for example, should strive to emancipate man 'from the various constraints imposed on him by the timidity of his own thought, by caste prejudices, by the authority of tradition, by the striving towards a common ideal and by all the obsolete lumber that prevents a living man from breathing freely and developing in every direction'.[29] His readers were exhorted to try to 'live a full life', without stifling what was *original* in them in order to accommodate the established order and the taste of the crowd. He urged the destruction, together with other old values, of that 'artificial system of morality' which crushed people from the cradle.[30] In short, Pisarev's doctrines are partially similar to those of Chernyshevsky; but, as Dostoyevsky jotted in his notebooks, probably under the impression of the article from which I have quoted, 'Pisarev has gone further'.[31] In *Crime and Punishment* Lebezyatnikov, claiming that he would argue even with Dobrolyubov were he to rise from his grave, makes the same point in similar terms. 'We have gone further in our convictions,' he says, identifying himself with Pisarev and his supporters. 'We reject more' (VI, 283; V, i).

Now it very often happened that ideas being expressed in the Russian publicism of the age were embodied in the fiction and that the fiction in turn stimulated the publicism. In fact between the publicism and the fiction there existed an intimate relationship; they responded to one another and moved forward together dialectically. And the freedom from traditional restraints already being advocated by Pisarev in 1861 found its fictional representation in Bazarov, the literary prototype of the new man to whom Turgenev applied the title 'nihilist'. Pisarev was delighted to accept Bazarov as an example for the new generation to follow, although in the second of the two substantial tracts he devoted to examination of Turgenev's novel he preferred the name 'realist'.[32] The mission of the new man, as Bazarov saw it, was not to build but to destroy what impeded new construction, 'to clear space',[33] and Pisarev gleefully proceeded to elaborate on the freedom the destroyer would enjoy. Armed with an extreme materialism that obliged him to acknowledge only what his five senses could apprehend, and governed only by personal whim and self-interest, Bazarov acted 'everywhere and in everything' only as he wished or as seemed to him 'profitable and convenient'. 'Neither over himself, nor outside himself, nor within himself does he acknowledge any regulator, any moral law, any principle.'[34] That such freedom might be a basis for anarchy Pisarev plainly foresaw, since he considered it necessary to answer the question as to why Bazarov does not turn to crime. But his answer was unconvincing. Only circumstances and personal taste, he wrote, make such men as Bazarov 'honest' or 'dishonest', 'civic dignitaries' or 'inveterate swindlers'. Nothing but personal taste, he continued in terms strikingly pertinent to *Crime and Punishment*, 'prevents them from killing and robbing' and nothing but personal taste 'prompts people of this stamp to make discoveries in the field of science and public life'. Pisarev did invoke rational egoism as a restraining factor: intelligent people realize that 'it is very profitable to be honest and that any crime, starting with a simple lie and ending with homicide, is dangerous and, consequently, inconvenient'.[35] But the die was cast. Pisarev, as Masaryk has put it, had 'vindicated for the nihilists the right to kill and to rob'.[36]

Those who are capable of exercising the new moral freedom possess great power, as Turgenev, Pisarev and Dostoyevsky all realized.[37] They enjoy an implicit superiority over those who remain bound by conventional restraints. In his essay on Bazarov, Pisarev underlined this division of humanity. On the one hand he saw the mass, whose members never use their brains independently. The mass 'neither makes discoveries, nor commits crimes'; it lives quietly from day to day 'according to the established norm'. On the other hand he saw the intelligent individuals who cannot come to terms so easily with all that the mass accepts. These individuals fall into three categories. Firstly, there are those who, being uneducated, are unable properly to take themselves in hand when they withdraw from the herd. Secondly, there are those who are educated but incapable of carrying their rebellion beyond a theoretical stage. And thirdly, there are those who are capable of implementing in practice their theoretical rebellion. These 'people of the third category' (*tret'yego razryada*) 'acknowledge their dissimilarity to the mass and boldly mark themselves off from it by their acts, by their habits, by their whole way of life...Here the individual attains his full self-liberation, his full individuality and independence.'[38] Chernyshevsky, at the end of his publicistic career, draws a somewhat similar distinction in *What is to be Done?* between 'ordinary people'[39] and those who are by implication extraordinary, although now the rational egoists Lopukhov and Kirsanov (who, as their names imply, have grown symbolically out of Turgenev's representatives of the young generation)[40] are themselves only ordinary before the epitome of independence, the iron-willed 'special man' Rakhmetov.[41]

Now Raskolnikov's speculative article on crime which is discussed in part III of *Crime and Punishment* owes much to current views such as Pisarev's on the division of mankind into the enslaved and the liberated. Indeed Raskolnikov says that what he is describing 'has been printed and read a thousand times' (VI, 200; III, v). Like Pisarev, as Dostoyevsky saw him, Raskolnikov has not merely flirted with rational egoism but has 'gone further'. He aspires, like Bazarov, to membership of that category of people who are bound by no moral law and who may waive those moral considerations that have generally restrained men from committing antisocial acts and continue to prevent the masses from doing so. Thus Raskolnikov has granted himself licence to destroy human life. He has committed the murder and robbery which Pisarev's destroyers might contemplate and has pondered the scientific discoveries and contributions to society which they might make if 'personal taste' disposed them to such actions. And he has murdered, it now appears, for no sound financial reason, but merely to confirm the freedom Pisarev had exalted. He is one of those who might be able to say a '*new word*' (VI, 200; III, v), the original contribution which Pisarev urged his readers not to stifle. His terms of reference are those of Pisarev too, although he has carried out a further simplification: the first category (*pervyy razryad*) is the mass, conservative by nature, which lives obediently; the second category (*vtoroy razryad*) consists of the 'extraordinary' men and women, the 'people of the future', the 'destroyers' (*razrushiteli*) (VI, 200; III, v). Finally, the elitism implicit in Pisarev's schema is reflected in Raskolnikov's pride, his arrogance towards 'ordinary' mortals. It is a trait which Dostoyevsky is concerned to underline at this particular point in the novel. Thus in the notes for part III he remarks that the 'thought of immeasurable pride, arrogance, and contempt for society' are expressed in Raskolnikov's personality;[42] and in the finished work Razumikhin tells Raskolnikov's mother and sister that his friend is 'arrogant and proud' (VI, 165; III, ii).

Raskolnikov, then, represents Dostoyevsky's conception of the man moulded by the new outlook and once all inhibitions have been properly stripped away. The self-will of this man accounts for a number of other traits in Raskolnikov's character which are brought out in the novel together with the explanation of the murder of Alyona as an attempt to test Raskolnikov's right to destroy, namely: the violence which threatens to erupt again at the expense of Luzhin; Raskolnikov's inflexible insistence on having his own way, manifested in his determination, of which his mother now speaks, to marry his landlady's crippled daughter (VI, 166; III, ii) and his demand that Dunya reject Luzhin (VI, 178; III, iii); and his own rejection of all authority, parental and divine, implied by his coolness towards and alienation from his mother and by spurning of prayer once he feels secure (VI, 147; II, vii). But most importantly, self-will finds expression in his attitude towards crime which now seems only a further logical consequence of the thorough rejection of all those 'constraints', 'prejudices' and 'traditions' execrated by Pisarev.

VI

As Dostoyevsky deepens the examination of the implications of current radical theory, so he broadens his consideration of crime, or more correctly, as the Russian word *prestupleniye* implies, of transgression. He now broaches important questions concerning the general rules by which the conduct of all individuals in a society is circumscribed, namely the laws. There thus begins in his work that profound debate on the nature and status of law which culminates in his last novel and crowning achievement, *The Brothers Karamazov*.

The word 'law', of course, may have not only a juridical sense of a 'body of enacted or customary rules recognized by a community as binding', but also, among many others, a moral sense of 'precepts' or 'binding injunctions' to be followed because they are dictated by conscience rather than by statute; and, thirdly, a scientific sense of 'correct statement of invariable sequence between specified conditions and specified phenomenon'.[43] The variety of meanings inherent in the English word 'law' is also available in its Russian equivalent *zakon*, although in Soviet lexicography the moral sense tends to be either blurred, merging with the morally neutral concept of a 'generally accepted rule',[44] or simply classified as obsolete.[45]

Numerous Western jurists have discussed the relationship of law in its juridical sense (which may be known as 'human', 'positive' or 'temporal' law) to law in some broader and more abstract sense.

They have considered whether there exists a 'natural law', that is a 'system of right or justice held to be common to all mankind',[46] and have asked themselves whether human law is an expression of such 'natural law'. Does human law then embody some principles of absolute, universal and permanent validity, can it be evaluated against certain immutable standards? Or does it merely reflect the values and needs of a particular society, and therefore have little or no relevance in other times and places?[47] (The debate is analogous to that on the question as to whether moral values are absolute or relative.) Now Dostoyevsky, as a Russian Orthodox writer passionately critical of most tendencies in Western thought, cannot be closely identified with any Western exponents or opponents of theories of natural law, but he is preoccupied with the sort of questions to which Western jurists have addressed themselves, and on one level *Crime and Punishment* represents his first major attempt to deal with them.

Law in its juridical sense – and it is with the 'juridical question' that Raskolnikov's remarks to Porfiry in part III begin (VI, 200; III, v); indeed Raskolnikov has been a student of this law – has little status for Dostoyevsky's anti-hero in his murderous frame of mind. It is clear that the concept lacks absolute authority for him, since he treats it in the same relativistic fashion as crime in part I and again in part III. All the great 'lawgivers' to whom he refers – the Spartan Lycurgus, the Athenian Solon, Mohammed and Napoleon (remembered in Russia not only as an invader but also as the promulgator of a new legal code on which Speransky largely based the code he was preparing for Alexander I)[48] – were at the same time 'criminals' by virtue of the fact that they destroyed orders sanctified by their forebears. Conversely, just as an act which might normally be deemed a crime was '"not a crime"' when seen from Raskolnikov's utilitarian point of view in part I, so the infringement of a law by a Lycurgus might with a similar change of perspective be seen as the establishment of a law. Lawbreakers or 'destroyers' might also be designated 'lawgivers' and 'institutors' (*ustanoviteli*) of mankind (VI, 199–200; III, v).

Historically speaking, the view that human law had some absolute validity, derived from the existence of an immutable moral law which it expressed, was weakened by the promotion of law in its third, scientific, sense. For thinkers like Comte, who accepted only those concepts which could be verified empirically, rejected as obsolete unproven hypotheses about the existence of God or the nature of man on which moral law rested. They were interested not so much in assumptions about how man ought to behave as in the description and classification of the ways in which he in fact did behave. Again Darwin, in demonstrating scientifically the adaptability of organisms in the struggle for survival, provided a biological precedent for thinkers who urged institutional and legal change in response to external pressures.[49] In this respect, therefore, he too helped to undermine the view that legal orders rest on some permanently valid principle.

The Russian radical thinkers of the 1860s, much influenced by Comte, Darwin and other Western writers who adopted a supposedly scientific approach to the problems that interested them, also treated as absolute and binding only the empirically verifiable scientific law and rejected any intuited natural *laws*. They insisted that a rational man could acknowledge only the empirical method of enquiry which proceeded along the lines of Comte's 'positive philosophy' and treated 'all phenomena as subject to immutable natural law'.[50] Such laws as had already been discovered in the natural sciences they propagated with enthusiasm and every effort was made to reveal equally immutable laws in disciplines such as the study of man's behaviour and even his aesthetic concepts, which had not previously been considered amenable to scientific treatment. Thus Chernyshevsky assured his readers that 'all the diversity' in human motivation and in human life in general sprang 'from one and the same nature in accordance with one and the same law' and set out to investigate the 'laws in accordance with which the heart and the will operate'.[51] Pisarev's thought is coloured by the same admiration of the natural sciences and the same faith in the universal applicability of the scientific method.

It is clear from the way in which Raskolnikov frequently expresses his thoughts in *Crime and Punishment* that he too, like many other members of his generation, is a devotee of the scientific method. Just as the student has done in part I, he presents in part III a mathematical equation, in which the discoveries of Kepler and Newton are weighed against the lives of 'one, ten, a hundred and so forth people who might prevent this discovery or might stand in the way as an obstacle' (VI, 199; III, v). He neatly divides humanity into 'two categories' and repeats the terms 'first category' and 'second category' and expresses qualifications parenthetically as if in a mathematical formula.[52] And towards the end of his monologue he uses an image already popular with Dostoyevsky to evoke the scientific approach (XIX, 131; V, 104; II, iv), alluding to the 'retort' in which the processes he has described are taking place.

He also says now that there must exist some 'law of nature' which determines the 'order of appearance of people, of all these categories and subdivisions'. He is convinced that an exact law governs the divisions of men into the categories he has postulated: 'there certainly is and must be a definite law'. Nor does the fact that such a law has not yet been discovered shake Raskolnikov's conviction that 'it exists and may subsequently become known' (VI, 202; III, v).

In appealing to scientific law Raskolnikov is in effect arguing not only that people who have a new word to say will inevitably break the established criminal law, but also that such people will inevitably appear. This scientific explanation of lawbreaking in turn diminishes the status of any moral law from which human law might have derived some authority. For the scientific inevitability of lawbreaking tends to reduce the culpability of the lawbreakers. A moral choice is valuable if there is freedom to make it. But if actions, in Büchner's words, are in the final analysis 'dependent upon a fixed necessity' and if therefore 'in every individual case free choice has only an extremely limited, if any, sphere of action', then criminals 'are rather deserving of pity than of disgust'.[53] And the smaller the degree of control a man has over his actions, the smaller becomes the burden of guilt he must bear for them. The legal implications of this argument were clear to the positivist criminologists of the second half of the nineteenth century, who 'instead of assuming a moral stance that focussed on measuring the criminal's "guilt" and "responsibility",. . .attempted a morally neutral and social interpretation of crime and its treatment'.[54] If crime was the result of abnormalities in the human organism or of inherited or environmental factors outside the control of the criminal, punishment was an inappropriate response to it. Raskolnikov himself, in invoking scientific law to confirm his right to kill, is brushing aside moral law and thereby detracting from his guilt: he seems, as the horrified Razumikhin notices (VI, 202–3; III, v), to permit the shedding of blood in accordance with the dictates of one's conscience, and he does not expect the 'extraordinary' man to suffer if he kills; indeed the greater the calculable utility of his act, the less significant will be the burden of moral responsibility he will bear (VI, 200; III, v).

The ascendancy of a scientific law, then, allows certain people to break the moral law as well as human law with impunity. Thus as law in one of its senses is promoted, so the status of law in another of its senses is diminished. The 'men of the sixties', who had shown such industry in redefining concepts and values such as the 'beautiful' and the 'good', had also shifted the emphasis of the concept of law from the morally binding to the scientifically inevitable. Indeed in so far as the 'extraordinary' men are granted free will, it had become morally binding, Dostoyevsky implies, for them to promote what was scientifically indisputable. For the establishment of scientific laws seems in part III of *Crime and Punishment* to have become the most pressing moral obligation. Kepler and Newton, to whom Raskolnikov refers in support of his thesis that 'extraordinary people' may 'step over' certain 'obstacles' (VI, 199; III, v), are unaggressive scientists whose association in Raskolnikov's mind with Napoleon seems at first sight strange. In fact they constitute classic examples of the discoverers of physical laws of motion of the sort admired for their apparent incontestability by the men of the sixties. (Thus in *What is to be Done?* Newton is extolled by Rakhmetov as the 'most brilliant and the most sane mind of all the minds known to us'.)[55] And to Raskolnikov the promotion of the discoveries of these scientists had evidently seemed so important that what might normally have been designated a 'crime' could have been in a sense quite legitimately committed in order to assist it. Raskolnikov seems to imply by his choice of examples, then, that the cause of the transgression of the law may be the need to establish a scientific law and even that such a transgression is obligatory. For although in one breath he denies that he insists, as he thinks Porfiry has insinuated, that 'extraordinary people inevitably must and always were bound to commit all sorts of excesses', he does in the next admit that a Newton, encountering obstacles to the dissemination of his discoveries, 'would have the right, and would even be obliged...' to eliminate the individuals standing in his way (VI, 199; III, v).[56]

VII

It is a repeatedly asserted or implied belief of Dostoyevsky's in the early 1860s that his radical contemporaries were wrong to concede omnicompetence to law in its scientific sense. By devising and upholding such law they neither provided an entirely accurate description of man's nature and conduct nor did they lay down sound rules about how he ought to behave.

Just as the observation of a utilitarian ethic tended to reduce to impersonal mathematical terms problems of human conduct which were properly speaking unquantifiable, so the attempt to bring all man's characteristics and behaviour under the jurisdiction of scientific laws resulted in an oversimplification of a very complex reality. In attempting to embrace reality in its entirety in some logically incontestable schema, the radicals failed properly to take into account aspects of man's being other than his reason; for phenomena which were not rational, or the existence of which could not be empirically demonstrated, did not seem to lend themselves to precise analysis. The exponents of the supposedly scientific doctrines, Dostoyevsky wrote in his notebook, were 'theoreticians' who wished to 'clip' man, to shear off him those parts of his being which did not accord with the soothing theories they had devised in the isolation of their studies or which might serve to obstruct the development of the utopias they envisaged.[57] There are references to such simplification in *Crime and Punishment* too: Razumikhin, for example, accuses the socialists of failing to take human nature into account when designing their phalansteries. 'All the mysteries of life' they try to accommodate 'on two printer's sheets' (VI, 197; III, v). In particular the radicals seemed to Dostoyevsky to ignore man's often irrational craving to assert his individuality, to preserve at least that illusion of free will so cherished by the Underground Man. They also failed to take into consideration conscience, the 'moral sense of right and wrong'[58] which might inhibit harsh treatment of one's fellows. Individual conscience, having no bearing on the general utility of an action, is not a faculty to which the student in part I of *Crime and Punishment* is prepared to devote serious attention (VI, 54; I, vi). And Raskolnikov, treating it more as an attribute of the oppressed mass than as an innate human characteristic, expects to remain free of the remorse it might arouse (VI, 203; III, v).

In opposition to the supposedly irrefutable scientific laws exalted by the radicals, Dostoyevsky puts forward certain laws of his own which seem to him more accurately to describe reality as he perceives it. There is a 'law of truth and human nature', he writes in his letter to Katkov, which leads the criminal voluntarily to accept 'torments'.[59] The suffering required by the criminal and described by Porfiry as a 'great thing' (VI, 352; VI, ii) contrasts with the pleasure which utilitarianism postulates as the only end of man's existence. It is a law of nature for Porfiry, moreover, that a criminal like Raskolnikov, pursued by psychological methods, and left at large in the uncertainty dreaded by the rationalist, will eventually trap himself (VI, 262; IV, v). And 'facts' – the investigator's equivalent of scientific data, which it is not really proper for him to question (VI, 346; VI, ii) – Porfiry treats with scepticism, for they may lead him into error no less than the 'abstract arguments of reason' which have so beguiled Raskolnikov (VI, 263; IV, v).

Not only does Dostoyevsky suggest the existence of psychological laws at variance with those accepted by the radicals (whose approach to psychology, as Dostoyevsky perceives it, is reflected in *Crime and Punishment* in the statements of Zosimov on the subject (e.g. VI, 159; III, i)). More importantly Dostoyevsky also reinstates the moral law which scientific law tended to ignore or to suppress. The moral law emanated not from the reason – only a 'twentieth part' of the Underground Man's capacity for living (V, 115; II, v) – but from the spiritual side of man's nature which, Chernyshevsky had categorically stated, did not exist.[60] In opposition to Chernyshevsky's supposedly scientific law, which asserted that egoism was the basic impulse of all human actions,[61] Dostoyevsky's moral law postulated in man a need for 'sacrifice', the submission of one's ego to others in selfless love.[62] It is clearly this law which Dostoyevsky believes will prevail in the final stage of human development, designated 'Christianity' and envisaged by him in plans for an article drafted shortly before he embarked on the writing of *Crime and Punishment*. The Christian phase would supplant and stand in opposition to a phase designated 'civilization', characterized by the extreme development of the individual consciousness and crowned by the advent of socialism.[63] And it is Christ's commandment 'Thou shalt love thy neighbour as thyself', observed in *Crime and Punishment* by Sonya, which ultimately prohibits acts based on the supposedly scientific precept approved by Luzhin, 'Love, above all, thyself alone' (VI, 116; II, v).

For Dostoyevsky the moral law, not any scientific law, is sovereign: there is 'one law – the moral law', he wrote in a rough draft of one of the scenes of the novel.[64] Beside this law human law pales into insignificance. Thus Porfiry, although he is the chief agent of the human law in *Crime and Punishment*, is manifestly 'less concerned with apprehending Raskolnikov as a criminal,' as Richard Peace has aptly put it, 'than with saving him as a human being'.[65] In any case the '[juridical] punishment for a crime,' Dostoyevsky wrote in his letter to Katkov, 'frightens a criminal much less than they [the lawgivers] think, in part because *he himself morally requires* it'.[66] But the unimportance of the human law beside the moral law does not entitle one to break it. For whereas the promotion of supposedly scientific laws tended to weaken existing legal codes by making crime a relative concept, the reinstatement of moral law strengthened them by making acts such as killing absolutely wrong.

Raskolnikov therefore does not have the right to disregard human law on the grounds that its authority is threatened by inevitable political, social or intellectual change; on the contrary, he is bound to obey it because it expresses a higher Christian principle.

VIII

The points I have made stand in need of three qualifications. Firstly, Dostoyevsky was not a singleminded publicist, like Chernyshevsky, but first and foremost an artist committed to faithful and full representation of reality as he perceived it; he did not therefore give definitive answers to the questions he posed. Secondly, some of the views implicit in *Crime and Punishment* were not fully developed by Dostoyevsky for more than another decade, until he presented that profound debate which takes place in *The Brothers Karamazov* on the relationship between the 'laws of Christ' and the laws of the state and on the need to punish the criminal by cutting off not a limb but a soul (XIV, especially 55–63; I, v). And thirdly, to read the novel primarily as a contribution to the intellectual life of the period is to illuminate it only partially and to leave out of consideration its artistic riches and other qualities.

Nevertheless it is true to say that Dostoyevsky, unlike Turgenev, did have passionate convictions which find expression in his novels. Moreover, Dostoyevsky's objections to the new radical *Weltanschauung* had on the whole become clear by the time he came to write *Crime and Punishment* in 1865. Most importantly, it was probably mainly out of a desire to state or at least to clarify these objections that Dostoyevsky now raised numerous important questions. Is man's behaviour determined by circumstances outside his control? Is he bound, if placed in certain conditions, to commit crime? Should criminals be considered blameless for their actions? Is it unjust that criminals should suffer punishment? Is the individual unimportant by comparison with the larger group to which he belongs? Do affirmative answers to these questions help to promote crime by destroying in the individual a sense of responsibility for his actions and love and respect for his fellows? And it is in no small measure from Dostoyevsky's examination of these questions – to which radical contemporaries seemed to give such crude and dogmatic answers – that *Crime and Punishment* derives its lasting and universal significance.

Notes

1. Dostoyevsky's reactions in the early 1860s to some of the views of the radicals are described in my article 'Dostoyevsky and Chernyshevsky', *Slavonic and East European Review*, 57 (1979), 509–30.
2. N. G. Chernyshevsky, 'Antropologicheskiy printsip v filosofii', in his *Polnoye sobraniye sochineniy* (Moscow, 1939–50), vol. 7, p. 240.
3. See *PSS* VI, e.g. pp. 16 (Lewes), 197 (reference to phalanstery of French utopian socialists), 280 (Fourier and Darwin), 283 (Dobrolyubov).
4. The relationship of *Crime and Punishment* to current polemics in Russia has not been very fully examined except by Joseph Frank, 'The world of Raskolnikov', *Encounter*, 26 (June 1966), 30–5. See also Richard Peace, *Dostoyevsky: An Examination of the Major Novels* (Cambridge, 1971), pp. 19ff.
5. E.g. the nos. for October 1864, February 1865, March, May and November 1864.
6. See Dostoyevsky's *Zapisnyye knizhki*, published in *Literaturnoye nasledstvo*, 83 (1971), 219.
7. See Katharine Strelsky, 'Lacenaire and Raskolnikov', *Times Literary Supplement*, 8 January 1971, 47. The transcript of the trial and Dostoyevsky's preface to it were published in *Vremya*, February 1861.
8. N. G. Chernyshevsky, *Chto delat′?*, in his *Polnoye sobraniye sochineniy*, vol. 11, p. 175.
9. Robert Owen, *A New View of Society* (Harmondsworth, 1970), pp. 99, 104, 106, 125. Owen's italics.
10. L. Büchner, *Force and Matter* (London, 1864), p. 246.
11. Chernyshevsky, 'Antropologicheskiy printsip', p. 266.
12. N. A. Dobrolyubov, 'Tyomnoye tsarstvo', in his *Sobraniye sochineniy v devyati tomakh* (Moscow/Leningrad, 1961–4), vol. 5, p. 47.
13. See F. M. Dostoyevsky, *The Notebooks for 'Crime and Punishment'*, ed. and trans. Edward Wasiolek (Chicago/London), 1967, p. 96 (*PSS*, VII, 71).
14. Rakhmetov comes to the fore in ch. III, sections XXIX and XXX of Chernyshevsky's novel; see esp. *Chto delat′?*, p. 207.
15. D. I. Pisarev maintained this point of view even in his review of *Crime and Punishment.* The cause of Raskolnikov's crime, he wrote, lay 'not in his brain but in his pocket'. (See Pisarev's article 'Bor′ba za zhizn″', in his *Sochineniya* (4 vols., Moscow, 1955–6), vol. 4, p. 324.
16. In particular see the discussion of *Crime and Punishment* in the light of classical utilitarian thought by A. D. Nuttall, *Crime and Punishment: Murder as Philosophic Experiment* (Edinburgh, 1978), esp. ch. III.
17. The letter is reprinted in Dostoyevsky, *Pis′ma*, ed. A. S. Dolinin (Moscow/Leningrad, 1928–59), vol. 1, pp. 417–21.
18. Chernyshevsky, 'Antropologicheskiy printsip', p. 286.
19. 'Arithmetic' and 'mathematics' are mentioned even more frequently, in connection with utilitarian morality, in Dostoyevsky, *Notebooks* (e.g. pp. 48, 53, 58, 65, 67, 69, 70) than in the finished novel.
20. Chernyshevsky, 'Antropologicheskiy printsip', p. 254.
21. N. N. Strakhov's comment, cited in the notes to *Crime and Punishment*

in Dostoyevsky's *Sobraniye sochineniy* (Moscow, 1956–8), vol. 5, p. 590. Dostoyevsky himself talks in similar terms in his letter to Katkov Dostoyevsky, *Pis'ma*, vol. 1, p. 418).

22. A lengthy examination of this polemic is contained in B. P. Koz'min's article, ' "Raskol v nigilistakh" ', reprinted in his collected works under the title *Iz istorii revolyutsionnoy mysli v Rossii* (Moscow, 1961), pp. 20–67. See also Frank, 'World of Raskolnikov'. On the book by Napoleon, see the notes in Dostoyevsky, *Sobraniye sochineniy*, vol. 5, pp. 582–3, and Peace, *Dostoyevsky*, p. 24.
23. 'Gospodin Shchedrin, ili raskol v nigilistakh', *Epokha*, May 1865.
24. E.g. the nos. for March 1864, pp. 339–43, and October 1864, pp. 1–9.
25. Peace, *Dostoyevsky*, p. 29.
26. Pisarev, 'Myslyashchiy proletariat', *Sochineniya*, vol. 4, pp. 7–49.
27. N. G. Chernyshevsky, *Esteticheskiye otnosheniya iskusstva k deystvitel'nosti*, in his *Polnoye sobraniye sochineniy*, vol. 2, pp. 5–92.
28. Pisarev, 'Razrusheniye estetiki', *Sochineniya*, vol. 3, pp. 418–35.
29. Pisarev, 'Skholastika XIX veka', *Sochineniya*, vol. 1. p. 103.
30. *Ibid.*, pp. 120, 122.
31. Dostoyevsky, *Zapisnyye knizhki*, p. 151. See also p. 167n.
32. Pisarev, 'Realisty', *Sochineniya*, vol. 3, pp. 7–138.
33. I. S. Turgenev, *Ottsy i deti*, in his *Polnoye sobraniye sochineniy i pisem* (28 vols., Moscow/Leningrad, 1960–8), vol. 8, p. 243.
34. Pisarev, 'Bazarov', *Sochineniya*, vol. 2, p. 11.
35. *Ibid.*, pp. 9ff.
36. T. G. Masaryk, *The Spirit of Russia* (London, 1919), vol. 2, p. 105.
37. It is perhaps significant that Dostoyevsky was one of the very few people whom Turgenev considered to have really understood *Ottsy i deti* (see Turgenev, *Pis'ma*, vol. 4, pp. 358–9, in *Polnoye sobraniye sochineniy*).
38. Pisarev, 'Bazarov', *Sochineniya*, vol. 2, pp. 15, 20–1.
39. Chernyshevsky, *Chto delat'?*, e.g., p. 227.
40. Bazarov in ch. XXI tells Arkady: 'iz menya lopukh rasti budet'. Arkady's surname, of course, is Kirsanov.
41. Chernyshevsky, *Chto delat'?*, p. 195. The expression 'people of the future' also became commonplace; it appears in the title of an article, 'Lyudi budushchego i geroi meshchanstva', published in 1868, by P. N. Tkachev, a revolutionary disciple of Pisarev, who had at one time contributed to Dostoyevsky's journal, *Time*. In this article Tkachev argues that the end (the happiness of mankind in socialist society) justifies means which may involve the transgression of commonly accepted morality (see his *Izbrannyye sochineniya na sotsial'no-politicheskiye temy* (Moscow, 1932–6), vol. 1, pp. 173–233).
42. Dostoyevsky, *Notebooks*, p. 188 (*PSS*, VI, 155).
43. The meanings cited are given in the *Oxford English Dictionary*, 5th edn (Oxford, 1974).
44. S. I. Ozhegov, *Slovar' russkogo yazyka*, 8th edn (Moscow, 1970).
45. *Slovar' sovremennogo russkogo literaturnogo yazyka* (17 vols., Moscow/Leningrad, 1950–65), vol. 4.

46. See the entry on 'natural law' in *Encyclopaedia Britannica*, 15th edn, *Macropaedia*, vol. 12, p. 863.
47. *Ibid.*, pp. 863–5; see also the entry on 'Western philosophy of law' (*ibid.*, *Macropaedia*, vol. 10, pp. 716–19).
48. See Marc Raeff, *Michael Speransky: Statesman of Imperial Russia* (The Hague, 1957), pp. 68–9.
49. *Encyclopaedia Britannica, Macropaedia*, vol. 10, p. 717.
50. Auguste Comte, *Cours de philosophie positive*, in his *Oeuvres* (Paris, 1968–71), vol. 1, pp. 11–12. Comte's italics.
51. Chernyshevsky, 'Antropologicheskiy printsip', pp. 283, 292; see also his *Esteticheskiye otnosheniya*, p. 6.
52. Compare the similarly mathematical syntax of D–503, when he is confident that all phenomena are comprehensible and explicable, in the early stages of Zamyatin's novel *My*.
53. Büchner, *Force and Matter*, pp. 240, 246.
54. See the entry on 'criminology' in *Encyclopaedia Britannica, Macropaedia*, vol. 5, p. 283.
55. Chernyshevsky, *Chto delat'?*, p. 197.
56. The pause indicated by the dots after the word 'obliged' in Raskolnikov's monologue seems to emphasize that he himself is aware that he is no longer talking about the possibility of transgressing but about the necessity or inevitability of doing so.
57. E.g. Dostoyevsky, *Zapisnyye knizhki*, p. 154. See also my article 'Dostoyevsky and Chernyshevsky', section III.
58. *Oxford English Dictionary*, 5th edn.
59. Dostoyevsky, *Pis'ma*, vol. 1, p. 419.
60. Chernyshevsky, 'Antropologicheskiy printsip', p. 240.
61. *Ibid.*, p. 282.
62. Dostoyevsky, *Zapisnyye knizhki*, p. 175.
63. *Ibid.*, pp. 246–8.
64. Dostoyevsky, *Notebooks*, p. 58 (*PSS*, VI, 142).
65. Peace, *Dostoyevsky*, p. 44.
66. Dostoyevsky, *Pis'ma*, vol. 1, p. 419. Square brackets enclose words written above the line in Dostoyevsky's manuscript.

3

Across the threshold: *The Idiot* as a Petersburg tale[1]

SIDNEY MONAS

The year and a half during which Dostoyevsky worked on *The Idiot* were for him high-pressure years. It was almost as though he were searching for some ultimate crisis, some last threshold of intensity, and if circumstances would not oblige him, he seemed exceptionally inventive in seeking them out. But even his marriage to a good, kind, self-effacing woman had its load of problems. His dead brother's family, including his adopted son, disapproved of the marriage. Shortly after the wedding, in a single day, he had two epileptic fits – to the horror of his new bride, twenty-five years his junior.[2]

While Anna Grigorevna was still working as his secretary, before they were married, he had told her he was 'standing on a boundary, and there were three roads before him: to the East, Constantinople and Jerusalem, perhaps to remain there forever; or abroad to Europe and plunge his whole soul into roulette-gambling which absorbed him so; or, finally, to marry a second time.[3]

Unfortunately, the third choice did not preclude the second. He used Katkov's advance for a novel he had not yet even conceived to pay off his debts, and he cashed in his wife's dowry to pay for their trip abroad.

There followed the period he called his second exile. He was ill; he was in debt; the gambling fever consumed him; everything he and his wife owned went into hock; and there came more and more money-demands from him to Katkov for the novel not yet written. Anna Grigorevna was stalwart, but she could not resist reading the letters he received from a former love. A daughter was born to them, but died in three months. Dostoyevsky borrowed money from Goncharov. He went to see Turgenev, whom he had borrowed money from years ago and never repaid. Deliberately, he set Turgenev up for a quarrel – an anti-type against whom he could formulate his sense of his own significance.[4]

No sooner had Dostoyevsky crossed into Europe than he wrote to his friend Maykov telling him how much he hated it.[5] Yet it was during this 'second exile' that he pulled himself back across the threshold of nervous collapse; it was there his second marriage took firm hold; and when he returned to St Petersburg in 1871, having pursued that 'illness' to its extremity, he left the gambling fever behind him. And he had finished one of his best novels, which he had written in a frame of mind somewhat resembling that of his gambling. Everything depended on it, it was all or nothing, only the novel could change his fate. He published the first part without knowing how it could go on from there. In the long-run – unlike his gambling – he brought it off.

Having left St Petersburg, he was the more obsessed by that city.[6]

In *Crime and Punishment*, published the year before he left for Europe, Dostoyevsky's Raskolnikov had stood on a Neva bridge overlooking a splendid urban panorama only to have a strange sadness come over him. The sense of Babylon, perhaps. Emptiness, hollowness made it sad. Its destiny was precisely to be used up – the city of the last end. Dostoyevsky's Underground Man had called it 'the most intentional', the most abstract city in the world. Yet as the capital and major port, it was the city into which everything Russian made its way, and everything European as well. It was the threshold-city, the window to and from the West, the *limen*.

The long dusk of St Petersburg was 'the suffused cheek of a tubercular girl'.[7]

St Petersburg was the city of rebellion on the one hand and submission on the other; arbitrary will and helpless acceptance; and strange 'cross-overs'. Filicide: the first political 'case' tried within the newly founded city was that of the Tsarevich Aleksey, who died of torture in the Peter–Paul. And parricide: for Dostoyevsky, any act of rebellion was implicit parricide, and St Petersburg was a city of would-be rebels. Aleksey's mother, Peter's first wife, confined in a nunnery, had laid her curse upon it, that it be 'empty', a city 'built on bones', a city of crumbling and 'accidental' families.[8]

Dostoyevsky subtitled *The Double* 'A Petersburg *Poema*' – an epic poem of St Petersburg. Golyadkin, the central figure, is on the threshold of schizophrenia, and the *poema* reaches a climax when Golyadkin's projected other self first appears to his deranged sensibility in a wild hallucinatory dance through the unreal city screened by falling snow. Doublings of sorts occur, too, in the language: puns, half-rhymes, alliteration. The use of mirrors; the watery element of rivers, harbour and canals that mirrors reveries; dreams, hallucinations, illusions, lies, tall tales (*vran'yo*), inventions, projections – these are the stock-in-trade, the *topoi* of the Petersburg tale.

The threshold, Bakhtin wrote, was the 'chronotope' of Dostoyevsky's novels.[9] For Bakhtin, 'chronotope' is the mode of expressing significant relations of time and space in a text, through which the reader may acquire a sense of the author's image of man and the authorial outlook on the world. While it is not the *only* chronotope in Dostoyevsky's fiction, Bakhtin points out how important the threshold (in its extended meaning) is.

First of all, literally: the scenes in doorways and through windows; at crossroads; in the public square where 'currents' or individuals coming from different directions meet; or in the living-room, which for Dostoyevsky, as Bakhtin points out, is often an analogue of the public square; on staircases, on landings and on platforms; at railroad stations or in a railroad car where people accidentally converge. The threshold-encounter is a kind of analogue, Bakhtin implies, for the phenomenon of dialogue – currents of thought that cross in speech.[10]

It is also an analogue for certain physical and psychological states – the boundary between life and death, the familiar and the strange, health and illness, reality and illusion, sanity and madness, waking and sleep, clearsightedness and hallucination, childhood and maturity. The sense of time that accompanies the meaningfulness of this kind of space is very different from that of developmental or biographical or continuous time. It is one in which specific moments are imbued with an intensity and significance that cause them to expand beyond any mode of abstract measurement; and the rest of time dwindles correspondingly into insignificance. It is, as Michael Holquist has put it, *kairos* as opposed to *chronos*.[11]

Time in a Dostoyevsky novel is always somehow discontinuous. Part I of *The Idiot*, which describes a period of less than twenty-four hours, takes 144 pages; and the six months which presumably pass before part II begins have only fragmentary and discontinuous moments of later reference. Myshkin, describing the heightened and illuminated visionary experience that comes to him before the falling phase of the epileptic fit, refers to that moment between the time a drop spills from the rim of a pitcher and when it touches the ground, which is sufficient for the prophet to contemplate all the kingdoms of Allah (VIII, 189; II, v).

The dream is the liminal state, psychologically speaking, in which themes moving from the unconscious to consciousness appear on the threshold of transformation.[12] Of all nineteenth-century novelists, it is Dostoyevsky who uses the dream most centrally and effectively as both a structural element in his novels and a profound revelation of character and intent. Ancillary to the use of dream is his use of the story within a story (one of the characters tells a story, which has great interest in its own right, but which also reveals the teller: Ivan's Legend of the Grand Inquisitor; Grushenka's tale of the onion) and of hallucination (Raskolnikov's projection of the landlady being beaten on the stairs). The threshold is always, in Dostoyevsky, a place of transformation; what transgresses is transformed; and to cross back over is to return transformed.[13]

If the dream is a liminal condition, St Petersburg is a liminal city where things happen 'as in a dream'. In St Petersburg, dream *is* the reality. Intentions crowd into the city and parade masked along the streets under the illusory streetlights, like the crowd in Gogol's 'Nevsky Prospekt'. The hallucinatory effect of the city is compounded by the fact that its thresholds are often disguised: what seems to be a wall turns out to be paper-thin, and words come across it that enter the mind transformed; a man falls asleep on a park-bench and dreams of one beautiful woman to wake up confronted with the presence of another.

St Petersburg is thus 'the most intentional city' in a double sense. It is the capital, city of conscious intent, sovereign will, itself the product of the Emperor's *fiat*, and from which the Empire is governed; it is also the dream-capital, the city of repressed intent, wishes unfulfilled, the city of poor clerks, impoverished students and ambitious dreamers. Both the natural setting and the architecture – the ensembles of palaces, the mannerist vistas, the watery surroundings, the fogs and tubercular climate, and the tricks of light of its far northern location – compound its ambivalences.

Though it begins under the sign of hope, a Petersburg tale is always sad.[14] *The Idiot* comes out of the most desperate period of Dostoyevsky's life, and it is surely the least buoyant, the least charged with hope and optimism of all the great novels. Its theme is, as Robert Hollander and others have eloquently demonstrated, apocalyptic.[15] Yet apocalypse is not only a revelation of the end, but also a veiled intimation of new beginnings. These are not lacking in *The Idiot*, but they are indeed thickly veiled.

Central to the novel and its problematics is the character of Prince Myshkin and the impact he has or doesn't have on those around him. We have Dostoyevsky's statement of intention – it emerges very late in the notebooks, it is true – to create 'a wholly beautiful [i.e. also 'good'] man'.[16] As Mochulsky put it, Dostoyevsky did manage to 'resist the temptation of writing a novel about Christ', yet still managed to create an immensely appealing if infinitely sad Christ-like figure.[17] But this figure has proved highly problematic, especially to recent criticism.

Guardini has emphasized Myshkin's resemblance to Christ. Malcolm Jones has tried to indicate the ways in which Myshkin differs from Christ, and to display something of what he calls his 'dark side'. Holquist insists on what he calls 'the failure of Heilsgeschichte', in spite of Christ and Myshkin, to bring peace, to persuade the lion to lie down with the lamb, or to convert *chronos* into *kairos*.[18] Indeed, almost all readers have perceived that Myshkin's passage through people's lives does little if anything to improve them; tends, on the contrary, rather to precipitate crises and make things worse. Some however interpret this as indicating the utter depravity of the world through which he passes, while others suggest that there is a certain talent for catastrophe, a certain malice hidden in Myshkin himself.[19] Still others, and among them the psychoanalytic critics, that the ideal of goodness that Myshkin sincerely and perfectly embodies is in itself deeply flawed and destroys both him and those he tries to 'save'.[20]

The hero of a Petersburg tale is always somehow caught on the threshold of the public and the private, the conscious and the unconscious, the real and the illusory. Pushkin's Yevgeny in 'The Bronze Horseman' was determined to lead a completely private life, only to be overwhelmed by the elemental public fact of St Petersburg itself. His aspirations to 'idiocy' – for as Blackmur reminds us, that was the original meaning of the word 'idiot', a completely private, a lay person, a mere subjectivity, outside the bonds of social hierarchy and professional status – are crushed by the ongoing wilfulness of the imperial project.[21] The hero of Gogol's 'The Nose' becomes an idiot when he wakes one morning to find himself deprived of that part of his body that symbolizes his aspiration to status, the part that looks *up* the hierarchical ladder, his nose. In Dostoyevsky's *The Idiot*, the split in personality has taken place before the novel in its finished form begins. We have a train moving from Warsaw to St Petersburg on a damp foggy day in late November 1867: 'In one of the third-class cars two passengers had been facing each other by the window since dawn, both of them young men, both with little luggage, both unfashionably dressed, both of rather striking appearance and each wishing finally to open a conversation with the other' (VIII, 5; I, i).

One is named Lev Myshkin, combining the royal and the humble in his very name, the lion and the mouse; the other Parfyon Rogozhin, another curious combination, the virgin, innocence intactus, combined with suggestions of diabolic horn, the roughness of bast cloth and the Rogozh Old Believers' cemetery near Moscow. One wears a European cloak much too light for the weather, the other a heavy peasant sheepskin. One is light, the other dark. One has a dreamy spiritual presence, the other a passionate look and a bodily magnetism. One physically resembles Othello, the other Iago, yet the roles are reversed – Iago is the spiritual one, the dreamer. What remains is the inseparable nature of their mutual dependence.

In the notebooks for the novel they were originally conceived as one. Before Myshkin became Myshkin, he was both Myshkin and Rogozhin, with perhaps a little of Ganya and some others thrown in.[22] He is conceived in the spirit of Dostoyevsky's archetypal 'great sinner' who *must* experience the utmost in sin in order to become, in the end, the great saint. In the first seven versions of the novel that Dostoyevsky sketched in his notebooks that is clearly the character of the central figure, an even more demonic Raskolnikov, in whose soul however redemption and blessedness slumber like a caterpillar in the cocoon. In the sixth plan of the novel, Dostoyevsky poses the vexing problem of the central character: 'Enigmas. Who is he? A terrible scoundrel or a mysterious ideal?'[23] And then (as Wasiolek puts it – 'a shaft of inspiration!'):[24] '*He is a Prince. Prince Yurodivyy.* (He is with children.)'[25] And the Christ-like Myshkin begins to emerge. By the eighth plan his character is integral and complete: 'The hero of this novel, the Prince, is not comical [this is to distinguish him from Don Quixote and Pickwick, two literary forerunners who figure prominently in his creation] but does have another charming quality: he is innocent!' (The word is boxed in the original.)[26] Correspondingly, Rogozhin is sensual, passionate, a man of the body, of the flesh – the shadow-self, in terms of the old gnostic tales. When Christ loses his shadow, in these tales, the shadow becomes the devil. And in the old German tale of Peter Schlemiehl, the man who loses his shadow loses his power to act effectively in this world.[27]

That Myshkin and Rogozhin are in some sense 'doubles' and inseparable has been noted by many critics, but it is Blackmur in particular who points out that it is only when they are together, acting upon and against each other, that the novel takes on its real fullness of being.[28] Others, especially Elizabeth Dalton, by far the best of the psychoanalytic critics, have pointed out that if Myshkin is all superego (a man cannot, of course, be *all* superego, and Dalton has acute things to say about what is or might be repressed in Myshkin's psyche, with her long chapter on 'The Epileptic Mode of Being' especially impressive) then Rogozhin is virtually all id; and what is missing between them is the ego, worldly wisdom, the sense of how to negotiate things in the given conditions of the world, the reality principle.[29] Murray Krieger goes even further than the Freudians in seeing the essential lack of ability for worldly accommodation in Myshkin as responsible for the murder of Nastasya Filippovna, for Myshkin's own relapse into mindlessness and for the general sense of catastrophe and/or impasse in which so many of the novel's characters are left at the end.[30] Harold Rosenberg acutely observes Myshkin's passivity, his unwillingness or inability to engage the action, the way in which the action rather seems to engage itself *through* him (VIII, 261; II, xi).[31] R. Lord goes so far as to see in the finalized character of Myshkin the cunningly hidden but nonetheless still present villain-intriguer of the early drafts.[32] Except for Lord, who is clearly mistaken, all these critics do point out, and some of them very acutely, essential things about Myshkin and the effect he has on the world around him. Except for Lord, these critics tend to see Myshkin and Rogozhin as polar opposites – their 'chance' meeting on the train to St Petersburg as the kind of chance that is the language of necessity – from whom a vital centre and an effectively functioning threshold are missing: worldly wisdom, the ego, the reality principle. Curiously enough, they all tend to look on Myshkin with the eyes of the Grand Inquisitor, which are the eyes of the ego and the reality principle.

There is a third significant passenger on the train that approaches St Petersburg – a sponger, toady and hanger-on, described as the kind of man who knows everybody, who makes himself useful and sometimes even indispensable by virtue of the fact that he knows everybody, the slick intriguer Lebedev. His name, which suggests a swan (*lebed'*, from the same ancient root-word as 'libido') and those fairytales in which erotic swans figure as transmogrified maidens, may also have a distant echo of one of the apocalyptic passages in the Igor Tale:

> Obida has come to Dazhbog's grandson and his men; like a girl she came to the land of Troyan; she wet her white swan's wings

> in the blue sea near the Don; and splashing her wings, she stirred up trouble.
>
> The princes had beaten the pagans, now they were beaten; and brother said to brother, 'This is mine; and that, too,' and the princes began to say of a little thing, 'It is a great matter', and to invent quarrels among themselves.[33]

A widower, genuinely devoted to his family (who include the near-saintly Vera and the poisonous nephew Doktorenko), a drunkard, a buffoon and above all a calculating intriguer, Lebedev is nevertheless a man of intelligence and imagination; his curious character serves Dostoyevsky both as a means for advancing the plot and as an ironical commentator on the depraved condition of Russian and especially St Petersburg society. For Lebedev has set himself up as an interpreter of the Apocalypse, of the Book of Revelation, and it is by no means the least irony in the novel that the man who seems to understand the Apocalypse best and apply the Bible most skilfully and imaginatively to the current Russian situation is himself a buffoon, a drunkard and an intriguer.[34]

In fact Lebedev serves beautifully to introduce overtly and explicitly into the novel those forebodings of the last end with which Dostoyevsky's 'second exile' was laden. Since their inception, he had been interested in the reformed Russian law courts, and of course he exulted in the fact that Russia had no death penalty – not everything was lost – and yet he was weighed down with the heaviest of premonitions. He followed crimes and murder-cases avidly, reading into them symptoms of the last end, yet trying to squeeze out of them at the same time some hidden sign of hope. The notebooks show how prominently the Umetsky case figured in his conception of *The Idiot*. And it is difficult to forget the explicit Russianness of the case Myshkin relates to Rogozhin, of the artisan who, before murdering a merchant-companion for his silver watch, addresses a prayer to Christ to forgive him for the crime he knows he is too weak to avoid committing (VIII, 183; II, iv). (Myshkin's point, of course, is that as long as there is faith, a common belief and a common idea, no matter what the personal weaknesses, there is still hope for the future.) There were also financial scandals, and scandals of mismanagement with regard to the railroads. Turgenev's novel *Smoke*, which Dostoyevsky hated, gave him a target – the rootlessness and homelessness, the un-Russianness of the Russian liberal. Less important – but he must have read it, for he never followed the thick journals more avidly than when he was abroad – some themes from Leskov's 'Waiting for the Moving of the Waters' (a preliminary version of the novel later to be called *Soboryane*, or *People of the Church*, or *Cathedral Folk*, which appeared in 1867 in *Notes of the Fatherland*) may have suggested some of the quotations from the Book of Revelation and almost undoubtedly the associations with Old Believers and sectarians that cling to Rogozhin.[35]

Lebedev interprets 'the star Wormwood' that casts a pall over the living waters in Revelation 8:11 as the network of railroads spreading over Russia. He hastens to explain that he doesn't so much mean the railroads themselves as the spirit behind the railroads, the spirit of self-seeking, capitalist enterprise, bureaucratic organization, speculation, large-scale external organization, the timetable, that is the organization of a large part of life by clock-time and external standards, and the fact that the Russian peasant bears the burden of the enormous cost of this first basic step in the industrialization of Russia on his overworn back, like the crushed peasant in Tolstoy's *Anna Karenina*. Lebedev sees the end at hand, very much as Myshkin, does, because the 'common idea', the common faith, is in danger of being lost as all pursue the goal of selfish interest in a war of all against all and only those with the mark of the Lord on their foreheads will be saved (VIII, 167–8; II, ii).

Lebedev is not slow to pursue his own self-interest. Indeed, he calculates beyond gain, engages in intrigues beyond even his concern for profit, and though one of his intrigues results in the death of his dearest friend and alter ego, General Ivolgin, for the most part they serve the end of opening things up and out, rendering fluid what might otherwise rigidify, keeping open what might otherwise close off, keeping things in motion, even though the motion doesn't lead anywhere, and the intrigues serve both ends against the middle. Only when he is with his family is he a different person, and also when interpreting the Apocalypse. Prince Myshkin sometimes brings out the 'better' Lebedev, yet sometimes he provokes the 'worse'.

Even within the family, there are two Lebedevs. There is the Lebedev who dotes on his new infant, on his beautiful daughter Vera and on his son. And there is the Lebedev who relates to, and perhaps one might even say 'produced' his wicked nihilist nephew Doktorenko. The latter is not much developed in the novel, but there is quite a bit on him in the notebooks. He is one of those figures who crowd into a Dostoyevsky novel, contribute to its energy and sense of charge and jammed-fullness, undeveloped as characters, but carrying with them a sense that development – a new novel – is somehow always with them; that they will cause something to happen, if not in this novel, then in another one. It is possible in this sense that Doktorenko may turn up later as Pyotr Verkhovensky in *The Possessed.*

There is a similar case with the Yepanchin girls. I suppose there are three of them because there are three Graces, and Dostoyevsky seems to have the Greek archipelago and 'the golden age' in mind when he writes of them. But Aleksandra is scarcely developed, Adelaida serves only as an occasion for Myshkin to tell her how to use her drawing talent – to paint the face of a convict about to be executed! Even Aglaya, whose Greek name suggests brightness, and who is chief of the three graces, though she is a powerful presence, has an uncertain development, as a number of critics, but especially Wasiolek, have pointed out.[36] Myshkin has told her that she is 'almost as beautiful as Nastasya Filippovna' (VIII, 66; I, vii). In the notebooks, Dostoyevsky attributes to her a number of deeds strikingly similar to those carried out by Nastasya in the novel:

> The Prince...wants to give Aglaya up. Frank discussions with Aglaya. Aglaya says all right and to avenge herself runs away with Ganya – on the eve of the wedding. The Prince is engaged to Aglaya...
>
> On the eve of the wedding Aglaya breaks everything off or else runs away with the count.[37]

Between the dark (Nastasya) and the light princess (Aglaya) there is a relationship strikingly analogous to that between Myshkin and Rogozhin. They are doubles; once, in the author's mind, before they became characters, they were conceived in terms of a psychological conflict which might (perhaps inadequately) be called 'submission vs. rebellion' or 'hate vs. love'; the two women were one conflict. Unlike Rogozhin and Myshkin however, who represent nearly polar opposites, Nastasya and Aglaya are each of them divided within themselves; the conflict lives on in each.

From the very beginning of the novel Nastasya Filippovna seems headed for the fatality that finally overtakes her. Most of the weight of the novel rests on it; nothing could seem more inevitable. So it is strange that the notebooks are full of ways that seem to be seeking to avoid that outcome, including even a putative involvement of Rogozhin with Aglaya! But Dalton is surely right in seeing these diversions as more frequent and more frantic just to the degree that the novelist's ruthless gift insists against his own apprehensions on the necessity and inevitability of the outcome that does finally occur.[38]

What clouds the characters of the two women is the uncertainty of their relationship to Myshkin and of their sexuality in general. Nastasya for a while sees Aglaya as an 'uncorrupted' version of herself, as the innocent beauty who deserves the prince. It is not clear that Myshkin sees her that way. In any case, Aglaya demonstrates her own demonic potential, beginning with her provocation of Nastasya and ending with what Dostoyevsky must have considered the ultimate act of rebellion, apostasy and transgression, conversion to Roman Catholicism and marriage to a Polish revolutionary count.

From the opening pages of the novel, on the train to St Petersburg, Myshkin carries with him 'something of the archetypal traveller...like the youngest son in a fairy tale, walking with an air of dreaming abstraction into the deep wood where some awful fate awaits him. Yet, like the youngest son, Myshkin turns out to be alert and courageous as well as ingenuous, and in fact his very ingenuousness disarms the ogres.'[39] But is he, as all the critics say, impotent? Rogozhin asks him if he likes women, and Myshkin stammers in embarrassment 'I? N-no! You see...Perhaps you don't know that, owing to my illness, I know nothing of women' (VIII, 14; I, i). Later he tells Ganya he cannot marry because he is an invalid (VIII, 32; I, iii). Rogozhin calls him 'a blessed innocent, and God loves such as you!' (VIII, 14; I, i). That doesn't prevent Rogozhin's fierce and intense jealousy later when it seems that Myshkin's relation to women is more obscure than at first appeared. Later, Myshkin and Nastasya live together for a month in the same flat – under what terms is not clear. Myshkin shows every sign of revulsion at the thought of Nastasya as a sexual object. 'For him, Myshkin, to love that woman with passion was almost unthinkable, for it would have been cruelty, inhumanity' (VIII, 191; II, v). And he tells Rogozhin, 'I don't love *her* with "love" but with "pity", as I told you. I think that's an exact way of putting it' (VIII, 173; II, iii). And Nastasya's sexuality is in itself ambiguous. She is a powerful beauty. Once she was a kept woman. In a certain social sense she can be and is regarded as sexually available. No doubt with this in mind, men respond to her. Even old General Yepanchin has 'plans' and buys her an expensive necklace. On the other hand, Dostoyevsky makes it clear that for five years, since she came to St Petersburg, Nastasya has had nothing to do with Totsky. Was she Rogozhin's mistress? Presumably she ran off to 'an orgy' with him, and lived with him for some time. But she confronts Myshkin: 'Ask Rogozhin whether I'm a loose woman, he'll tell you!' (VIII, 474; IV, viii). A number of times, and with considerable authority, her virtue is insisted upon.

Her withholding herself from Rogozhin is no doubt part of her invitation to his knife. The invitation stands because she cannot accept Myshkin's pity for her, and pity, Myshkin comes to insist, is all he can feel. At the same time, he assures Aglaya that for her his feelings are different; he pities Nastasya, but loves her. Later, Nastasya intervenes by writing to Aglaya and urging her to marry Myshkin.

Is Myshkin impotent with Aglaya, too? Is she perhaps his 'cure', so that he may marry after all, and have a future? Or is it also love of the 'charity' kind, and if so, can Aglaya be blamed for her irritability or even her dark suspicion that maybe all is not just charity between Myshkin and Nastasya Filippovna?

Nastasya and Rogozhin, the dark princess and the dark prince, seem clearly made for each other, as the seven-inch garden-knife purchased by Rogozhin in the cutlery shop seems made to be used. In Rogozhin's house, Nastasya has left a book for Rogozhin to read. The books she leaves behind her seem to bear the weight of her understanding as well as her taste and literacy. In her apartment, before setting off on her final rendezvous with Rogozhin, she left for Myshkin to find in his frantic search Flaubert's portrait of that other 'misplaced' and suicidal beauty, *Madame Bovary*. For Rogozhin, in his dark house that seems removed from time and history, a Moscow house in the middle of St Petersburg, with its *raskol* associations, its idiot mother-spirit (Rogozhin's mother), and its hints of murder and savagery, the suggested smell of some forgotten corpse hidden under the floor, Nastasya has left a volume of Solovyov's *History of Russia* – Dostoyevsky does not tell us which one, but surely it was the volume on Peter the Great, of whom and of whose 'civilizing' state-mission Solovyov was a celebrant. Myshkin notices the book, but is fascinated by the knife. As if absent-mindedly, he picks up the knife and stares at it. Rogozhin takes it away from him. He picks it up again. Finally, Rogozhin removes it by placing it in the book, punctuating the history of Petrine secularization with both a murderous and phallic thrust that has not been lost on an astute psychoanalytic critic like Dalton.[40]

She points out, too, Aglaya's parallel or analogous gesture, when she inserts Myshkin's somewhat unconventional letter into her copy of *Don Quixote*. Aglaya has identified Myshkin with 'the poor knight' of Pushkin's poem, which is in turn based on *Don Quixote.* Reading the poem aloud, she substitutes for the letters A.M.D. (Ave, Mater Dei), which the knight in Pushkin's poem has emblazoned on his shield, the letters N.F.B. (Nastasya Filippovna Barashkova) and tends to see the Prince's idealism in the project she imagines him undertaking of turning 'Maria Magdalena' (Nastasya) into a self-respecting, noble, ladylike Dulcinea del Tobosa (or the Madonna) (VIII, 209; II, vii). Of course, Don Quixote becomes in the end disenchanted with his project, and on the way to his death reconciles himself with the terrible nature of the real world in order to leave it for a better one. Myshkin's letter is presumably thrust somewhere between the project and its disillusionment.[41] It is also just possibly from this time that Aglaya begins to consider the Prince as 'hers'.

In the fevered atmosphere of Pavlovsk, just after Ippolit's botched suicide attempt in the early morning hours, Myshkin wanders distractedly through the park, having half forgotten his appointment with Aglaya, but sits down on the very bench (the 'green bench' she had pointed out to him) where he was to have met her:

> At last a woman came to him; he knew her, knew her to the point of suffering; he could always name her and point her out, but, strange to say, her face seemed completely different from the one he had always known and he felt it as tormenting to recognize her as the same woman. There was such remorse and horror in this face that it seemed she must be a great criminal and had just committed a terrible crime. A tear trembled on her pale cheek; she beckoned to him and placed a finger on her lips, as if warning him to follow her silently. His heart stopped beating; not for anything, not for anything in the world did he want to admit that she was a criminal; but he felt that something dreadful was about to happen, something that would mark his whole life. She seemed to want to show him something, not far from there, in the park. He got up to follow her, and suddenly near him he heard a bright, fresh laugh; he felt someone's hand in his; he seized the hand, pressed it hard, and woke up. Aglaya stood before him. She was laughing out loud. (VIII, 352; III, vii)[42]

Half remembering Aglaya, he dreams of Nastasya, and then bumps into Aglaya, who laughs. Though one woman is dark and the other light, though one weeps and the other laughs, one has suffered and the other is as yet inexperienced, they do not involve opposite choices. The beauty of the Madonna which is to save the world and the beauty of Sodom which damns it contend in both women, and it is not the Madonna who wins in either case, but self-will, rebellion and self-destruction.

Ippolit, a youth of seventeen or eighteen, precocious, rebellious, whose great gifts will not make it to maturity because he is dying of consumption, is the only character in the novel beside Rogozhin, Nastasya and Lebedev who is not diminished by the Prince even while presumably being enhanced by him. Like Rogozhin, he is a kind of alter ego, a double to the Prince, but where Rogozhin seems to represent the rebellion of the flesh against the spirit, Ippolit represents the mind. Like his namesake in Euripides and Racine, he is a tamer of the wild horses of intellect; like him, he is in love with his own virtue, convinced that the universe has committed a kind of crime against him, and that since he has been excluded from the life of the world by the 'death sentence' that has been imposed upon him, he must make a drama of his exclusion in which he may appear however briefly as the director of the play instead of its puppet.

Critics like Wasiolek who come down hard on Ippolit for his vanity tend to overlook his age, which is that of Narcissus.[43] His mind is in many ways grown up; certainly, it is brilliant. He is just in process of discovering its powers when he receives what he calls his 'death sentence'. One cannot help thinking of Myshkin's account of the condemned man's attempted escape into timelessness; or the possibilities of the timeless moment of the severed head, also described by Myshkin. Ippolit seems to move in the opposite direction; to exult in his captivity to chronological time. The ticking clock is as much his enemy as it was Baudelaire's, but before smashing it, Ippolit feels he must exalt it. Thus he exalts his own plight.

It has been argued that, after all, the basic conditions of mortality are the same for all. No one knows when he is going to die. It could be a long time from now or in the next few minutes. The mature man lives as he must regardless of the time of the end. That is assuredly a good existentialist position. (Ippolit, after all, turns out to be quite mistaken about the hour of his death.) But Ippolit is not a mature man; he is an adolescent on the threshold of fully conscious life. Only Nastasya and the Prince understand and sympathize with his rebellion; Rogozhin understands, but disapproves of the style.

Ippolit cannot accept his fate; with what Dostoyevsky considers to be the typically rebellious psychology of the gambler, he refuses to accept it. The laws of nature are devouring him: that is not the way he would choose to be a part of nature. The green trees of suburban Pavlovsk are a symbol of life – Myshkin offers them to him that he may 'breathe easier', and at first he refuses. He talks about 'Meyer's wall', the dingy brick wall that faces the window of his apartment. 'Yet that wall is dearer to me than all the Pavlovsk trees,' he says (VIII, 326; III, v). In *Notes from Underground* Dostoyevsky's narrator used the image of a brick wall as a symbol for the laws of nature which the narrator refuses to 'accept'. At the same time, the wall – any wall – is a natural symbol of exclusion: a wall is designed to keep at least some people out. So Ippolit broods upon his exclusion, except as victim from the laws of nature. Roger Cox writes that the apocalyptic references in *The Idiot* are sufficiently strong and numerous to suggest also a resemblance between Meyer's wall and the New Jerusalem that descends in the Book of Revelation. It too has a wall around it, and presumably the wall excludes unbelievers.[44]

Like most adolescents, Ippolit is indecisive. He winds up in Pavlovsk after all. In telling stories about himself, he dwells both on destructive-rejective incidents and acts of exceptional charity. He cannot make sense, or an identity, out of either. Myshkin and Rogozhin contend for his soul. Ippolit points out that since he is doomed to die very soon in any case, there is nothing to deter him from committing a gratuitous act of murder of the kind Dostoyevsky was reading about in the Russian papers. He could kill ten people. Myshkin smiles at the thought of Ippolit killing ten people. Rogozhin does not smile.

In Rogozhin's house there is a 'good' copy of Holbein's painting of Christ just after he has been taken down from the cross. Blackmur calls it the dominant icon of that house, and it is surely an image that has resonance throughout the novel.[45] Myshkin remembers having seen and been appalled by it in the museum at Basel. 'Looking at that picture, a man could lose his faith,' Rogozhin says. It confronts the viewer with the overwhelming fact of death, of mortality, the agony of suffering and the improbability of resurrection. It is Ippolit who describes it in detail:

> It seemed altogether the corpse of a man who has borne infinite agony even before crucifixion, who has been wounded, tortured, beaten by guards, beaten by the people when he carried the cross and fell beneath its weight, and who, finally, has suffered the agony of crucifixion lasting for six hours (by my calculation, at least)...a man who has *just* been taken

> down from the cross; that is, a face which still retains much warmth and life; nothing in it is rigid yet, and the suffering seems to continue in the face of the dead man as if he were still feeling it (the artist has caught this very well); on the other hand, the face has not been spared in the least; *it is no more than nature itself* [my italics]...His body on the cross was fully subject to the laws of nature...A certain curious question arises: if such a corpse (and it certainly must have been like that) was seen by all His disciples, by those who were to become His chief apostles, by the women who had followed Him and stood at the foot of the cross, by all who believed in Him and adored Him, how could they believe, gazing at a corpse like that, that this martyr would be resurrected? (VIII, 338–9; III, vi)

Holbein's picture represents Ippolit's 'tarantula-god' – the ruthlessness, the imperviousness to human desire, the inflexibility to the point of seeming malice of the laws of nature – a role roughly analogous to the 'more than natural' stench produced by Zosima's body in *The Brothers Karamazov*. A more direct analogue in *The Idiot* is Ippolit's Kafka-like dream of the tarantula-god's attack upon him in the form of a kind of scorpion-snake, into which Hollander reads the image of Antichrist, and it must be said that the laws of nature seen as a malign being and invested with godlike power indeed provide a fitting image for the Antichrist.[46]

The other form that the tarantula-god takes for Ippolit is Rogozhin himself. There are three characters whom Rogozhin haunts like a spectre, and he drives them all to despair – Nastasya, Myshkin and Ippolit. They see him most often as a pair of burning eyes. But Ippolit sees him too as a hallucinated presence – literally a ghost sitting in a chair beside his sickbed, silently staring at him. It is that presence which precipitates his decision to commit suicide.

Ippolit needs to die eloquently, as Radomsky puts it. He is full of literary flourishes, and also self-ironic asides, commentaries on the flourishes. 'And suddenly, quite unexpectedly, he pulled from his inner pocket a large envelope sealed with a large red seal...This unexpected action produced a sensation among the company, which was by now fortified for anything, but not for that' (VIII, 318; III, v). Breaking the seal like the angel of the Apocalypse, Ippolit announces: 'Tomorrow "there will be no more time!"' and laughs hysterically. He reads what he calls 'My Necessary Explanation', to which he had placed the epigraph, '*Après moi le déluge*!' Then he adds: 'Could I seriously have put such a stupid epigraph?' Of course, it is an extremely adolescent gesture, adolescent self-inflation. It says: look, I am about to die, and you really should be taking this much more seriously than you seem inclined to, because my death is but the harbinger of the larger death to come, which will include your own. Or even perhaps: my end is the end of all. Ippolit squirms in self-irony as he catches the pitiful, helpless, appealing, adolescent forced bravado of all this. He even anticipates Rogozhin's bitter grin: 'That ain't the way it ought to be handled, lad; not like that' (VIII, 320; III, v). But he goes on.

Two things are worth noting here. First, that at one point in his notebooks Dostoyevsky seemed inclined to let the whole weight of the novel rest on the character of Ippolit.[47] Clearly, this notion was superseded like so many others. Yet clearly the reading of the 'Necessary Explanation' is one of the high points of the novel, and it follows the apocalyptic speculations and interpretations of Lebedev. It converts the Prince's party from a celebration to a doomsday foreboding, and the play of deep sincerity with sham adolescent hypocrisy does not diminish its impact. Secondly, '*le déluge*' besides fitting into the apocalyptic imagery joins associations of the French Revolution, of mass rebellion against injustice and denial of 'rights' with that most archetypal Petersburg image, the flood. It should be pointed out too that in Pushkin's 'The Bronze Horseman', the original Petersburg tale, the St Petersburg flood of 1824 is linked through Pushkin's imagery with a rebellious bandit-cossack horde, so that rebellion and *le déluge* are doubly bound together. Pushkin's hero, Yevgeny, is both the creature of St Petersburg and its victim – like Ippolit.

The Book of Revelation tells us that 'those who are neither hot nor cold shall be spewed forth', and Dostoyevsky disposes of such characters as the Ptitsyns and Ganya (for whom in the notebooks there were a number of other plans!) by referring in an unusual and magisterial authorial aside to their 'middling' calculating natures. For Ganya, after all, the 'King of the Jews' was Rothschild! But Ippolit too refers to Rothschild as 'King of the Jews', and it cannot be said of Ippolit that he is 'neither hot nor cold'. In any case, Rothschild is a role that the tarantula-god has denied him, and he can only rail at others who presumably have a full lifetime at their disposal and do not become Rothschilds. Ippolit is a waverer – he cannot move decisively one way or the other – but in his wavering he is intensely passionate. He is attracted to the Prince and revolts against him: '"Let me tell you that if there's anyone I hate here –"

he started yelling, with a rattle and shriek and a sputter of spray from his mouth, "and I hate you all, every one of you! – it's you, you treacly, Jesuitical soul, idiot, philanthropic millionaire, it's you I hate more than anyone or anything in the world!"' (VIII, 249; II, x). He is repelled by Rogozhin, and fascinated and haunted by him. He begins glued to 'Meyer's wall', yet he ends up in Pavlovsk after all. He does not commit suicide. He does not die as or when he anticipated, yet soon enough, after all. An adolescent, he stands on the threshold where his posture points passionately first in one direction and then in the other; yet he cannot move across.

Myshkin thinks that beauty will save the world; Rogozhin stands as his reminder that it is beauty that needs to be saved. A man of flesh, of passion, Rogozhin is also a man of will. Indeed, it is through the manifestation and operation of will that he makes his presence so powerfully felt in the novel. After a characteristically brief physical description of him on the train (dark hair, pale face, pallor enhanced by a still burning fever) Dostoyevsky allows his physical appearance to fade almost completely away and he appears most often in the rest of the novel as 'a pair of burning eyes' or simply as an undescribed physical presence. And this presence tends to make its impact on the reader as much by what it does not do, by its exercise of impassioned restraint, as by what it does. After having sent his minions scurrying about St Petersburg to raise a million roubles in cash for Nastasya Filippovna, he stands by impassively, not moving a muscle as she throws the million-rouble bundle into the fire. During the horrendous confrontation of Aglaya and Nastasya, with Myshkin as the object of contest, Rogozhin stands silently by, knowing that he will lose Nastasya again, and when she dismisses him, he leaves without a word. He looms as destructive and threatening largely through the grim-lipped and foreboding silence he maintains.

As a Dionysian, orgiastic figure, he maintains a band of ruffians and rowdies who spy for him and do his bidding. One is given several reminders that the passion of his father and his brother Semyon had been for accumulation. Their association is with the Old Believers and the *skoptsy* (a heterodox religious sect that practised self-mutilation), more as a hint of pervasive superstition, set-apartness, closed-offness, than as a commitment to religious feeling. Nevertheless, the symbols and traces of religious feeling never entirely disappear. The religion of the household, however, the tie that binds, is possession. For old Rogozhin and for Semyon that religion is money, gold, goods – the avarice framed in superstition of an old merchant family, an avarice beyond mere commonplace miserliness, an avarice like that of Pushkin's 'Covetous Knight', an avarice that is monomania for possession comparable to a desert saint's passion for God. Semyon cuts off the gold tassels from old Rogozhin's coffin that they not go to waste. ('I could have had him put away for blasphemy,' comments Parfyon (VIII, 10; I, ii).)

Rogozhin's passion is not for gold or goods but for flesh; rather, not for flesh either. It is not the whore Nastasya that attracts him, but the saint. Unlike Myshkin, he cannot believe in her innocence; but it is her suffering that he must possess, her soul. He cannot merely live with it – he must have it. He cannot possess it with his penis; and so he buys a seven-inch knife. It is his visible lust for the possession of a soul that causes consumptive Ippolit to identify him with the tarantula-god. The singlemindedness of Rogozhin's passion, however, removes him from concern with appearances, gentility, society, social life, hierarchy; he is not among those at the last end, the 'neither hot nor cold' who shall be 'spewed forth'. He is set apart from the corrupt society of St Petersburg that he contemptuously dominates; he is a criminal, and a potential saint.

With Myshkin, from the very beginning, Rogozhin has a special relationship. Dalton, approaching the text psychoanalytically, with Myshkin at the centre, sees Rogozhin as a sadistic father-figure, with Nastasya as the 'abused' mother, and Myshkin placing himself in a masochistic-feminine relationship to the father. She interprets the scene on the stairs of Rogozhin's attempted murder of Myshkin as a wishful-guilt-ridden re-enactment of the primal scene.[48] But what would happen if one put Rogozhin at the centre of the analysis? At their first meeting, he is somewhat condescending, one might say paternal; yet clearly drawn to, fascinated by, apprehensive of Myshkin. In his 'dark-green house' Rogozhin takes the initiative in the exchange of crosses and symbolically he and Myshkin become brothers; green, the colour of jealousy which no doubt seeped into *The Idiot* from Dostoyevsky's reading of *Othello*, from which something of the 'double' relationship between Othello and Iago carried over into the novel, atmospherically surrounds Rogozhin and plays a role in the novel somewhat analogous to dark yellow around the old pawnbroker in *Crime and Punishment*. After that, he takes Myshkin to his idiot-mother to be blessed. 'It takes an idiot to bless an idiot,' as Blackmur notes.[49] The mother is beyond human communication and she haunts the house more as a kind of presiding spirit than as a personality. Rogozhin tells Myshkin that, as she is beyond communication, if she had not spontaneously had the impulse to bless him, Rogozhin's oral request would have had no effect. They are now twice-brothers. But as they part, Rogozhin wryly remembers the origin of the cross he is wearing – it was palmed off on Myshkin by a soldier who thought he was cheating him, and he remembers the other story Myshkin told about the artisan who killed the merchant. 'Though I took your cross, I'm not going to knife you for your watch!' he mutters half to himself (VIII, 185; II, iv).

Meanwhile, Myshkin has told him that he 'lives in darkness', and that he is very like his father. He has observed that Rogozhin is a fighter and is trying to 'force' back his lost faith – to capture, to possess, to rape it. As long as Myshkin is with Rogozhin, Rogozhin believes, but when Myshkin leaves, his faith deserts him. ('Parfyon, you live in darkness.') Not long after they part, Rogozhin tries to kill Myshkin, and only the onset of an epileptic seizure saves him from the knife. Later, Myshkin takes upon himself the blame for the assault. Just as, with Ganya, he took upon himself not only the slap (originally intended for Varvara) but also the guilt for the slap, he somehow associates the attempted murder with his own doubts about Rogozhin.

Several times, Myshkin calls Nastasya 'mad'. He comes to the conclusion that Rogozhin too is 'insane'. His worst fears are realized. In the end, Rogozhin comes to him and in an extraordinary, almost liturgical sequence – I will not dwell on it here, but it is surely one of the most powerful and moving passages any novelist has ever produced – they undergo their nightlong siege beside the hardening corpse, hornlike foot protruding from the sheet that covers her, of Nastasya Filippovna. It is here that Myshkin slips quietly back across the sill of consciousness into the idiocy from which, at the beginning of the novel, he had but recently emerged.

What is the sum of the Prince's 'Russian mission'? What has he accomplished? Devastation, say a number of critics. But his mission was, after all, not to placate the world but to change it. Dostoyevsky wrote in the notebooks, 'Humility is the most terrible force that can ever exist in the world!' And shortly following:

> N.B. The Prince has had only *the slightest effect* on their lives. But everything he might have done and undertaken perishes with him...
>
> But wherever he even made an appearance – everywhere he left a permanent trace.[50]

Everywhere, the Prince responds to children. He is a child himself.

In Switzerland, he attempted to organize a band of children somewhat in the manner of Alyosha at the end of *The Brothers Karamazov*, a kind of alternative society, in which suffering does not corrupt innocence yet at the same time produces and heightens consciousness, a world in which the ego and the reality principle are not the lodestones. It is to the child in everyone that Myshkin appeals, and to the possibility of a resurrected childhood in an adult world.

Myshkin comes to Russia from Switzerland, in an awkward and inappropriate foreign cloak. We know that Dostoyevsky hated Switzerland, which is where he was living at the time he wrote *The Idiot*, but in the novel it is a kind of never-never-land, an idyllic landscape, associated with Rousseau and Pestalozzi, with the education of children, in which that education is closely bound up with sensitive responses to nature, with an attempt to overcome the human feeling of separation and alienation from nature. Early in the novel, Myshkin tells how he overcame his own feeling of estrangement:

> I remember the sadness I felt was unbearable. I even wanted to cry, everything surprised and bewildered me. What impressed me terribly was how alien everything was. I understood this. This foreignness was killing me. I completely recovered from this depression, as I recall, one night after I had reached Switzerland and was in Basel, when I was awakened by the braying of a donkey in the market-place. The donkey made a great impression on me and for some reason pleased me intensely, and at the same time everything seemed to clear up in my head. (VIII, 48; I, v)

Myshkin may or may not be impotent, but his sense of belonging to the world of physical nature is reawakened and reinstated by the animal that has been since the time of Apuleius and through the time of Shakespeare and the tradition of carnival the symbol of the lower bodily parts. When the Yepanchin girls are prompted to laugh at Myshkin, Madame Yepanchin looks at them angrily. 'Any one of us might fall in love with a donkey,' she tells them (VIII, 48; I, v).

During his travels in Russia, at the same time that he acquires the tin cross from the soldier, Myshkin comes across a mother with her new baby. When the baby smiles at her, she crosses herself, and explains to Myshkin that God feels the same joy when he hears a prayer that a mother feels at her baby's first smile. Myshkin constantly affirms an identity with the life-process itself, and with a maximum of spontaneity in responding to it. The contrast between the world of children and the world of adults has its analogue in the formlessness and openness of the Russians compared to the inherited polished forms and closed-offness of the ways of Europe.

Recently, an astute and learned critic, Grigory Pomerants, has noted that Myshkin's speech at the Yepanchins in which he sees a mission for the Russian aristocracy, and in which he also denounces the Roman Catholic Church as Antichrist, can be imagined as a speech of Dostoyevsky's (after all, it expresses what were to become some of his favourite and most often repeated doctrinal statements) but scarcely as a speech of Myshkin's.[51] I do not wish to deny that there is something inappropriate about the speech on the Prince's lips – many other critics, after all, have agreed with Pomerants – but what if one posits the presence of an external or internal censor and, bearing such a presence in mind, changes the terms just a little bit?

In expressing a mission for the aristocracy, Myshkin is of course being utterly oblivious to the used-up, blasé nature of the people he is addressing. But what he is advocating is, after all, not hierarchical privilege, but a spiritual elite of the dedicatedly humble! He is asking them to be as little children. Of course, they are amazed. With regard to the Roman Church, let us look at what he sees as the Antichrist in it. Clearly, it is the temptation of worldly power – the triumph of hierarchy, law and individuation in the service of physical, worldly power – at the expense of the communal and the spiritual. Is this charge levelled more appropriately at the Catholic Church or at the Petrine State? It was Peter, after all, who set himself up deliberately as the Antichrist, who surely with some degree of consciousness spoke the language of Antichrist, attempted to endow the State with religious awe and with powers deemed appropriate in the past only for religious institutions. It was Peter who completed the subordination of the Church to the State, and who did his best to create a religion of the State, with its own carefully articulated hierarchy of authority.[52] Perhaps Myshkin is attacking Rome; but perhaps at the same time he is also, like Yevgeny in Pushkin's poem, confronting the Bronze Horseman? In any case, the Prince's impact on high society is minimal. On Ippolit, it is great, but indecisive. There is the following illuminating passage concerning Ippolit and Myshkin in the notebooks:

> There is a terrible voluptuousness in opposing oneself to an immense power, no matter how insignificant you are.
>
> Or else:

> Since I am insignificant, I want to oppose immense power. There is a voluptuousness in subjugating oneself to immense power. In the Prince's speech: 'Here's to the sun, here's to life.'[53]

But Ippolit cannot break with the tarantula-god.

Mme Yepanchin, whom the Prince has several times blessed by calling her 'childlike', has been much moved by his fate, is moved to visit him in Switzerland and is stunned by his idiocy. After her 'good Russian cry' however she falls back on being 'reasonable', and concludes that Europe is unreal. Aglaya joins a committee for the restoration of Poland. Radomsky, on whom the Prince has indeed had some effect, has nevertheless become a superfluous man in Russia and lingers abroad. Kolya, Burdovsky and Keller, all minor characters, have clearly been profoundly affected by the Prince and something within them has indeed changed. Given the perpetually unresolved, or at least unfixed nature of character in a Dostoyevsky novel, the crowding of character and characters against the framework of any one of his novels, their pressure against the frame as if trying to break out of it and their propensity to appear under different names again in later novels, the least one can say is that we leave them expecting something from them.

But the character who haunts the novel and beyond is Rogozhin. True, he is a murderer. So was Raskolnikov. But as the Prince slips from clairvoyance to insanity, falling across the threshold into that timeless and pointless realm where Rogozhin's mother also sits, Rogozhin crosses the threshold in the other direction. After having survived 'two months of brain-fever', he stands trial:

> On every point, he gave direct, exact and fully satisfactory testimony, as a result of which the prince was kept completely out of it from the very beginning. During his trial, Rogozhin kept silent...He was sentenced, in view of extenuating circumstances, to fifteen years of hard labour in Siberia, and he heard out the sentence grimly, silently and 'dreamily'. (VIII, 507–8; IV, xii)

And it was perhaps out of that 'dreamily' of Rogozhin's presence at the trial that Dostoyevsky began to project an immense novel, about the life of a great sinner who would perhaps someday become a great saint, a great *Russian* saint who would bring back into the world the terrible force of humility and the clairvoyance of children, a novel that he would never, however hard he tried, and no matter how much his material conditions improved, be able to finish.

Notes

1. Translations from *The Idiot* are my own. A number of English translations are available; my own preference is for the translation by Olga and Henry Carlisle, published by Signet Books (New York, 1969). Beyond works specifically cited in the notes, this essay must acknowledge an intellectual debt to Norman O. Brown, the works of Mikhail Bakhtin and O. M. Freidenberg, and Alex de Jonge's *Dostoevsky and the Age of Intensity* (London, 1975).
2. Anna Dostoevsky, *Dostoevsky: Reminiscences*, trans. and ed. Beatrice Stillman, with an Introduction by Helen Muchnic (New York, 1975), pp. 25–76.
3. *Ibid.*, p. 30.
4. Konstantin Mochulsky, *Dostoevsky: His Life and Work*, trans. Michael Minihan (Princeton, 1967), pp. 326–9.
5. Dostoyevsky and his new wife went abroad in April of 1867. He wrote to Apollon Maykov on 2 August, from Geneva, 'justifying' his departure. F. M. Dostoyevsky, *Pis'ma*, ed. A. S. Dolinin (4 vols., Moscow/Leningrad, 1928–59), vol. 2, Letter no. 279, p. 26.
6. See especially the letters to A. Maykov of this period. See Yevgeniya Sarukhanyan, *Dostoyevsky v Peterburge* (Leningrad, 1972). Of an entirely different order – splendid works of the imagination that capture and trace the mythological hold of St Petersburg on the mind and imagination of Dostoyevsky and others – are the books of N. P. Antsiferov, *Dusha Peterburga* (St Petersburg, 1922; reprinted in Paris, 1978), and *Peterburg Dostoyevskogo* (St Petersburg, 1923). Dostoyevsky had several residences in St Petersburg, but obsessively sought out a certain pattern: all were quite near a church, and all had a balcony that opened out on a crossroads.
7. Quoted from 'White Nights' (*PSS*, II, 105: First night) by N. P. Antsiferov, *Dusha Peterburga*, p. 137.
8. See George Ivask, 'The vital ambivalence of St. Petersburg', *Texas Studies in Literature and Language*, Special Russian Issue, 27 (1975), 247–55.
9. M. M. Bakhtin, *The Dialogic Imagination*, ed. Michael Holquist, trans. Caryl Emerson and Michael Holquist (Austin/London, 1981), p. 248. 'It [the threshold] can be combined with the motif of encounter, but its most fundamental instance is as the chronotope of *crisis* and *break* in a life.' See also Bakhtin, *Problems of Dostoevsky's Poetics*, trans. R. W. Rotsel (Ann Arbor, 1973). The Rotsel translation leaves much to be desired, and a new translation by Caryl Emerson is scheduled for publication within the next year or so by University of Minnesota Press. There are further remarks on Dostoyevsky in the posthumous Bakhtin collection, M. M. Bakhtin, *Estetika slovesnogo tvorchestva* (Moscow, 1979), pp. 181–7, 308–27. Conceived in this way, the 'threshold' is intrinsically dramatic. For the dramatic, dramatizing impulse in Dostoyevsky, see George Steiner, *Tolstoy or Dostoevsky* (New York, 1959).
10. The criss-crossing of speech-lines in dialogue is one of Bakhtin's most

important notions, and central to his thought. It is precisely what he takes to be Dostoyevsky's gift for 'multi-voicedness' and 'polyphony' that makes Dostoyevsky in turn one of his most important literary subjects. This is contrary to the view expressed by R. Wellek in his 'Bakhtin's view of Dostoevsky: "Polyphony" and "Carnivalesque" ', *Dostoevsky Studies*, 1 (1980), 31–9.

11. Michael Holquist, *Dostoevsky and the Novel* (Princeton, 1977), pp. 102–23.
12. The mask, not as a disguise or something to hide behind, but as a symbol of transformation, metamorphosis from one state to another, as used in primitive dance and ritual, is a favourite notion of Bakhtin.
13. One cannot help recalling the play on *prestupleniye–perestupaniye* (crime–transgression) in *Crime and Punishment*. See also Mochulsky, *Dostoevsky*, p. 326.
14. 'Pechalen budet moy rasskaz . . .' ('Sad will be my tale . . .') from A. S. Pushkin, 'Mednyy vsadnik' ('The Bronze Horseman').
15. Robert Hollander, 'The apocalyptic framework of Dostoevsky's *The Idiot*', *Mosaic*, 7 (1974), 123–39.
16. F. M. Dostoyevsky, *The Notebooks for 'The Idiot'*, ed. Edward Wasiolek, trans. Katharine Strelsky (Chicago/London, 1967), p. 129 (*PSS*, IX, 200); at the end of the Sixth Plan, and even in the Seventh Plan, there is some falling back to the notion of a 'mixed' Prince. See also Dostoyevsky's letter to A. N Maykov of 12 January 1868, in his *Pis'ma*, vol. 2, Letter no. 292, pp. 59–66, and his letter of the following day to his niece, S. A. Ivanova, *ibid.*, Letter no. 294, pp. 69–73.
17. Mochulsky, *Dostoevsky*, p. 350.
18. Romano Guardini, 'Dostoevsky's *Idiot:* a symbol of Christ', trans. by F. X. Quinn, *Cross Currents*, 6 (1956), 359–82; M. Dzhouns (M. Jones), 'K ponimaniyu obraza knyazya Myshkina', in *Dostoyevsky: Materialy i issledovaniya* (Leningrad, 1974–), vol. 2 (1976), pp. 106–12; Holquist, *Dostoevsky*, p. 122.
19. The most extreme position is taken by Robert Lord, *Dostoevsky: Essays and Perspectives* (Berkeley, 1970). But also by Murray Krieger, 'Dostoevsky's "Idiot": the curse of saintliness', in his *The Tragic Vision* (New York, 1960), pp. 209–27; Philip Rahv, 'The other Dostoevsky', *New York Review of Books*, 20 April 1972, 30–8; but even, to some degree, by such a splendid interpreter of Dostoyevsky as R. P. Blackmur, '*The Idiot*: a rage of goodness', in his *Eleven Essays in the European Novel* (New York, 1964), pp. 141–63, in which Blackmur touches on the impulse in Dostoyevsky that seems to need 'humiliation' as a prerequisite for 'humility'. Harold Rosenberg, while avoiding the pejorative slant, also emphasizes the passivity of Myshkin in his interesting Introduction to the Signet edition of the Olga and Henry Carlisle translation (see note 1 above).
20. Simon O. Lesser, 'Saint and sinner – Dostoevsky's *Idiot*', in Leonard and Eleanor Manheim (eds.), *Hidden Patterns: Studies in Psychoanalytic Literary Criticism* (New York, 1966), pp. 132–50; Elizabeth Dalton,

Unconscious Structure in 'The Idiot': A Study in Literature and Psychoanalysis (Princeton, 1979).

21. Blackmur, '*The Idiot*', p. 143.
22. Dostoyevsky, *Notebooks*, pp. 23–137 (*PSS*, IX, 133–208).
23. *Ibid.*, p. 124 (*PSS*, IX, 200).
24. *Ibid.*, Wasiolek's Introduction, p. 14.
25. *Ibid.*, p. 129. The *yurodivyy*, or 'Holy Fool' or 'Fool in Christ' is a Russian version of the Greek Christian *salos.* It is inspired folly and/or childlike wisdom, that disregards hierarchy, social status etc., and speaks alike to all. It has a certain kinship to madness, and surely involves a valuation of the unconscious untrammelled by the reality principle.
26. *Ibid.*, p. 191 (*PSS*, IX, 239).
27. For the significance of the shadow and the shadow-self, see Carl Jung, *The Undiscovered Self* (London, 1958), pp. 8–9, and *The Collected Works of C. G. Jung* (20 vols., New York, 1953–79), vol. 9, pt 2, ch. 2; and vol. 12, pp. 29ff; see also his 'Battle for deliverance from the mother', *Collected Works*, vol. 5.
28. Blackmur, '*The Idiot*', p. 159.
29. Dalton, *Unconscious Structure*, pp. 123–44.
30. Krieger, 'Dostoevsky's "Idiot"', pp. 209–27.
31. 'His self-abnegation makes him an impersonal witness even during his most earnest participation.' Rosenberg in his Introduction to F. M. Dostoyevsky, *The Idiot*, trans. O. and H. Carlisle, p. viii. Radomsky tells Myshkin, 'A great deal has happened *through* you.'
32. Lord, *Dostoevsky*, pp. 81–101.
33. 'The Tale of Igor's Men', trans. Sidney Monas and Burton Raffel, *Delos*, 6 (1970), 8–9.
34. Hollander, 'The apocalyptic framework', p. 121. Hollander points out that in addition to what might be called Dostoyevsky's normal apocalyptic preoccupations, his friend A. N. Maykov, with whom he was in correspondence, had just published a translation of the Book of Revelation; Hollander, 'The apocalyptic framework', p. 129.
35. See Hugh McLean, *Nikolai Leskov: The Man and His Art* (Cambridge, Mass., 1977), pp. 173–90.
36. Edward Wasiolek, *Dostoevsky: The Major Fiction* (Cambridge, Mass., 1971), pp. 85–109. It should be pointed out however that Akira Kurosawa's film version of *The Idiot* (1952), which completely 'Japanizes' the text while remaining remarkably faithful to it, contains not a single Christian reference yet retains much of the power and 'sense' of the original.
37. Dostoyevsky, *Notebooks*, p. 165 (*PSS*, IX, 216).
38. Dalton, *Unconscious Structure*, pp. 185–208.
39. *Ibid.*, pp. 68–9.
40. *Ibid.*, p. 109.
41. While full of admiration for Dostoyevsky's novel, and quick to see the degree to which it conforms to his theory of 'triangular desire', René Girard tends to see Dostoyevsky's references to *Don Quixote*, and

his use of that novel as a kind of subtext, as a 'typical' Romantic misinterpretation of Cervantes' novel (*Deceit, Desire and the Novel: Self and Other in Literary Structure* (Baltimore, 1965), pp. 256–89).

42. The dream is repeated (VIII, 377; III, x).
43. Wasiolek, *Dostoevsky*, pp. 92–100.
44. Roger Cox, *Between Earth and Heaven: Shakespeare, Dostoevsky and The Meaning of Christian Tragedy* (New York, 1969), pp. 190–1.
45. Blackmur, '*The Idiot*', p. 160.
46. Hollander, 'The apocalyptic framework', p. 135.
47. Dostoyevsky, *Notebooks*, p. 236 (*PSS*, IX, 277).
48. Dalton, *Unconscious Structure*, pp. 107–17.
49. Blackmur, '*The Idiot*', p. 46.
50. Dostoyevsky, *Notebooks*, p. 193 (*PSS*, IX, 242).
51. G. Pomerants, 'Knyaz′ Myshkin', *Sintaksis*, 9 (1981), 120.
52. See the brilliant and too little known article by Michael Cherniavsky, 'The Old Believers and the new religion', in M. Cherniavsky (ed.), *The Structure of Russian History* (New York, 1970), pp. 140–88. Also the essay by Boris Uspensky, 'Historia sub specie semioticae', in Henryk Baran (ed.), *Semiotics and Structuralism: Readings from the Soviet Union* (New York, 1974), pp. 64–75, in which he maintains that Peter knowingly spoke the language of Antichrist. One often feels in reading Slavophile attacks and critiques of Roman Catholicism that it is really their hatred for the Petrine State, which of course they see as derived from the spirit of Rome, that commands their language, tone and direction.
53. Dostoyevsky, *Notebooks*, p. 173 (*PSS*, IX, 223).

4

The Devils: the role of Stavrogin

R. M. DAVISON

In the three major works by Dostoyevsky which precede *The Devils* there is no doubt about the identity of the central character. In *Notes from Underground* the Underground Man himself may be petulant, spiteful and unheroic but he is unequivocally central. In *Crime and Punishment* Raskolnikov may be *manqué* as a Napoleonic hero but he is ever-present and the way in which he is pulled towards opposing extremes does at least draw attention to his centrality. Myshkin continues the catalogue of characters who do not come up to the mark as heroes but compensate for this by occupying most of the reader's time. His heroic qualities are unlikely to detain us for long but the clearest pointer to his centrality is that he actually is himself the title of his novel *The Idiot*.

What, then, of *The Devils* in this respect? The title gives no pointer other than to what limited potential for heroism and centrality may be presumed to reside in a doomed collective of Biblical pigs. It seems to be commonly held by the characters in the novel that the leading light in their sordid, seething little town is Stavrogin. The distinction may indeed be a dubious one but it is difficult to find any other candidate on whom to confer it. Stavrogin has a respectable history of dramatic deeds and duels; he exudes an air of Romantic mystery; he has great promise as a heroic character. Yet by the end of the novel it will be sensed that although the spirit of Stavrogin broods over everything he is himself curiously absent. This change, from the unheroic central character, as in *The Idiot*, to the heroic character who may not be central, is a major one and creates at least as many problems as it solves. Dostoyevsky does not make things any easier for himself by yet again trying to write two novels at the same time. He had done this already in *Crime and Punishment* (the Marmeladov and Raskolnikov stories) with ingenuity and success. Although the creative history of *The Devils* is quite different, the novel as it finally emerges still contains two distinct stories: the anti-nihilist pamphlet about the political conspiracy of Pyotr Verkhovensky, and Stavrogin's moral quest. The aim of the present essay will be to define Stavrogin's role in the narrative which Dostoyevsky welds together (or perhaps, as will appear, merely strings together) from these two parts. The aim is not primarily to consider the ideology of the character nor to scrutinize Dostoyevsky's usually inscrutable purposes so much as to examine the literary effects, the aesthetic consequences of how in the end he does present Stavrogin. It may well be, for instance, that some of Stavrogin's deficiencies can be attributed to the fact that Dostoyevsky had long been thinking of Pyotr as his major figure before he decided, as he thought, to give central importance to Stavrogin, but such considerations will be neglected here in favour of an examination of Stavrogin as he is.

It will be argued that there is in fact some radical deficiency in Stavrogin as a central character; that we must not try to find ways around this deficiency but must accept it; that the novel is about the problems which arise when a character with good claims to a leading position in the world between its covers does not match up to his promise; and that his place in the literary structure reflects this theme as it is presented in the developing narrative. In brief, the story is about Stavrogin's loss of centrality in his world and it is told by making him lose his centrality in the structure of the novel.

The first point to establish is the one which Dostoyevsky leaves to his last page: that Stavrogin is not mad (X, 516; III, viii). It may induce a degree of irritation in the reader, who has struggled through several hundred pages of labyrinthine narrative under certain pardonable misapprehensions, to be told in the very last sentence that he is wrong, with the implication that he ought to go back to the beginning and start again, but it will be seen that the arrangement has its advantages. It is important to note the source of the information about Stavrogin's sanity and the point can perhaps be made most clearly by comparing the case of Captain Lebyadkin who endearingly declares, in a sentence pregnant with awful promise, that he will go mad one day but is not mad yet (X, 141; I, v, 4). As a clinical diagnosis this has about as much claim on the reader's attention as the drunkard's habitual assertion of his sobriety; in terms of Bakhtin's polyphony it sounds distinctly like a wrong note. By contrast, the assertion of Stavrogin's sanity is said to be the verdict of doctors who 'utterly and completely reject the possibility of madness' (X, 516; III, viii) and it comes through the comparatively neutral narrator. Unless we attend to this verdict the whole of our interpretation of Stavrogin will be off-key. Nor are we straying from the principle of disregarding Dostoyevsky's purposes in favour of his results: this particular instruction on how the character is to be understood comes entirely from within the novel of which it is a part. In fact the final sentence of the narrative ensures that, despite Stavrogin's best and most eccentric efforts, the earlier remarks in the novel about his sanity are not overlooked.

When he seizes Gaganov by the nose, 'unexpectedly but firmly' (X, 39; I, ii, 2), it is said that 'no one in the whole town attributed this wild action to madness' at the time, though people later recollected that at the crucial moment Stavrogin looked 'as though he had gone out of his mind'. The issue is also raised by Stavrogina who says, with a clear indication of what she truly fears, 'Of course I am not speaking of madness. There could never be any question of that!' (X, 81; I, iii, 6) and asks Liputin about the state of her son's mind. The reader is not told of the consoling answer for another two pages but meanwhile Liputin puts the same question to Kirillov, who says that there is something strange about Stavrogin and, as Liputin sapiently remarks, 'If Kirillov thinks he's a bit odd then there really must be something up, mustn't there?' (X, 82; I, iii, 6). Captain Lebyadkin too thinks that Stavrogin is mad. There is however a countervailing stress on Stavrogin's rationality. The narrator thinks that he 'never knew those outbursts of blind rage which make it impossible to think rationally' and that even his malice 'was cold and calm and, if one can put it thus, *rational*, that's to say the most revolting and dreadful kind of malice there can be' (X, 164; I, v, 8). *Prima facie*, rationality is not consistent with madness, yet for Dostoyevsky being rational is not always the same thing as being sane: Raskolnikov reasons himself into an act of criminal folly; Ivan Karamazov uses his brain so hard that it conjures up for him visions of the Devil; Kirillov reasons himself to a self-destructive conclusion.

Dostoyevsky does not take the easy way out, which would be to announce at an early stage that Stavrogin was mad and then use this circumstance as a licence for all manner of unmotivated excesses, as had, in effect, happened with some of his earlier characters. The Underground Man for instance embodies a philosophical principle of constant negation so far removed from normality that, however great the value of his ideas, he forfeits our interest as a literary creation; the behaviour of Myshkin is rarely dictated by normal human considerations and thereby acquires a quality of apparent caprice, of unapproachable arbitrariness which makes him too much less considerable as a literary character. If Dostoyevsky does not take the easy way out for himself, by the same token he does not make it easy for the reader to interpret the omens. Liputin's remark about Kirillov is double-edged: on the one hand, a character more unbalanced than Kirillov must indeed be unstable; on the other, do you set a madman to catch one? If Kirillov thinks Stavrogin is mad could this not paradoxically be seen as a possible pointer to Stavrogin's sanity? Captain Lebyadkin's insecure footing in reality will likewise cause the reader to take his words with a pinch of salt, but not perhaps to dismiss them altogether, for the gallant Captain shows himself, surprisingly and intermittently, to be in quite close touch with what is going on, and at moments of public uproar he often *is* what is going on.

All of these doubts are swept away by the concluding sentence of the book, which offers an authoritative, clinical judgement on the matter. To return to the musical image, this is a note sounded by the tuning-fork to establish the pitch. The practice of giving the pitch of the performance at the end of the concert is inconsiderate but, translated into literary terms, it is crucial to the success of Dostoyevsky's enterprise in two ways. First, the reader is in doubt until the end; since the issue is of rather more significance than identifying the murderer in a detective story (though the parallel is suggestive) it follows that the course of the narrative is attended by a sense of unease, of being pulled and pushed in opposing directions. It will later be seen that this is just one of many areas of instability in the reader's response to the novel. Second, the verdict is in the event one of sanity, so that if Stavrogin is indeed absent from the central place in the novel we cannot escape from the problem which this poses by arguing that, as a madman, he is of little account.

One problem in assessing Stavrogin's character is the difficulty of getting close enough to him. At all stages of his career he is notable for his coldness and air of detachment. Whatever impels him it is certainly not elemental explosions of the kind to which Captain Lebyadkin is prone. When he pulls Gaganov's nose he is described as 'thoughtful' and in the ensuing uproar he looks at everybody 'with curiosity' (X, 39; I, ii, 2). After some one hundred and fifty pages of preparation he is eventually noticed standing in the background with a gaze which is 'stern, thoughtful and somehow absent-minded' (X, 145; I, v, 5); amidst the great excitement produced by his arrival he appears 'altogether indifferent, even languid' (X, 157;

I, v, 7); he listens to Pyotr Verkhovensky 'very lazily and absent-mindedly' (X, 160; I, v, 7). Similar treatment awaits Pyotr later when Stavrogin 'looks at him absent-mindedly without saying anything' (X, 237; II, iv, 1). At the end of 'The Fateful Morning' Stavrogin is again 'unusually absent-minded' (X, 352; II, x, 3). Other characters tell the reader what they know Stavrogin once thought or what they think he now thinks, but until his letter of explanation to Dasha Shatova in the 'Conclusion' Stavrogin presents his own character largely through his actions, whether the dramatic ones of the early stages or the more negative ones of the later stages. At the same time his absent-mindedness makes it quite clear that he is detached from the responses which these actions evoke, thereby implying that the reasons for the actions are his own and may differ from those which observers impute to the actions. A well-known example is his outburst to Kirillov, 'To hell with your approval, I'm not seeking it from anybody' (X, 228; II, iii, 3), when Kirillov has hazarded an explanation of Stavrogin's behaviour in the duel with Gaganov's son. The reader is rarely given an insight into the strictly private world of Stavrogin's reasoning and must usually content himself with an air of mysterious indifference; but even on this inadequate basis of information it is possible to avoid the error of explaining Stavrogin's actions in terms of the reactions of the other characters: there is a difference between their view of Stavrogin and his own view of himself. Again there is an area of instability, of enigmatic half-suggestion, where any sort of definitive explanation is carefully kept away from the reader. Stavrogin's actions are for the world at large, but his reasons are for himself alone. We must resign ourselves to being kept at a distance.

Remoteness and cold detachment are ostensibly in contrast with the dashingly Romantic elements in his character. Stavrogin's earlier years were misspent in rowdyism, duels and exile, which is reminiscent both of Lermontov and of Pechorin. He has the proper worldly characteristics of the Romantic hero: he is strong, handsome, elegant and clever. It is tempting to see his Prince Harry period as mere youthful rumbustiousness which is naive in Schiller's sense of the word; but Stavrogina prefers for her son the more reflective role, more sentimental in Schiller's sense, of Hamlet (X, 151; I, v, 6). (If only in passing, it should be noted that the venomous caprices of Stavrogina's impetuous and imperious character ought not to blind us to the perspicacity of her observations. Her purpose in life is to make a misery of it for everybody else, in which she achieves great success partly by sheer devotion to duty, but in part also by a shrewd assessment of where her victims' weak points are to be found.) In the event the relevant chapter (X, 34ff; I, ii) has 'Prince Harry' in its title, which very firmly moves it away from the narrower, more specifically Russian and nineteenth-century suggestions of a title such as 'Pechorin'. This is part of a pattern, for Stavrogin's Romanticism is not a public, historical phenomenon: it is an element of his private life, of his personal search for morality. Even though it occurred a few years before the main action of the novel (which is roughly contemporary with its writing, say 1870), Stavrogin's Romantic period is certainly too late to fit in with Russian Romanticism, which may be seen as an indication that Stavrogin is in this respect not a 'historical' character of his own time, an indication strengthened by his association with Prince Harry, who was even farther removed from contemporary developments. An aesthetically satisfying consequence of making Stavrogin a late-flowering Romantic is that it nicely balances the clash between him and young Verkhovensky as antithetic coevals.[1] However, the balance is promptly upset as the very historicity of Pyotr Verkhovensky (a nihilist alive at the right time) draws attention to the lack of historicity in Stavrogin (a Romantic alive at the wrong time). The true historical clash is between the generations, between Stepan Trofimovich Verkhovensky the liberal father and Pyotr Stepanovich the nihilist son. Stavrogin cannot be part of this public, political conflict because, as will later be seen, he is so closely identified with his 'intellectual father' Stepan Trofimovich, even though he is the same age as his 'intellectual brother' Pyotr, whom he comes to oppose. If it is accepted that Pyotr's conspiracy is the main propulsive force of the narrative, then the effect of the chronological manipulations under discussion is to keep Stavrogin separate from the main narrative because of his opposition to Pyotr. A further effect of this farraginous arrangement of conflicts between like and unlike, between history and non-history, between fathers (who are not necessarily fathers and may be the same intellectual age as their sons) and sons (who are not necessarily sons) is to leave the reader in a state of almost irretrievable muddle. From the muddle we can however salvage the significant contradiction between the promise of colourful action in Stavrogin's early Romanticism and the reality that it was a transient, external phenomenon, not to return in the main action of the novel.

Before putting the question of Stavrogin's Romantic features behind us, we should say something about the umbrella which he takes with him on his excursions during the night (X, 166ff; II, i–ii).

This object serves a symbolic purpose in linking Stavrogin with Fedka, whom it shelters, and with Stepan Trofimovich Verkhovensky, who sets out in search of God armed with an umbrella. Yet it remains an absurd accoutrement for a Romantic hero, for a possible Nietzschean superman. Did Pechorin worry about getting wet? Would Zarathustra use an umbrella? Although it clearly was a useful literary device, it is a relief (and not at all surprising) that Dostoyevsky was equally aware of its ridiculousness. Lebyadkin wonders whether he is worthy to borrow Stavrogin's umbrella and Stavrogin observes crushingly that 'everybody is worth an umbrella'. Quick to see the possibilities of humiliation in this proposition, Lebyadkin responds with masochistic satisfaction, 'You define at a stroke the minimum of human rights' (X, 213; II, ii, 2). The umbrella is yet another sign that the Romantic Stavrogin precedes the action of the novel and that the man whom we see in action is advancing towards the middle age of his 'intellectual father' Stepan Trofimovich Verkhovensky. Only the physical shell of his earlier years remains, to remind the reader and to confuse him. This confusion however is valuable, since it helps towards an understanding of why other characters in the novel are themselves confused about the difference between Stavrogin's past and present.

The peculiar chronology of Stavrogin's intellectual kinship with Stepan Trofimovich, discussed above, is only one of a number of pointers to the close affinity between the two characters. Although Stepan plays tutor/parent to Stavrogin, Dostoyevsky explicitly draws them closer together than this might be thought to imply: 'it somehow turned out quite naturally that there was not the slightest distance apparent between them' (X, 35; I, ii, 1). Then Stepan himself, despite further dislocations of chronology, becomes as a son to Stavrogina, which must make him a brother of Nikolay. The two draw even closer with Stavrogina's typically bossy plan to marry Stepan to Dasha Shatova to cover up Stavrogin's sins. Peace has further identified the two characters with a careful analysis of the narrative, which shows how Stavrogin comes to the end of his metaphysical road after the night with Liza just as Stepan sets out at the beginning of his road, of his final pilgrimage.[2] The narrative is split between the two men but has an essential continuity. This connection is of considerable structural importance as one of the few instances where Stavrogin, here through his alter ego Stepan Trofimovich, is drawn into a response to the public conspiracy which goes beyond mere negation. Against this must be set the subtlety and complexity of the connection between the two characters which make it elusive. Furthermore, even if we do identify Stepan Trofimovich and Stavrogin, the clear implication of the way in which the former takes up the journey is that the positive contribution is to come from him since all that we have had from Stavrogin has been negative. The very fact that Stavrogin has come to the end of his journey and cannot in any sense, metaphorical or otherwise, accompany Stepan Trofimovich on his final pilgrimage is a decisive indication of his negative role.

If this symbiotic tie turns out to be negative, how much more is this true of Pyotr Stepanovich's parasitic attachment to Stavrogin. He refers to Stavrogin as his 'better half' (literally 'main half') (X, 408; III, iii, 2) and venerates him as a new revolutionary saviour of the world, in repayment for which his hero grabs his hair and flings him to the ground, forces him to walk in the gutter, regards him as mad and listens to him with amazement. The vigour and determination with which Stavrogin rejects Pyotr are an acknowledgement that he represents an unwelcome side of Stavrogin's own self, of his rational, speculative, atheistic self. It is Pyotr's role to bring to its logical conclusion in public action one side of what Stavrogin had been and, by his rejection of Pyotr, Stavrogin rejects also a public role for himself.

We have seen, then, that Stavrogin is not mad, which implies that there is some sense to be found in his actions and attitudes. We have seen that he is so detached from his actions that his reasons for them may well not coincide with the explanations offered by the observers of the actions. The significance of the Romantic elements in his character is obscured by complex considerations of chronology but in the final analysis he is moved further from the main, public narrative both in psychological terms (because his Romanticism is personal) and in time (because his Romanticism is, when he finally appears on the scene, a thing of the past). Oddly, our clearest view of Stavrogin is to be obtained through a prism, through his 'double' Stepan Trofimovich Verkhovensky; this indirect image is also the most stable but, ultimately, it too reveals Stavrogin's negativity. His relationship with Pytor Stepanovich distances him further from the public events of the novel and completes the elegant irony that Stavrogin is closer to Verkhovensky *père* than either is really aware and is much further from Verkhovensky *fils* than the latter would wish. But as Stavrogin retreats further into his private life it might be wondered how the question of centrality arises at all.

A crucial component of the answer to this question is: time. *The*

Devils is some five hundred pages long and Stavrogin does not enter into the action of the present until about one hundred and fifty pages have gone by. He appears in the text long before this but only in his past. The extraordinary length of this build-up for the entrance of one who may be the central character ensures both that the reader pays great attention to the Stavrogin of the past (who is, after all, the only one available at the time) and that he has very clear expectations of the character. (Presumably the technique also had a healthy effect on the circulation of *The Russian Messenger* in which the novel was serialized.) Here is a man who has bitten the Governor's ear, who has pulled a respectable gentleman's nose and kissed a less respectable gentleman's wife, who has married, it is darkly hinted, a half-crazed cripple. This is promising stuff indeed – and what follows is anticlimax. It does not always feel like it as the novel drags us along in its hectic course of murder, suicide and arson, of drunkenness and death, of riots and salvation; but anticlimax it is, both literary and moral, writ large and writ small.

It is first writ small in Stavrogin's actual entrance into the drawing-room (X, 142ff; I, v, 4–5). The bell is heard to ring downstairs, the butler announces that Stavrogin has arrived, feet are heard approaching and even Captain Lebyadkin as he looks at the door ('dreadfully stupidly') is struck dumb: 'then there suddenly flew into the room – not Stavrogin at all but some completely unknown young man'. Not to mince words, this is corny; it is taken from a shilling shocker and, as with so many of Dostoyevsky's outrageous vulgarities, what really annoys the fastidious modern reader is that it works. It can hardly be accident that it is the 'false entry' of Pyotr Stepanovich which distracts us from Stavrogin: his public bustle, as represented in his political activities, is to be a constant source of distraction from Stavrogin's mysterious, private concerns.

The literary anticlimax is immediately extended to the real appearance of Stavrogin, who contrives to come in without actually being noticed. It is continued in the intense drama of Stavrogina's challenge to him, for she is not one to underplay a scene, about his marriage, a challenge which he patiently and gently deflects by kissing his mother's hand. The real broadening of the anticlimax is to be seen in the nature of Stavrogin's main actions in that part of the narrative which we now observe for ourselves. They are, in Peace's expression, acts of 'self-effacement'; although Peace is concerned with a moral analysis, the term is equally apt for the present narrowly literary approach.[3] The act of marrying the cripple belongs to the past, but the confession of it belongs to the Stavrogin whom we see; the duel with Gaganov's son is arranged so that no one shall be killed; the public blow from Shatov's fist ('big, bony and heavy, with red hairs and freckles' [X, 164; I, v. 8]) is accepted. Whatever inner moral crisis for Stavrogin may be involved in these acts, externally they are negative.

Even Stavrogin's suicide is negative, dramatically speaking. Kirillov goes out to the accompaniment of a loud bang and a dreadful scream of agony (the latter from Pyotr Verkhovensky who has almost had his finger bitten off in a parting gesture), closely observed by the reader, albeit through a glass darkly, because the candle gets knocked over in the excitement. Stavrogin's death is hidden, sordid and furtive: he hangs himself behind the door in the loft and it might be thought that, as a nobleman, he ought at least to have shot himself. Moreover, this second suicide serves no useful political, public or social purpose (as does Kirillov's, which is stage-managed by Pyotr Verkhovensky as part of his conspiracy and is in any case designed, with what success it is difficult to say, to prove a point for Kirillov himself). The absence of public purpose and significance in Stavrogin's suicide is given literary expression in the way in which it is communicated to the reader: not in the main body of the novel, which effectively finishes its development with 'The Last Pilgrimage of Stepan Trofimovich', but in the scrappy and perfunctory 'Conclusion', which is more in the nature of a postscript. Here Dostoyevsky ties up the loose ends of the narrative (not that there are by now so many, since most of his characters have been converted to corpses) and disposes of Stavrogin. The most unsatisfactory aspect of the 'Conclusion' is that Dostoyevsky briefly loses his nerve: having portrayed Stavrogin for several hundred pages through his actions and lack of them, he now seems uncertain whether the reader will have grasped what has been going on and produces the letter to Dasha Shatova in which Stavrogin retrospectively explains the theoretical basis of his behaviour; and finally he produces the doctors' verdict on Stavrogin's sanity. Both of these definitive, objective attempts to make up the reader's mind for him are at variance with the hazy, hinting uncertainties of the rest of the novel. If however the 'Conclusion' is deficient in this particular respect, there can be no literary complaint about the accommodating there of Stavrogin's death, for it is in dramatic terms no more than a pendant to the narrative, the logical conclusion of Stavrogin's negative contribution once he actually appears on the scene.

Dostoyevsky even takes the negative side of Stavrogin so far as to suggest that he is as good as dead before he kills himself. This would seem to be the implication of the uncanny sleep into which he falls before going out on his excursion into the night: 'his breathing could scarcely be perceived. His face was pale and severe, but it seemed frozen and motionless; his brows were somewhat drawn together and he was frowning; decidedly he looked like a lifeless wax figure' (X, 182; II, i, 4). While this may well be seen as an indication of Stavrogin's moral death, we are more concerned here with the contribution that it makes to the general air of enigma and sinister mystery which surround him. Other elements in this aspect of Stavrogin's role are the repeated references to his pallor, to his strength and to the sense of unease evoked by his curious nocturnal excursions through the mud of the back streets. The essence of the enigmatic is that it does not explain itself, that the mystery is not resolved. It might seem that in the present case the explanatory letter to Dasha Shatova cancels the enigma of Stavrogin, but that letter is in its effect, whatever its creative history and intention, so much an afterthought and so out of tune with the style of presenting the character that it does not count for a great deal in literary terms.

It is, however, a fact that some kind of Stavrogin is alive inside the shell. That he now belongs only inside this shell and will not be brought into the arena of public events is most tellingly conveyed in the episode of the fête which is the culminating point of these events in the novel. It brings together in a brilliant dramatic inspiration nearly all the characters and lines of development, but the reader will rack his brains to no purpose in trying to recollect Stavrogin's contribution. This is a public display or exhibition and there is no place in it for one whose problems, whose tragedy and whose death are all for himself alone. The difficulty in which we find ourselves is that we have to explain away the absence from the central scene of the novel of the supposedly central character.

In this long anticlimax of the undramatic and the negative, of the enigmatic and the absent, the crucial element is time, for all hinges on the moment of Stavrogin's entry into his mother's drawing-room. Up to that point the reader, like the characters in the novel, has had reason to expect a particular sort of Stavrogin and the very extent of the preparation ensures that the image is well established, but from then on hopes are systematically disappointed. So far from conducting himself like a more intellectual version of Captain Lebyadkin, he turns out to be distressingly like Myshkin's ghost. As time moves on, Stavrogin recedes in dramatic effectiveness; having arrived on the public scene, he retreats from it. The expectation of a lively hero is not fulfilled; aesthetically, we are disillusioned.

This is all as nothing by comparison with the moral anticlimax, the moral and ideological disillusionment of the other characters, which hinges on the same moment in the narrative and is equally dependent on the passage of time. Its principal concern for us is that it is also dependent on Stavrogin and therefore has literary import as an aspect of the relations between Stavrogin and the others, an aspect of the way in which he is integrated into the narrative. The main part of the novel is a chronicle of disillusionment, of disappointed hopes, of vanished ideals. Jones has commented: 'The breakdown of personal ideals...is a recurrent motif. In several cases these personal ideals are projected on to one man – Stavrogin – and his indifference causes one disillusionment after another.'[4] This is all summed up in Marya Lebyadkina's crazed and laughing cry into the darkness: 'Grishka Otrepyev! Anathema!' (X, 219; II, ii, 3). Her falcon is no more, her Prince is a pretender, a fake, and she speaks for them all.

It is Pyotr Verkhovensky who cherishes the loftiest illusions and thus has the farthest to fall. Disagreeably located halfway between crime and socialism, Pyotr is himself concerned to ruin ideals: his frenetic activities in the town are devoted precisely to this end. The culmination of these activities will, he supposes, be a demoralization so general and so complete as to leave the situation ripe for the establishment of a new ideal, of which Stavrogin is to be the arch-representative. He has toyed with the notion of enrolling the Pope in the part and observes in his remorselessly chatty fashion, 'the old boy would agree in a flash' (X, 323; II, viii). However that may be, Stavrogin declines the role. Pyotr has made the mistake of failing to notice that Stavrogin has changed with the passage of time. 'What the hell do you want me for?' exclaims Stavrogin. 'Take a good look at me once and for all: am I your man? And leave me in peace' (X, 320–1; II, viii). Even the narrator had noted when Stavrogin returned that there was something different about him: 'Was there now perhaps some new idea reflected in his gaze?' (X, 145; I, v, 5). This had apparently escaped Pyotr in his headlong pursuit of moral destruction. When his 'sacred and remarkably absurd hopes' (X, 511; III, viii) in Stavrogin as the new saviour are mockingly thrown back at him or simply ignored, he is at first beseeching 'like a man whose most valued possession is being taken away, or has been taken away, and who has not yet recovered' (X, 321; II, viii). Then he erupts into gibbering abuse: '"You aren't interested! I knew it," he exclaimed in a blaze of flaming rage. "You're lying, you trashy, lecherous, broken-down little squib of a nobleman"' (X, 326; II, viii). We hear the characteristic note of the biter bit: Pyotr, the priest of disillusion, is disillusioned in his own god of disillusion. The subtlety and absurdity of this proposition is that Pyotr invents a Stavrogin to suit himself, knows that it is an invention and not the real thing, yet is annoyed when the real Stavrogin declines to accept his invented persona. When Stavrogin suspects what is going on he asks Pyotr if he has been presenting him as some sort of leader: 'Pyotr Stepanovich looked at him quickly. "By the way," he went on, as though he hadn't heard and trying to smooth it over as quickly as possible' (X, 178; II, i, 3). Clearly Pyotr realizes that he has created an unwelcome role for Stavrogin, but it sustains him to believe in it. He knows that, like Frankenstein, he has created his own Stavrogin – 'I invented you abroad; I invented it all while looking at you' (X, 326; II, viii) – but blames Stavrogin, not himself, when the part is found not to fit and the central role in his plans is unceremoniously declined. Here again we see precisely contrived misunderstanding within the novel of what Stavrogin's role is. Pyotr's ravings are of extraordinary value because of the irony that he sees through them even as he continues to believe in them, thereby depriving the reader of any excuses for being deluded.

The absence of irony increases the pathos of 'Night', where Dostoyevsky portrays the disillusioning of Kirillov and Shatov. They tell Stavrogin separately how much he has meant in their lives and both use the past tense: he *has* meant much (X, 189, 191; II, i, 5–6). They have adored and venerated him, perhaps no less than Pyotr Verkhovensky does now, but they have seen that the light of their sun has gone out; they have seen that the ideas which Stavrogin implanted in them no longer command his own conviction. 'I assure you,' Stavrogin says to Shatov, 'this repetition of my former ideas makes a very unpleasant impression upon me. Will you stop it?' (X, 198; II, i, 7). The man of limitless will who inspired Kirillov to his apotheosis of the individual and the preacher of a distinctively Russian religious morality who inspired Shatov are scarcely to be seen in the reputed debauchee who seeks humiliation and self-effacement: 'Why are people always thrusting banners on me?' (X, 201; II, i, 7), asks Stavrogin in response to Shatov's forlorn lament, 'You, you alone could have raised the banner!' The disillusionment of these two halves of the Stavrogin that was is more pathetic than that of Pyotr Verkhovensky because they are, for all their idiosyncrasies, a great deal less obnoxious than Pyotr; nor have they aggravated their despair by a refusal to accept the evidence of the change.

It is this change, wrought in Stavrogin by the passage of time and the sterility of his experience, which allows us to speak of the two halves of Stavrogin and simultaneously to agree with Jones that he 'is not one of Dostoyevsky's great dualistic characters'.[5] Yet again, attention must be drawn to the importance of time: Stavrogin as he was is presented split between Shatov and Kirillov; Stavrogin as he is now is neither of them, for he has abandoned both sides of what he was. It is therefore misleading to attempt to reassemble Stavrogin from those parts of him which are reflected in other characters; these reflections reveal to us only what Stavrogin was. The figure thus re-created can be seen as central only at the expense of distorting the crucial time factor. It makes for a tidier novel at the expense of truth, because the 'ideal in him [Stavrogin] has lost its effectiveness'[6] and he now has nothing to offer in place of what he used to be; he has no better ideology than to negate the hopes of those who had faith in him. The touchstone of virtue has been permanently in retreat from him as he has stretched out to find his limits and he has come eventually to be disillusioned in himself: he kills himself because he has seen through all his ideals. It was argued earlier that his sanity differentiates him from the Underground Man, but the way in which the Stavrogin whom we see in the action of the novel is against everybody does compare with his predecessor's wilful and predictable negation. The views of his which live on are rejected by him; the role of saviour, of a new god, does not appeal. Recalcitrant, he retreats into isolation.

The present argument makes no attempt to re-establish Stavrogin's centrality but is more concerned to trace the course of his disappearance from the novel in a series of deepening anticlimaxes from a fake entry into the drawing-room to a non-appearance at the fête. Side by side with the anticlimaxes marches the increasingly disastrous sense of disillusionment, from Pyotr's high hopes to Stavrogin's faith in himself.

It would be naive to suppose that the erosion of Stavrogin's centrality is as straightforward as it has been presented up to this point. The second crux of the problem was mentioned at the beginning of this essay and has been neatly formulated by Jones: 'Stavrogin nevertheless remains the central figure among the main characters in the fiction, if only because everyone else seems to consider him to be.'[7] The most important feature of this formulation is that it implies at least two perspectives: one for the characters and another for the reader.

Jones's proposition is by no means inconsistent with the sequence of disillusionments traced above. The glory that has departed, the ideal now tarnished, the perfection once known all remain a potent influence, especially when Stavrogin's presence, an embodiment of Plato's anamnesis, is a constant reminder of a better past and thus maintains a positive sense of loss. Though *stavros* ('the cross') keeps before us Stavrogin as he is now, Nikolay ('the conqueror of nations') Vsevolodovich ('master of all')[8] does not allow us to forget him as some once saw him. (Dostoyevsky would presumably have balked at a Jewish name for his hero but Ichabod ('departed glory') has its merits.)

The reader, however, is less convinced of Stavrogin's heroic capacities because much of what he learns about him is acquired at a remove through the agency of several characters who are now losing, or have lost, their own certainty on the issue. Our literary disappointment at Stavrogin's deficiencies is of a different order from Dostoyevsky's portrayal of the dashing of their personal hopes. Only the rare reader will honestly echo Shatov's passionate and pathetic 'I can't tear you out of my heart, Nikolay Stavrogin' (X, 202; II, i, 7).

There is, in fact, yet a third perspective and this is Stavrogin's own. As is seen principally in his refusal to accept the role assigned to him by Pyotr Verkhovensky and in his absence from the fête, Stavrogin declines to regard himself as central. His own perspective is not so very far from that of the reader but does differ inasmuch as he is less concerned to understand why he is not central because he has put his past behind him more firmly than, in differing measures, either the reader or the other characters have done.

These shifting perspectives make it difficult to focus the vision and compose the picture. They are however only one group out of a number of comparable devices which conspire to the same end, and we will briefly widen our discussion to consider some of these.

The most unsettling effect on the narrative is brought about by the arbitrary shifts in Dostoyevsky's own imputed viewpoint.[9] He adopts no consistent approach in distinguishing between the omniscient author and a narrator, Mr G—v, subject to normal human limitations. Perhaps he intermittently forgot what he was doing (and we do know that by the time he got to the end of writing *The Devils* Dostoyevsky had himself fallen prey to normal human limitations and had forgotten what happened at the beginning).[10] Be that as it may, as the narrator lurches from his comparatively stable earlier condition of knowing only what a participant would know to his later condition of being able to tell us what Stavrogin looked like when there was nobody to observe him, the effect is to 'undermine further the stability of the novel's structure'.[11]

The question of time has already been discussed. Why is Stavrogin a Romantic at the wrong time? What is the chronological relationship between him and his 'intellectual father' Stepan Trofimovich Verkhovensky? Although the basic time progress of the novel is probably quite normal, it is not easy for the reader to keep track of where he is supposed to be at any point of the narrative: is this something which happened two years ago, or four and a half, or seven? Since the sequence of time is a primary element in determining the relationship between cause and effect, the fragmentation and readjustment of time disrupt the chain of causality. This is seen to perfection in a minute comical incident of surpassing triviality. Shatov and Stavrogin are standing talking. Stavrogin 'sat down on a chair. "Sit down!" shouted Shatov and somehow suddenly sat down himself' (X, 195; II, i, 6). In the face of this it is not easy to know if one is coming or going.

Most analyses of the novel concentrate, quite properly, on tracing the lines which connect the major figures. Behind this pattern however is another appallingly complex set of relationships. Liza Tushina is engaged to Maurice Drozdov, and her mother is a Drozdov. The Drozdovs are related to Yuliya von Lembke (who had dallied with Maurice Drozdov). She is related to the 'great writer' Karmazinov. Kirillov, the Lebyadkins and Shatov have lived in the same house. Shatov's wife has a child by Stavrogin and Shatov's sister has an affair with him. Drozdova does not help by enquiring, some four hundred and fifty years too late, after Prince Harry. And Shigalyov is, of course, Virginsky's brother-in-law. Second marriages, substitute fathers, the remoter degrees of consanguinity, indiscriminate fornication and a motley assemblage of hangers-on ensure that the reader will remain uncertain to the end whether he has pinned down the last tentacle of the octopus. It is all very difficult to cope with, rarely advances the narrative and is frequently tedious, but we should not underrate the contribution which it makes to creating a general sense of claustrophobic turmoil and an atmosphere fraught with crepuscular potentialities.

As though the novel were not sufficiently eventful there is a further category of pseudo-events. Consider, for instance, the dinner in honour of Gaganov, who had his nose pulled. Within the space of a very few lines a good head of enthusiastic steam is worked up for Gaganov – he becomes highly esteemed, people call on him, embrace him – and a public dinner is planned in his honour, when the populace suddenly comes to a collective realization that there is nothing to celebrate (X, 39; I, ii, 2). Or consider the case of Avdotya Tarapygina, the poor woman who saw the Spigulin workers being flogged, declared 'Disgraceful!', spat, and was flogged herself for her pains. The story was printed in the newspapers and the narrator even contributed twenty copecks to a fund for her. It was then established that she did not exist. 'So,' says the narrator, 'I am particularly mentioning this non-existent Avdotya Petrovna because the same thing nearly happened to Stepan Trofimovich (in the event that perhaps she really did exist)' (X, 343; II, x, 1), from which it appears that a non-existent person can exist and that what did not happen to someone who does exist is most conveniently defined by reference to what did not happen to someone else who did not exist. Whilst this (or most of it) is logically coherent, it is an uneconomical way of explaining the matter and, yet again, leaves the reader not knowing whether he is coming or going. As so often in Dostoyevsky, important principles can be illustrated by the most trivial examples: consider for instance the four broken legs which Liza and her mother might have sustained if they had gone to Matveyeva last week, which they did not; and if the potential of that incident is exhausted by being in the past, then Liza immediately torments herself with the pleasurable prospect of breaking both her legs in the future if she should fall off her horse (X, 157; I, v, 7). Even more absurd is the incident where Liputin asks Lebyadkin whether he thinks Stavrogin is mad and Lebyadkin leaps up, says Liputin, 'just as if I had suddenly lashed him with a knout from behind without his permission' (X, 83; I, iii, 6). The alternative possibility gratuitously suggested in the last three words is another of the bizarre events which, like Gaganov's dinner, do not take place, but the effect is to hold over the reader the threat of realizing the potential of these absurdities. It is not an idle threat: the fête is its realization.

In this slight broadening of the discussion we have moved from the multiple perspectives on Stavrogin's centrality to other techniques used to create muddle, doubt, turmoil, to disorientate us in our attempts to grasp the reality of 'our town'. If Dostoyevsky has been changing the rules in the course of the game, in the fête he makes it plain that there are no rules: there are no rules because there is no Stavrogin.

Dostoyevsky had previously achieved his greatest success in portraying a scandalous public uproar with Marmeladov's funeral feast in *Crime and Punishment*. Under the combined influence of foreigners, alcohol and torment of the soul, all semblance of logic, causality and decorum was abandoned. In *The Devils* however the sheer scale of the scandal is significant: there is more at stake here than the landlady's spoons. The fête itself turns into a ghastly cauldron of balefully seething social and moral bathybius. Stepan Trofimovich rises to unknown heights of incoherent eloquence; Turgenev is roasted over a slow fire; Captain Lebyadkin is less than sober; an itinerant mad professor makes the sort of contribution that such persons familiarly do; von Lembke is terminally unhinged by the sight of Lyamshin walking upside down in a dress-suit with tails; the town is set on fire. This literary *tour de force* of sustained hysteria and imaginative intoxication sets the pattern of the structure and is the most representative moment in the novel. The pattern is one of arbitrariness, misunderstanding, confusion; it is one in which the regular sequences of causality are disrupted, in which the world falls apart, because all we know of the world from the fiction is 'our town'. The fête is the fulfilment of Pyotr's plan as outlined to Stavrogin: 'We'll proclaim destruction...We'll start fires...We'll spread legends...Yes, indeed, and then the confusion will start! There'll be such an upheaval as the world has never seen...' (X, 325; II, viii).

At this point in his fantasy Pyotr will present the Crown Prince, Stavrogin, to the world; but with neither ideals nor illusions, ignorant of where to look for a lead, with no sense of purpose, 'soured and sick, cynical and faithless, but with a passionate longing for some guiding idea' (X, 518; III, viii), our town does not turn to Stavrogin, for he is the greatest disillusionment of all. Stavrogin pre-empts the failure to turn to him by being absent from this most central of all occasions; he is attending to his private concerns with Liza. At long last the perspectives are adjusted and all are agreed that the central position is vacant.[12]

There is no denying that *The Devils* leaves most readers obscurely dissatisfied even after many readings. It is no purpose of the present essay to bring about any radical change in that state of affairs. The confusion and dissatisfaction can however be turned to more constructive effect in understanding Dostoyevsky if they are seen not as an adverse critical reaction but as a positive response to the way in which the novel is put together. At the beginning of this essay we undertook not to attempt to divine Dostoyevsky's intentions but simply to look at the consequences of what he did. An exception must be made for one famous notebook entry which is too tempting to be omitted: 'All the rest moves around him [Stavrogin], like a kaleidoscope' (XI, 136). The constantly changing pattern of unstable images, sometimes with a space at the centre, suggested by the kaleidoscope, offers an instructive comparison: does any one viewer ever see the same pattern as any other? How can we tell whether they do? Jones expresses a similar idea in an entirely different way when he writes of the 'sensation of a world built upon shifting sands'.[13] Perhaps there is also something to be learnt from the affinities between Dostoyevsky's techniques in this novel of around 1870 and Wagner's forays into the murky world of slithery chromaticism in *Tristan und Isolde*, first produced in 1865, whose harmonies embarked on a rough sea from the third bar and never regained dry land, with the same unsettling effect for those making the voyage as is to be found amongst readers of Dostoyevsky. Consider by comparison the clean, diatonic progressions of Turgenev, in whose novels we always know where we are, not least because we have been there so many times before.

We must not impose upon *The Devils* a shape which would make it more manageable. An assertion of Stavrogin's centrality would give it such a shape but the evidence points in the opposite direction. As he becomes increasingly negative the others become more disillusioned and Stavrogin eventually vanishes from the public stage just when disillusion is at its lowest depth and he is most needed. Mystery and enigma have partially masked the growing apprehension that there was no longer a centre to the world, but finally it is understood that the Stavrogin who was is no more; that the Stavrogin who is has retreated deeper and deeper into the personal, where he remains central only to himself until, in terminal disillusion, he is bereft of even that centrality. There is nothing to regret in this and much to admire in the ingenuity with which the story of the gradual souring of hopes and loss of ideals is reflected in and reinforced by the structure of the novel, as it uses a complex arrangement of graduated anticlimaxes and shifting perspectives to push the source of those hopes and ideals even further from the centre. What we are left with in the end is a convincing demonstration of how to maintain artistic coherence in telling a story explicitly devoted to disintegration.

Notes

1. Richard Peace, *Dostoyevsky: An Examination of the Major Novels* (Cambridge, 1971), pp. 154–5.
2. *Ibid.*, pp. 201ff.
3. *Ibid.*, p. 180.
4. Malcolm V. Jones, *Dostoyevsky: The Novel of Discord* (London, 1976), p. 134.
5. *Ibid.*, p. 142.
6. *Ibid.*, p. 142.
7. *Ibid.*, p. 142.
8. Peace, *Dostoyevsky*, p. 180.
9. Jones, *Dostoyevsky*, pp. 146ff.
10. Peace, *Dostoyevsky*, p. 324.
11. Jones, *Dostoyevsky*, p. 147.
12. There are several revealing parallels here with Wagner. First, the attempt to portray the whole world: 'The story told in *The Ring*, undeniably, is the history of a whole world' (Deryck Cooke, *I Saw the World End: A Study of Wagner's Ring* (London, 1979), p. 248); and as Wagner himself said of the work 'it contains the beginning and end of the world!' (*ibid*, p. 248). Second, the emphasis on witnessing the collapse of the enterprise: the title of Cooke's work is taken from Wagner's definitive 1872 text of *Götterdämmerung.* Third, the association of the final cataclysm with love: Stavrogin is with Liza; Wagner carries us aloft on what he himself admitted was the illogical reintroduction of the Redemption by Love leitmotiv, closing the cycle with an inspiration of ecstatic bliss. 'But,' says Newman, 'how to express it in words was a problem that always baffled and finally defeated him' (Ernest Newman, *Wagner Nights* (London, 1977), pp. 667–9). It also baffled Dostoyevsky and the best he could manage was the 'conversion' of Stepan Trofimovich Verkhovensky.
13. Jones, *Dostoyevsky*, p. 146.

5

Ivan Karamazov

F. F. SEELEY

It is widely agreed that *The Brothers Karamazov* represents the 'synthesis' and culmination of Dostoyevsky's work, in which we are presented with the latest and richest developments and combinations of themes and types which have evolved through his earlier writings. Thus Ivan Karamazov is the last of a line sometimes designated in Russian 'philosophizing doubles' because of their intellectual preoccupations and split personalities. His genealogy can be traced back through such 'heresiarchs' as Kirillov and Raskolnikov to the Underground Man, and beyond him, in Dostoyevsky's pre-Siberian period, to such progenitors as Golyadkin (in *The Double*) and Ordynov (in 'The Landlady').[1] However, it may be argued that this literary ancestry is less interesting and significant than his biological inheritance.

Though it is often claimed that Dostoyevsky wrote in terms of 'coexistence and interaction' as opposed to 'becoming', this formula will not fit *The Brothers Karamazov*, in which we can follow not only the processes of heredity working itself out from one generation to another, and not only the psychological maturation of, at any rate, Mitya Karamazov, but the evolution of Ivan's thinking over a six-year period. And, in view of the attention traditionally focussed on Ivan as a 'thinker', it may be well to start here by outlining this evolution before turning to an analysis of its biological and biographical foundations.

I

By most critics the character and content of Ivan's thinking are examined mainly within the limits of his 'Legend of the Grand Inquisitor'. This is hardly surprising: the 'Legend' forms the climax of Book V of the novel and Dostoyevsky himself declared Books V and VI to be of pivotal importance.

Some critics have vouchsafed a glance at Ivan's article on the ecclesiastical courts. This, like the 'Legend', is summarized by Ivan himself and is the subject of comments by other personages in the novel; but it occupies so few paragraphs, and is sandwiched so modestly between much more vivid and dramatic scenes, that very little has been made of it.

But the 'Legend' and the article represent only two out of the four recorded stages of Ivan's thinking, and the four need to be considered together and in sequence if one is to obtain an over-all view of its evolution. Dostoyevsky does nothing to encourage such an enterprise: he presents them to his readers out of chronological order and puts two of them into the mouth of a personage whose reliability may be a matter of dispute.

In chronological order – that is in the order in which they were produced in Ivan's mind – the four phases of Ivan's thought are embodied in the 'legend' of the 'philosopher' who refused to believe in paradise, the 'Legend of the Grand Inquisitor', the article on the ecclesiastical courts and the 'Geological Upheaval'. These span the period between Ivan's high-school days and his father's murder, that is between his eighteenth and his twenty-fourth year. As might be expected, there is continuity between all four phases, especially in the problems addressed, but there are radical differences between the hypotheses propounded as solutions to the problems – and between Ivan's self-image in his teens and in his twenties.

The 'legend' of the philosopher who refused to believe in a future life; refused for a thousand years to accept the penalty imposed on him for his unbelief; and finally, after walking a quadrillion kilometres in darkness, became convinced that two seconds in paradise was worth a walk of a quadrillion quadrillions raised to the quadrillionth power – is related not by Ivan in his own person, but by his 'devil'. But since this devil is also our main source for Ivan's final construct, the 'Geological Upheaval', it is necessary to consider his credibility as a source.

Ivan's Mysterious Visitor complains that he is a 'much maligned person'; if he could have foreseen how Dostoyevsky's critics would treat him, his complaint might have been even louder! Most of them approach him either in religious terms, as the Father of Lies, or else in psychological terms, as Ivan's 'double', but uncritically swallowing Ivan's assertion that this double comprises only the basest and the stupidest, the most vile and vulgar elements of his self, and mainly of his past self at that.

However, this is grossly unfair to Ivan's devil, who is a most interesting personage in his own right. It is true that he embodies some of Ivan's characteristics of which Ivan is ashamed, such as 'Romanticism'; but he also criticizes or mocks such characteristics in Ivan, if not in himself too. Certain other characteristics of Ivan's, to which Ivan clings in spite, perhaps, of some underlying ambivalence, are unhestitatingly deplored by the devil in relation to himself: what Ivan calls 'my Euclidean mind' becomes, in the devil's terminology, 'common sense...that most unhappy attribute of my nature'. Indeed, the devil has positive qualities of his own: he is sociable and equable, which Ivan is not; and, above all, he reveals a homely sense of humour, of which Ivan shows no trace in any other context.

Of course, as an emanation of Ivan, he cannot have in him any element which is not in Ivan; so we must posit in Ivan a 'repressed' sense of humour. And we may wonder just when that sense of humour was repressed. Was Ivan still capable of laughing at himself at the time when he thought up the legend of the unbelieving philosopher? From what we know of his childhood and adolescence, most probably not. The way in which the story is told in Ivan's nightmare is, in that case, the devil's; but we have Ivan's word for it that the story is his own, and he lays particular stress on its originality: it had emerged from the depths of his being.

So too we have at least partial corroboration of the devil's account of the 'Geological Upheaval', where Ivan confirms, in Zosima's cell, that belief in God and in the immortality of the soul is an indispensable basis for morality, and the lack or destruction of such belief a sanction for immorality. Moreover Ivan does not, in his nightmare, challenge any part of the devil's account of the 'Geological Upheaval'; so we must assume that – in regard to these two myths – the 'Father of Lies' is a 'witness of truth'.

Ivan's teenage 'legend' of the unbelieving philosopher marks a stage just short of the 'dead point' in his struggle between faith and unbelief. Faith is still able to tip the balance – but only barely able: it takes a thousand years and a quadrillion miles to bow that stiff neck and subdue that stubborn heart. The 'philosopher' is, like Ivan, a scientist (he is, in fact, Ivan), and it is clearly implied that it is modern science which has destroyed faith. Science believes it has all the answers: our 'philosopher'–scientist values the *a priori* principles of his science above his direct experience – of life after death. Only the direct experience of paradise does, at last, overwhelm the arrogance of the *a priori* and burst the bounds of mathematics and cosmology. The way the devil tells the story foreshadows – or rather, parodies – the way Ivan had told the story of the Grand Inquisitor. This myth of the unbelieving philosopher is also a 'legend', and as Ivan prefaced his 'Legend' with references to mediaeval literary models, so the devil claims that his 'legend' dates from the Middle Ages of hell: for hell, like earth, has had its Middle Ages and has its religious fanatics. Ironically, the devil defines his mission as the very opposite of that of the Grand Inquisitor, who claims to provide happiness for billions at the price of the unhappiness of one hundred thousand elect: the devil sees himself as appointed to 'destroy thousands so that one may be saved'. And the piquancy of the parody is further enhanced by the total difference in content and style between the two 'legends'.

The 'Legend of the Grand Inquisitor' dates from about a year before Ivan declaims it to Alyosha. So there had been an interval of five years between the composition of the first and the composition of the second legend. Studies and interpretations of the 'Legend of the Grand Inquisitor' are legion; at this point, three comments are in order as germane to our outline of the evolution of Ivan's thought.

First: although the 'Legend' is almost everywhere treated as the measure and peak of Ivan's intellectual achievement, it does not in fact represent the ultimate stage of his thinking, and it is interesting that he should present it to Alyosha as if it did. At the date when the two brothers met for their fateful conference, the 'Legend' had been supplemented, or modified, by Ivan's article on the ecclesiastical courts, and had been – or was about to be – virtually superseded by the 'Geological Upheaval'. Ivan is driven to bring up his Grand Inquisitor in order to meet Alyosha's challenge: how would your rebel against God's world deal with the person and teaching of Christ?

Secondly: who can fail to be struck by certain dissonances or incongruities between the revolt against God's world of Ivan himself in the chapter entitled 'Revolt' and the rebellion of the Grand Inquisitor – just such incongruities as would be likely if the 'Legend' expresses attitudes and assumptions which Ivan had partly, or largely, transcended in the intervening year. The Grand Inquisitor rebels against Christ's teaching out of love and compassion for humanity; Ivan revolts against the order of the universe out of love and compassion for little children. It would seem that in the course of twelve months Ivan's revolt has broadened in scope while his sympathies have narrowed. The Grand Inquisitor proclaims the happiness of mankind as his objective; Ivan's clamour is for justice, without which his life will not be worth living. The Grand Inquisitor will devote his energies and his life to organizing society in peace and prosperity; Ivan returns his ticket to eternity and proposes to spend his life, or at least his youth, in the pursuit of personal satisfactions. Within the last year, he has exchanged the humanitarian goals of utopian socialism for the individual goals of private hedonism.

And thirdly: Ivan, who at eighteen had imaged and projected himself as a unitary figure bent on mastering experience with the armoury of science, was imaging and projecting himself at twenty-two as irremediably split into a would-be rational and realistic votary of order (heir to Vergil's Rome!)[2] and a prisoner, a forlorn victim of his own romantic cult of freedom.

The article on the ecclesiastical courts, written and published within months of the composition of the 'Legend of the Grand Inquisitor', can hardly have involved any significant changes of position: the time interval was too short. It seems plausible to regard it as an appendix or supplement to the 'Legend', or perhaps – better still – as an experiment to find out how society might react to an adumbration of the regime of the Grand Inquisitor. Such testing of his theory or 'idea' is characteristic of each of Dostoyevsky's heresiarchs, but is, of course, doubly appropriate in Ivan, whose training had been in the natural sciences.

Finally, our hero is caught up in the 'Geological Upheaval' consequent upon the breakdown of belief in the existence of God and the immortality of the human soul. Our main source here is again Ivan's devil; we are entitled, if not bound, to accept his account as reliable, but unfortunately it is only fragmentary.

Like the 'Legend of the Grand Inquisitor', the 'Geological Upheaval' offers two fundamentally irreconcilable answers to the question 'How is Man to live?' Only, in the latter myth the answers are presented not as simultaneous alternatives – not in confrontation – but as sequential, so that their contradiction is blurred or masked. The two answers are re-evoked from earlier writings of Dostoyevsky's: Versilov's vision of men's ultimate state in a sort of Elysium or Isles of the Blessed, preceded, during an interim period of indefinite duration, by Kirillov's fantasy of the 'man-god' who is bound to substitute his will as the supreme law for the law which has prevailed hitherto.

Ivan's thought has come a long way in these six years of emergence from boyhood into manhood. He envisions himself first as a scientist, who rejects God and immortality as incompatible with his science, but who ends by capitulating to the direct experience of immortality and God. Five years later he has concluded that questions such as those of the existence of God and the immortality of the soul are not to be resolved by feeble human wits; the most that man can hope to do is so to organize human society as to do away with the worst of human suffering. A year after this, during or shortly before his visit to his father's house, he has lost confidence in the possibility of such a utopia. He plays with a dream of individual salvation in the form of at least a respite of private joys – 'till the age of thirty'. But he is one 'to whom the miseries of the world / Are misery and will not let him rest'; and he is torn apart between the urge to live and the need to understand what life is for. As his prospects of achieving either purpose appear more and more dubious, his hold on reality weakens: he is standing on the brink of an abyss, over which he projects new fantasies in desperate attempts to light up the darkness beyond.

On a superficial view it might seem as if this six-year mental struggle could be fitted into a dialectic, or at least a spiral pattern. At first there is the psychological unity and assurance, the life lived out and 'justified' in the pursuit of the one 'Truth' (with the collapse into faith relegated to some quite inconceivably remote future); next, the antithesis of the Euclidean (or Aristotelian) 'either–or': the stark choice between the 'happiness' of peace provided by order and the suffering which is a necessary condition of freedom, which in turn is a necessary condition of love; then, Euclid / Aristotle transcended in a 'both–and': both the freedom of the man-god, to whom 'all is permitted', and the happy peace and togetherness of the future Golden Age.

But on closer inspection, this synthesis is seen to be just a pseudo-synthesis. Not only is there no place for the man-god in the earthly paradise, but the era of the man-god cannot possibly lead up to an era of earthly paradise. For the essence of the man-god is 'self-will', whilst at the core of the earthly paradise is a harmony of wills, minds and hearts. How, then, could such a society ever be evolved out of any proliferation of man-gods?

The devil himself raises the question how far his host could truly believe in the realization of an earthly paradise with nothing beyond (and it does indeed fly in the face of Ivan's conviction that it is impossible to love one's neighbour here on earth), and caps this query with the barbed suggestion that the concept of the man-god is merely what would today be called a 'rationalization' of Ivan's urges to escape from the shackles of traditional morality.

Ivan's reply to these insinuations is none the less eloquent for dispensing with words: he hurls a glass of tea at his visitor. This is evidently to admit that the devil has a point – or even, that his taunt has struck home. But what Ivan is acknowledging is not necessarily the charge of bad faith; what would be apt to enrage him even more would be the opening of his eyes to the incoherence to which his proud intelligence is being reduced by the human relations and problems in which he has involved himself. To clarify these relations and problems, we must turn back to his heredity and upbringing.

II

Dostoyevsky was opposed, on principle, to all varieties of psychological determinism: that is, to any theory claiming that individual behaviour is determined by character which is itself determined by external material factors, whether environmental or genetic. In the 1860s, his main attack is on theories which cite environment as the prime cause of crime and antisocial personalities. And accordingly, till the mid-1870s we never have a portrait of both parents of any of his major characters; in many cases, we learn virtually nothing of either parent.

But in the wake of Darwinism, heredity came to be widely regarded as a second major factor – beside, or before, environment – in shaping character. And *The Adolescent* is the first work in which Dostoyevsky gives us full-length portraits of his protagonist's father and mother. But the stress here is not yet on heredity; this was a year or more before Dostoyevsky is supposed to have 'discovered' Zola, who had defined his Rougon-Macquart series as 'Histoire naturelle et sociale d'une famille...' and who, in the Preface to *La Fortune des Rougon*, had laid it down that 'la famille que je me propose d'étudier, a pour caractéristique le débordement des appétits, le large soulèvement de notre âge, qui se rue aux jouissances'. And in Dostoyevsky's last novel 'the Karamazov inheritance' is a constantly recurring motif.[3]

Nevertheless, critical reflections on the heredity of the Karamazov brothers have remained sparse and mostly superficial. It seems obvious that Alyosha is predominantly his mother's son; indeed, if it were not for his confidences to Rakitin and Mitya, few readers would charge him with any resemblance to his father; even the confidences are sometimes discounted as a fine concern not to seem better than other people, not to wound their susceptibilities. But this is to overlook the 'absurd, frantic modesty and chastity' (*dikaya, isstuplennaya stydlivost' i tselomudrennost'*), a transparent reaction-formation, into which he had 'sublimated' his inheritance of sensuality. Dostoyevsky, who must have destined Alyosha for sins of the flesh as well as other sins in the unwritten second volume of the Karamazovs' history, was far too good a writer not to have supplied advance evidence of his hero's latent disposition. Nor is sensuality, perhaps, the only trait which Alyosha may have owed to his father. There is a strange lability in his religious faith, even before it has been really severely tested by life. To Lise he says, 'Now, perhaps I don't even believe in God' (XIV, 201; V, i). At the first demonstration that the world is not run according to his idea of justice, he is ready to rise up against its Maker and is saved from sin only by a chance complex of circumstances. Old Karamazov's beliefs about God, the Devil, and the next world are obviously much more shallow-rooted and kaleidoscopic; but at Alyosha's age and in his circumstances, even the minor fluctuations are noteworthy.

In Smerdyakov, one could say that his father's amorality has combined with his mother's idiocy to produce a moral idiot, or psychopath, devoid of moral sense and human affections (though he does, oddly, claim to have 'loved' Ivan: this may perhaps connote a mixture of fascination with a superior intelligence and attraction to a figure perceived as a potential ally). In a combination of such disparate elements, it makes little sense to try to quantify the respective contributions of father and mother.

But Mitya – contrary to his own assumptions, to those of the other personages in the novel, and to those of most critics – has more in him of Adelaida Miusova than of Fyodor Karamazov. The Karamazov elements are by no means as limited in Mitya as they are in Alyosha, but they appear to account for a good deal less than half of his psychic make-up. This widespread misconception is all the more curious because a majority of personages and critics, if asked directly, 'Do you, then, see Mitya as the same kind of man as his father?' – would almost certainly answer, 'No: a very different kind of man.'

Why, then, this general obsession with Mitya's 'Karamazov inheritance'? To understand this, it is necessary to draw a distinction which is blurred everywhere in the novel, and subsequently in a good deal of the critical literature (although it was noticed by at least one critic over a hundred years ago).[4] All the Karamazov boys use the same word, *sladostrastiye*, to designate their father's instinctual disposition and their own. This is a mistake (which Dostoyevsky shares with them – or which, at any rate, he does nothing to challenge). Old Karamazov *is* a *sladostrastnik* – a voluptuary. His lust for pleasure is both exorbitant and undiscriminating; it has swamped his inhibitions, his respect for higher values, his capacity for love (not quite completely, as is shown by his attitude to Alyosha): in short, it impoverishes and destroys rather than enhances life. Mitya is not a voluptuary, but a sensualist, greedy for life and enjoyment, but by no means without inhibitions and discrimination. We see him capable of devoted, even chivalrous love – which would seem to have been beyond Fyodor Pavlovich even in his youth. Admittedly, there is in Mitya's sensuality a streak of excess and a streak of obsession; but, from his infancy up, he had been starved of affection, and such starvation is apt to engender such avidity: in a happy marriage Mitya has every chance of achieving a more normal emotional range and balance.

With *sladostrastiye* safely out of the way – what has Mitya taken from his father, and what from his mother? From both parents, 'le débordement des appétits'. The dissipation of Mitya's army days is the male analogue of the 'life of complete emancipation' into which Adelaida had plunged in St Petersburg: Mitya, like his mother, is simply following the fashion of his time and place. It is perhaps only when he encounters Katya and, later, Grushenka, that Karamazov elements are superadded.

From his father, the vein of meanness (*podlost'*) that brings Katya to his rooms and toys with the idea of humiliating her there; the vein of silliness or muddleheadedness (*bestolkovost'*) which however does not in Fyodor, as it does in Mitya, extend to business affairs; and the shamed sense of his own 'foulness' (*bezobraziye*), which drives both men to misbehave, though in quite different ways.

From his mother: the physical courage and aggressiveness displayed in her fights with her husband; the careless generosity with which she abandoned her dowry to him; the impulsiveness and the inability to respect or conform to social norms; the warm-heartedness; and the Romantic 'idealism'.

Ivan's inheritance differs from that of his brothers, Alyosha and Mitya, in two crucial and fateful respects.[5] If Alyosha's psychic make-up is overwhelmingly, and Mitya's is predominantly, derived from their respective mothers, Ivan's nature is compounded about equally of paternal and maternal elements. This would be the almost inescapable inference from the intellectual and emotional deadlock in which he comes before us; but it is actually corroborated in the text of the novel also. Smerdyakov says to Ivan: 'You are like Fyodor Pavlovich, of all his children, sir, you have turned out likest him, with the same soul, sir' (XV, 68; XI, viii). But old Karamazov, speaking to Alyosha, says of Ivan: 'I can't recognize Ivan at all [as my blood]. Where did such a man spring from? His soul is nothing like ours' ('*Da ya Ivana ne priznayu sovsem. Otkuda takoy poyavilsya? Ne nasha sovsem dusha*') (XIV, 159; IV, ii). Smerdyakov, having a good deal of Fyodor in him, recognizes Fyodor's traits in Ivan, and stresses them, both because he senses that this will be odious to Ivan and, perhaps, by way of hinting at Ivan's affinities with himself. Fyodor, who has just discovered that he is even more afraid of Ivan than of Mitya, now perceives him as wholly alien; he does not connect this alien character with his second wife, Ivan's mother, because, as he had shown only the day before (XIV, 127; III, viii) he does not think of Ivan as Sofya's son. So Smerdyakov sees Ivan as essentially Karamazov, while Fyodor sees him as essentially not-Karamazov.

But Ivan's predicament is even more tragic. Not only is he split 'fifty-fifty' between his father's nature and his mother's, but he is unwilling to accept either half as his own. Alyosha is quite content to have inherited his mother's nature, and struggles against such marginal traits in himself as lust or doubt – not because they come from his father, but because they threaten the unity of his being and the system of his values. Mitya's position is more difficult. The paternal component in his nature, though not predominant, looms large; and not only is Mitya aware of it, but he exaggerates its scope, is ashamed of it and detests it. On the other hand, he has no knowledge or clear remembrance of his mother; and though he has, romantically, enshrined an image of her in his heart, so that in a supreme crisis he can attribute his sparing of his father's life to his mother's intervention, yet that image is doubtless too shadowy to serve as a stable focus for identification or a strong counter-centre in his struggles for 'the ideal of the Madonna' against the 'ideal of Sodom'. In fine, Mitya consciously rejects his father while unconsciously identifying with his mother.

Ivan's loathing and rejection of his father is much more intense than Mitya's, in proportion as the Karamazov elements occupy a greater part of his psyche: Ivan wants his father dead, whereas Mitya only wants to neutralize his rival with Grushenka.

Ivan's rejection of his father is direct, open, unambiguous. His rejection of his mother is indirect and probably unconscious in the main. He rejects the world made by (his mother's) God. He strives to reject (his mother's) God. He mobilizes his Karamazov 'love of life' in plans to bury or shelve – at least till the age of thirty – all consideration of ultimate questions (*proklyatyye voprosy*). Above all, he chooses and sets out to adopt a life-style – science, writing, scepticism – equally remote from his mother's simple religion as from his father's debauchery, avarice and laodiceanism. He sets one half of his nature against the other – Karamazov earthy passion against Sofya's otherworldliness and passivity, and Sofya's muted rebelliousness against Karamazov licence and foulness (*bezobraziye*) – and aims to transcend both.

What, then, are the attributes which Ivan owes to his parents? To Sofya, his involvement with religion, his powers of attraction and his rebelliousness. Obviously, they appear in him transmuted. In Sofya, religion is 'natural', a force pervading her being and her life, from which she draws comfort and the strength to endure her sufferings. In Ivan, religion is under constant attack, both from his intellect and from his Karamazov passions, battling for survival, if not at times completely submerged. To him it is a source not of comfort, but of torment. Sofya arouses in rough Grigory a devotion which nerves him to stand up to his master on her behalf. Reactions to Ivan are more various. He is 'loved' by personages as different from him and from one another as Alyosha, Katya and – Smerdyakov. But Mitya is awed by him, old Karamazov is afraid of him, Lise is fascinated by him, and Katya's aunt dislikes him. In Sofya, revolt against the constant outrages to her heart and human dignity are muted by her religion or converted by her helplessness into hysteria (*klikushestvo*); only on one occasion – when her husband lets Belyavsky come courting her and submits to his blow in her presence – does it become overt and explicit. Ivan's revolt stops at nothing: it condemns his father, challenges Christ's teaching, indicts the order of the universe.

The qualities in Ivan which may be traceable to his father are also transmuted, and usually intensified and refined. It is a far cry from Fyodor's uglier appetites to Ivan's ardent thirst for life and joy, from Fyodor's, mainly practical, shrewdness to Ivan's speculative intelligence, from Fyodor's desultory reading to Ivan's scientific and literary culture, from Fyodor's random fantasies to Ivan's creativity in writing and myth-making. The shame to which Zosima, endorsed by Fyodor himself, attributes Fyodor's clowning and general misbehaviour, has in Ivan become excruciating: he is ashamed of his father, ashamed of his father's spirit in himself (and arguably, of more than his father's spirit), and he vents this shame in rage: against his father, against Mitya and Smerdyakov with whom he shares so much of that abhorred spirit, and against himself. Zosima also warned Fyodor against 'the lie in the soul', self-deception. And on two capital issues at least – his feelings for Katya and his desire for his father's death – Ivan is caught up in such a tissue of contradictions that it is a moot point how far he is deluded and how far self-deluded: that is, whether he is shutting his eyes to what he could see if he wanted to, or whether these are 'blind spots' due to repression of key materials into his unconscious.

And it may be relevant to recall here that, in Zosima's cell, old Karamazov allows himself to wonder whether he may not have a devil – if only a low-grade one, since he deserves no better! – and that when Ivan's devil makes his appearance, it is in the guise of a parasite, that is, in the very role in which Fyodor Karamazov had taken the first steps in his career. Thus symbolically Ivan identifies his devil with his father, and rams the point home by insisting (mistakenly, as we have argued) that this devil embodies only the basest and stupidest, the most vile and vulgar elements of his self.

Finally, one might discern in Ivan's pride a composite of his mother's integrity and sense of honour (as evidenced, for example, in the Belyavsky incident) and his father's arrogance, which is the obverse of his shame at his own *podlost'* and *bezobraziye*. The maternal aspect of it is most evident in his refusal to indulge his passion for Katya at Mitya's expense (that is till Mitya is definitely out of the running) and in the bitter struggle with his false pride which issues in his testimony at the trial; but it may be recognized too in the demand for independence (*nikomu ne klanyat'sya*) attested to by Smerdyakov.

III

It is a truism among educationists that it is the first seven years of life which set an indelible stamp upon the character and personality of the individual; and the rule certainly proves valid in regard to Ivan Karamazov. Though we are told nothing of how Ivan lived through those years, there can be no question of their effects on the formation of his character and thinking.

Why does Alyosha, who was only three when his mother died, remember her and preserve her image as a guiding light, while Ivan, who was seven at the time, is allowed no memories of her? Was it because Alyosha was the favourite child? Or because he was too young to realize much of what was going on in his home? And does Ivan really remember nothing of those first seven years: that is, have his memories been repressed into the unconscious, as commonly happens with very unhappy or traumatized children? Or does he remember but, unlike Alyosha, refuse to share his memories? These are questions which cannot be answered; but fortunately our interpretation of the influence of those years on Ivan's development need not depend on being able to answer them.

Ivan must have been a highly intelligent and sensitive child, and he cannot have failed to sense and 'understand' – with his heart, if not with his head – how unhappy his mother was, that his father was the cause of her unhappiness, and how ugly his father's behaviour was. The seeds of his hatred of his father and of all cruelty, of his compassion for victims of human cruelty, and of his revolt against an order of things which gave such fathers unlimited power to inflict such cruelty – were certainly sown in those years, irrespective of whether his memories of them remained conscious or not and irrespective of whether he identified with his mother or rejected her also in his heart. If he identified with her, then his later rebelliousness was rooted in an instinctive grasp of the significance of her hysteria and a transmutation of it, later, in terms of his own powers and circumstances. But it is more likely that he 'rejected', or tried to 'reject' her (if he had identified with her, he should, like Alyosha, have had no difficulty in 'accepting' her God) and, despising what seemed her submission to tyranny, adopted his revolt not as a variation on her attitude, but as an alternative to it.

Of course, in those seven years Ivan's emotional and intellectual development was being conditioned not only by the relations between his parents, but equally if not more profoundly by his own plight and that of little Alyosha. From his father he will have had neither affection nor attention; and though Fyodor may never have punished nor even shouted at his children, Sofya's fear of him cannot but have communicated itself to the growing boy. His mother will have loved him, and, in his earliest years at least, with a full, warm, healthy love, however it may have been chequered later by preoccupation with the baby and by the fits of hysteria during which the servants felt that even the baby was not safe in her hands.

But what is remarkable is how closely Ivan's adult conception of the world is patterned on the experiences of his first seven years. He cannot conceive the possibility of loving one's neighbour, i.e. the people around one, because there had been so blighting a lack of love between the adults in his childhood world. Yet he loves children – because his mother loved him. But not all children – not all who are young and inexperienced and vulnerable; his attitude to Lise, whom Alyosha sees as a sick child, is one of brutal cynicism. He loves only children under seven, that is up till the age at which he lost his mother and, with her, all love. And these little children he not only loves, but idealizes. Under seven there are no ugly children. And children under seven are innocent: they have no knowledge of good and evil. There is a terrible gulf (*strashno otstoyat*) between them and the rest of humanity: they seem quite different beings, with a quite different nature. And so it is their sufferings (not those of wicked adults) which are intolerable, for which Ivan must and will call God to account, for which he must have justice and, since justice is impossible in regard to them, because of whom he will return his ticket to eternity. But surely it was Ivan himself who (in his unconscious memories) was, till the age of seven, beautiful and innocent, because loved – but not happy, for he suffered with his mother's sufferings – and at the age of seven was stripped of all he had and cherished. Like Job, he was delivered by God into the hands of Satan, for no fault of his; but unlike Job, he does not bless the name of the Lord in his affliction. When he rejects God's world on account of the suffering of little children – it is, unconsciously, his own sufferings, his own wrongs that he cannot forgive.

But at seven, revolt is not practicable. Ivan withdrew into himself. In Grigory's primitive home, in the grand but loveless house of the General's widow, in the family circle of Polenov, he held aloof, nursing his grief and his shame: shame for his father, shame for his own dependence. He concentrated on study, perhaps as the quickest path to independence, and proved a brilliant student; later, left to work his way through university on his own resources, he not only achieved independence, but developed new talents – literary and critical – which brought him notice and the respect he craved.

Still, his mind is a battlefield. At eighteen he had imagined he could find in science an escape route, at least for the duration of his life, from the 'frenzied and indecent' thirst for life of the Karamazovs and the religious obsession and precarious mental and emotional balance of Sofya. But university and the world beyond have extended his perspectives. The problem of his own salvation is now seen to be bound up with the destinies of humanity. Who among men is capable of freedom? The masses are not, and left to themselves, they will perish miserably. They can be saved only by the rule of superior intelligences; and would it not be nobler for these to devote themselves to establishing their weaker brethren in security and 'happiness' than selfishly to seek their own salvation either in the 'serene temples' of scientific wisdom or in the solitude of a desert? And so the Grand Inquisitor is conjured up. Here too the main features of the picture – the opposition between unlimited paternal power and helpless childlike submission – are extrapolations from Ivan's first seven years. But the Grand Inquisitor is a 'good' father: he uses his authority and power to make his children 'happy' and he takes the sufferings of the world upon himself.

This fantasy does not satisfy Ivan for long, though as a good scientist he proceeds immediately to test the 'idea' by writing and publishing his article on the ecclesiastical courts. His own doubts about the basic conception may be inferred from the ambiguity of his presentation, which leaves room for the most varied interpretations. And Ivan hardly waits to study the reactions before starting to search for another creed.

Reasons for this switch of interest are not far to seek. The 'Legend' was likely to occur only to a solitary such as Ivan then was. It presents in the foreground only the two selves of Ivan, with the mass of mankind somewhere in outer darkness. But within a few months Ivan had become involved, for the first time since his childhood, in personal, emotional relations with other human individuals. He had been drawn into Mitya's imbroglio with Katya and had fallen passionately in love with her. And to follow up this affair – to mediate between Mitya and his father – he had returned to his childhood home. What was needed now was a myth, or rather, two myths: one for the immediate present, the other for the near future. Ivan hated his father with a deadly hatred (perhaps, largely unconscious); he detested, despised, and was jealous of, Mitya; and he loved Katya. He wanted Katya for himself; so he wanted Mitya out of the way, as he would be if he married Grushenka, and he did not want the old man to marry Grushenka, which would have made it more difficult for his pride to woo Katya, in view of the disparity between her wealth and his prospects. So what was required was, first, a myth to legitimize the removal of Mitya and Fyodor and his own union with Katya; and then, a myth to establish that, although love of one's neighbour has been impossible until now, a time is at hand when it will become possible for humans to love one another and to be happy in doing so. Hence the twin myths – of the man-god, to whom 'everything is permitted', and of the earthly paradise to follow. If it be objected that this is to assimilate Ivan's myth-making *ante litteram* to Freud's theory of dreams, objectors might reread the exposition, by no less an authority than Ivan's devil, of the scope and artistry of 'dream-work'.

Did he actually want Mitya to kill their father, which would have removed both of them from his path, perhaps no less effectually? The evidence here is complicated and contradictory. On the one hand, we have Alyosha's categorical and repeated 'It wasn't you who killed him' (XV, 40, 87; XI, v and x), which can only mean, 'You didn't intend to have him killed', for the intention would have been equivalent to the sin.[6] On the same side we have Ivan's assurance to Smerdyakov at their last meeting: 'I swear I was not as guilty as you thought, and perhaps I wasn't inciting you at all' (XV, 66–7; XI, viii). The most that Ivan will admit here is that he may have had an unconscious desire (*taynoye zhelaniye*) for his father's death. But on the other hand, there are his words to Alyosha before the murder: 'One reptile will devour the other, and serve them both right!'; and: 'who has not the right to desire... even the death [of another]?...As to my desires, I allow myself full scope in this matter' (XIV, 131, 132; III, ix).

To harmonize these pronouncements, especially in the light of Book V ('Pro and Contra'), one might assume that the sensual-rationalistic Ivan wanted his father dead, while the would-be Christian Ivan did not, and that the desire continued to play hide-and-seek with Ivan's consciousness, as it is not uncommon in neurosis for 'unacceptable' desires to remain in consciousness so long as they carry no emotional charge (and therefore no potential for action), but to fade from consciousness in proportion as they become emotionally charged, and to disappear from consciousness completely when the emotionally charged desire, or intention, is ripe for translation into action. Thus after Mitya's assault on their father Ivan can speak coolly to Alyosha of desiring the old man's death, while assuring him that he will not allow any killing to take place, and be perfectly sincere in this. Whereas next day, in his colloquy with Smerdyakov outside the gate, Ivan is in effect talking with two voices, of which he himself hears only one, while Smerdyakov hears only the other: Ivan thinks he is only satisfying his curiosity by his detailed questions about the danger to his father, while Smerdyakov, intent on not mistaking his young master's meaning, clearly hears behind the spoken words unspoken signals of approval for the crime.

What has happened within the last twenty-four hours to convert Ivan's conscious wish into unconscious will? Only two things: his break with Katya and his communion with Alyosha, which immediately precedes this splitting of his consciousness. The process must actually have begun during that meeting of the brothers, for the chapters entitled 'The Brothers Get Acquainted' and 'Revolt' are full of contradictory utterances; but at that point Ivan is still conscious of everything he says and means what he says while he is saying it. Whereas in the talk with Smerdyakov, there are no contradictions, but the unitary utterance is so refracted that one part of the spectrum of meaning is perceived by Ivan, the other part by his interlocutor. No doubt, Smerdyakov hears what he wants to hear, but he does not want to misunderstand Ivan. Ivan wants to understand his father's situation; but part of the meaning of his words is screened from his consciousness (though not from his unconscious: hence the repeated flares of temper). And the splitting of consciousness continues to the end of the novel, escalating into hallucination in 'Ivan's Nightmare' and lapsing ultimately into something like brain fever.

For sixteen years, since the death of his mother, Ivan has remained locked up inside himself, avoiding all close personal ties (as witness his admission to Alyosha that he has no friends). Suddenly fate throws him up against a girl and three men who arouse powerful emotions in him. But he distrusts emotions – positive ones even more than negative – and he will not give his free play now. He insists on treating Katya as his brother's fiancée, and for months he keeps Alyosha at arm's length, ignoring the boy's mute appeals for a *rapprochement*. Yet he believes himself in love with Katya and declares more than once that he 'loves' Alyosha.

These emotions, churning inside him, have been eroding the fragile unity of the personality he had so long striven to construct on the basis of the two disparate halves of his nature. The Karamazov elements, in particular, have been straining to break loose and establish an ascendancy over the rest. This is evidenced in the 'Geological Upheaval': whereas the myth of the earthly paradise, like the earlier myths of the unbelieving philosopher and the Grand Inquisitor, are creations of the whole personality, the myth of the man-god is essentially a Karamazov myth. (And, in accordance with his usual practice, Ivan has started to test it, flaunting the principle that 'all is permitted' before society and before Smerdyakov, in whom he finds an apt pupil. Mitya too is interested, but finally cannot stomach the major premiss, the non-existence of God.)

Now, the dykes are breached. In a single day the emotions held down and caged in for months have burst out and found utterance, first in his declaration of love for Katya, then, more abundantly, in his 'confession' to Alyosha. And this release of feeling into expression marks a turning-point: from here on, the Karamazov in Ivan will have a voice of its own, an 'independent' voice – outside the purview of Ivan's central consciousness. That is what we hear in the colloquy with Smerdyakov at the gates, in Ivan's three visits to Smerdyakov after he returns from Moscow and in his final appearance in court. And not for nothing is the headlong passion for Katya, to which he 'abandons himself totally' after his return from Moscow, defined by the epithets 'burning' (*plamennoy*), 'insane' (*bezumnoy*) and – 'new' (*novoy*) (XV, 48; XI, vi). The devil in Ivan's nightmare expresses – despite Ivan's endeavours to equate him with Fyodor – not one but all sides of his nature; but in the following chapter, 'It Was He Who Said That', in which Ivan attributes to his vanished devil a series of sneers designed to deter Ivan from proclaiming his guilt in court next day, this invented (as distinct from hallucinated) devil is a Karamazov product.

From the time he leaves home (at the end of Book V) to the end of the novel, Ivan is engaged in strenuous if sporadic efforts to re-establish the integrity of his being: we have glimpses of them in his last-minute decision not to go to Chermashnya (Chermashnya represents Smerdyakov, Moscow – escape from Katya and temptation); in his judgement on himself, 'I am a scoundrel' (XIV, 255; V, vii), when he reaches Moscow; in his repeated, if twice aborted attempts to elicit the truth from Smerdyakov; in his despairing struggles to understand his own motives on the eve of the trial; and in his public proclamation of his guilt, half-hearted and unconvincing though it sounds.

IV

In his meeting with Alyosha in Book V Ivan sets out to 'make himself known' to his 'little brother', to pour out before him his inmost thoughts and feelings.[7] What erupts is a bewildering chaos of contradictions: 'acceptance' of God while rejecting His Creation; thirst for life and repudiation of the world; exaltation of 'stupidity' and of 'facts' while he castigates intelligence and disowns understanding; although love of one's neighbour is an impossibility, there will be individuals he will love; no one is guilty, but he will kill himself if he cannot see justice done on whoever inflicts suffering on the innocent; he is convinced that the eternal harmony can and will 'undo the done', yet he must return his ticket, 'even though I be wrong'. Even on the level of immediate practicalities: he does not want to subvert Alyosha's faith – but he will not yield him to Zosima. Perhaps this study should be rounded off by a consideration of some of the more puzzling or paradoxical terms and antinomies in Ivan's confession.

To start with the least difficult: love of one's neighbour is 'impossible' to a Karamazov and in terms of Ivan's childhood experience; but his adult experience has recently taught him that it is possible for him to love – in different modes – Alyosha and Katya. What he does not yet know is whether he, warped as he is, will be capable of constructing a close and enduring relationship on the basis of those feelings; and since he is on the point of abandoning both Katya and Alyosha, his hopes of love must be, at best, tenuous.

Next: as a scientist, he can accept that nobody is guilty, that men are what life has made them; as Sofya's son, he can accept that the eternal harmony will – like the paradise of his teenage myth – bring complete and perfect compensation for all suffering; yet he will kill himself, he must return the ticket! It is worth quoting his own, startlingly revealing words: 'I would rather remain with my [*sic*!] suffering unavenged and my indignation unappeased, *even if I were wrong!*' (XIV, 223; V, iv).[8] Whatever the healing power of the harmony, he will not forgive what was done to him (and to his mother?) in the first seven years of his life. This is a measure of the rebelliousness he has developed as a transmutation of his mother's covert revolt – or as a protest against her overt meekness.

The stupidity–intelligence and facts–understanding antinomies are more intricate. On the face of it, one would expect intelligence to go with understanding and with facts, and all three to be opposed to stupidity. And indeed, elsewhere in the novel Ivan's attitude to stupidity and intelligence is the reverse of his attitude here. In his nightmare, for instance, he showers his devil with cries of 'Fool!', 'Ass!' and the like; the word 'stupid' and equivalents occur a dozen times or more in as many pages, and the devil snipes back deriding the excessive value Ivan sets on intelligence as the mark of a very young man. And Ivan's last significant words, at Mitya's trial, are, 'Why is everything that exists so stupid!' (XV, 118; XIII, v). With his life in ruins and his reason about to desert him, the most damning word he can find to sum up his world is 'stupid'. For Ivan the scientist and philosopher intelligence *is* the measure of worth. But in the chapter 'The Brothers Get Acquainted' Ivan has shed, for a brief half-hour, his science and philosophy. It is a half-hour of unprecedented – and unrepeated – tenderness, in which he presents himself as an inexperienced boy, confides in lyric tones his surging love of life, exults in his freedom (from love and Katya), appeals for Alyosha's friendship, and ends up with the paradox about accepting God but not His world. In such a context one can, and Ivan does – for half an hour – find intelligence to be an encumbrance and 'stupidity' – that is, artlessness, directness, simplicity – the shortest and therefore best way to the heart of his problems.

But, at a deeper level, this new attitude has other ramifications. It connects with Ivan's words in the following chapter ('Revolt'): 'The world is founded on absurdities, and perhaps without them nothing would come to pass in it' (XIV, 221; V, iv). And these are in the same key as the devil's admonition that the truth is very seldom 'clever' (*ostroumna*), as his scorn for Ivan's cult of intelligence (after all, the devil is part of Ivan), and as his dream of achieving faith in the body of an eighteen-stone merchant's wife, which is a caricature of Ivan's unavowed yearning for religious certainty. There is scriptural warrant for a link between religion and 'stupidity' ('Blessed are the poor in spirit'); and if the 'stupidity' extolled by Ivan in 'The Brothers Get Acquainted' is a metonym for 'religion', surely there could be no directer way to Alyosha's heart. All this is the spirit of Sofya speaking through Ivan, whether he knows it or not.

For the opposition of 'fact' to 'understanding' ('I don't understand anything. . .and now I don't want to understand anything. I want to stay with facts. . .If I try to understand anything, I shall immediately be false to the facts') (XIV, 222; V, iv)[8] and Ivan's refusal to understand, the context is different and his mood has changed between chapters. But it is still to his childhood we must turn for explanation. Facts are the materials of science and the food of the scientist, and Ivan has here reverted to his role of scientist. But the scientist does not 'understand' facts: he discovers, collects, knows, accepts them. He asks: 'What? when? where? how?' – not: 'Why?' 'Why?' involves the heart; it is the heart that pants to understand, as the child Ivan must have laboured to understand his mother's sufferings, and her death, and the collapse of his seven-year-old world. The facts feed not only Ivan's scientific brain, they feed too his 'unslaked indignation'. Understanding might soften his anger, might take the edge off his will to justice – and that must never be. He is committed to clamour for justice for his wrongs, and his mother's wrongs; and so he is doomed to be the eternal rebel, as his devil is doomed eternally to negate.

And lastly: what does Ivan mean when he says he 'accepts' God, and why does he accept Him? Since he does not accept God's Creation, it is clear that he does not accept God with his heart, with love. Does he, then, accept God intellectually? That would mean: either as a 'working hypothesis' or as a 'fact'. But from the presentation of Christ in the 'Legend' and from Ivan's paean to the eternal harmony etc., it is plain that God is much more to Ivan than a working hypothesis. Yet He cannot be a fact either: from the viewpoint of a scientist of the mid-1860s, God cannot be fitted into the world of facts (any more than the devil could, when he tried to get his tribute to Hoff's malt extract published). But if God is to Ivan neither an object of love nor a fact (i.e. an object of knowledge-that-it-is-so) – what is He? To answer this, we must look again at Ivan's attitude to the world. Or rather, not at Ivan's attitude, but at Ivan's attitudes. The child Ivan rejects the Creation because it is defiled by the sufferings of innocent children, and because it is unintelligible; the man Ivan loves 'life' – the sticky little leaves, the blue sky, a man here, a woman there, great human achievements ... (XIV, 210; V, iii). Ivan's judgement condemns the Creation; Ivan's 'inside and belly' cleave to life – or would do, if they were not paralysed by the judgement. So too Ivan seeks and 'accepts' God – not with his heart, not with his head, but with his deepest, visceral instincts. He needs God, and with a twofold need: as a focus for his 'unslaked indignation' and rebellion, and as the indispensable condition of morality, Who, as such, can alone save him from his nightmare of turning into another – perhaps more bestial, perhaps more criminal – Fyodor Karamazov.

Ivan Karamazov is the most complex, the most richly gifted and the most tragic of Dostoyevsky's 'split thinkers'. Staggering under the load of his heredity, haunted by the spectres of his childhood, he wages a heroic fight, in utter loneliness, against despair: seeking to transcend, since he cannot reconcile, the warring halves of his nature, to evolve a faith to live by, and to relate himself to life through joy and love. The first and second acts of his drama end in disaster, and Dostoyevsky did not live to narrate what followed.

Notes

1. See F. F. Seeley, 'Towards a typology of Dostoevsky's characters', *Annali dell'Istituto Universitario Orientale di Napoli* (*Sezione slava*), 16–17 (1973–4), 1–12.

2. Tu regere imperio populos, Romane, memento;
Hae tibi erunt artes – pacique imponere morem,
Parcere subiectis et debellare superbos. (*Aeneid,* VI. 851–3)
3. The details of genetic processes were of course unknown in Dostoyevsky's day. Even today there is no consensus as to the scope of physical factors in determining psychological qualities and biases. Dostoyevsky would, in any case, have been disinclined to distinguish between genetic and environmental (socio-cultural, educational) determinants of personality. In this study, inheritance is used in the same loose sense, as roughly equivalent to: 'what the child owes to the parent(s) at birth and through his earliest years'.
4. The critic referred to is L. Alekseyev in *Russkoye Bogatstvo,* November–December 1881 (chapter 7, *passim*).
5. Smerdyakov is not amenable to comparison, in view of the already mentioned impossibility of assessing the proportions of his debt to each parent.
6. Cf. 'But I say unto you, That whosoever looketh on a woman to lust after her hath committed adultery with her already in his heart' (St Matthew 5:28).
7. Ivan no doubt wanted, and tried, to be candid; but apart from having misled Alyosha on the status of his 'Legend', he finds cause to upbraid himself, as he walks home, with having failed to speak his mind fully (*ne sumel vyskazat'sya*).
8. Both here, in Ivan's determination to 'stay with' his indignation, *even if he be wrong*, and in the quotation below, in his resolve to 'stay with' the facts, even if that rules out understanding, there is a striking identity with the pattern (though, of course, not with the content and implications) of Dostoyevsky's own thought in the famous 1854 letter to N. D. Fonvizina: 'Nay more, if anyone proved to me that Christ is outside the truth and it were *really* the case that the truth is outside Christ, then I would rather stay with Christ than with the truth.' (F. M. Dostoyevsky, *Pis'ma*, ed. A. S. Dolinin (4 vols., Moscow/Leningrad, 1928–59), vol. 1, pp. 141–4). Ivan will survive his brain fever as Dostoyevsky survived Siberia; but will he, like Dostoyevsky, triumph over his past, or are the dice of his inheritance loaded too heavily against him?

PART TWO

6

The religious dimension: vision or evasion? Zosima's discourse in *The Brothers Karamazov*

SERGEI HACKEL

The prophet acclaimed

Dostoyevsky took pleasure in telling his wife that he had been acclaimed as a prophet by at least some of his Muscovite audience on 8 June 1880 when he gave his celebrated Pushkin speech.[1] He had conjured up an atmosphere of euphoria and exultation: the epithet was not necessarily intended to survive the occasion. And yet it has survived. In various contexts and with various qualifications Dostoyevsky's 'gift for prophecy' is still discussed. Although Dostoyevsky himself occasionally felt impelled to speak of a capacity for foresight,[2] it is more often a gift for prophetic insight which will be attributed to him.[3] But whatever the nature of the gift, its mere possession would not guarantee judicious use of it. The best heresies are likely to be propagated by prophets, whose identity as 'false prophets in sheep's clothing' may not be perceived until it is too late. If Dostoyevsky is indeed to be designated as prophet in some sense, how Orthodox – indeed, how Christian – was his message? Questions of this kind were already being posed by such contemporaries of his as Konstantin Leontyev.[4] A century later there is still room for a fresh consideration of them.

The cry 'prophet' could not have startled Dostoyevsky unduly on 8 June since he had already been receiving some acclaim as such on the eve. Members of the audience, so he told his wife, came crowding in on him during the interval of yet another ceremonial meeting. 'You are our prophet,' they told him. 'You made us into better people when we read the Karamazovs.' 'In a word,' added Dostoyevsky in his letter home, 'I was left convinced that the Karamazovs have colossal significance.'[5]

Dostoyevsky's own association of the designation 'prophet' with *The Brothers Karamazov*, the nature of the book, the place it occupies at the very peak of his career, together help to justify its being singled out for study when his religious views require to be discussed. In its turn, that section of the novel which Dostoyevsky – in an unprecedented fashion – segregated from the narrative proper and limited largely to religious discourse cannot but provide a natural focus for a discussion of this kind.

The text within the text

The passage in question, which consists of the elder Zosima's memoirs and admonitions, is exceptional also in its undisguised didacticism. At several removes the speaker may be said to participate in some kind of dialogue and dialectic with other characters in the novel. But in itself the passage manifestly lacks that vitality and polyphonic richness in which the novel as a whole abounds. Bakhtin attempted to define the section as 'hagiographical': Dostoyevsky was using his '*zhitiynoye slovo*' ('hagiographical discourse').[6] The phrase presumably referred less to the form of the section than to its manner and assumptions. In particular Bakhtin might have noted the author's manifest dependence on the credulity of his readers or, equally important, his manifest aim to make them into 'better people'.

Dostoyevsky himself certainly claimed to have such an aim. The blasphemy of Ivan Karamazov, he assured N. A. Lyubimov on 10 May 1879, was to be 'triumphantly rejected': he was working on its refutation ('The Russian monk') with 'fear, trepidation and awe', for his task was to be considered as nothing other than 'a civic feat' ('*grazhdanskim podvigom*').[7] Statements of this kind could be quoted from other letters of the time, some addressed to the same correspondent (his publisher's editor), others to K. P. Pobedonostsev, all of them commanding some respect.

Dostoyevsky's 'fear, trepidation and awe' involved a certain anxiety about his future audience. In one of his letters to Pobedonostsev, written in August 1879 when 'The Russian monk' was about to appear, he mentioned Zosima's teachings 'at which people will simply shout that they are absurd, since too elated'. He added, 'They are of course absurd in the everyday sense, but in another, inner sense, they seem justified.' But he concluded, 'In any case I am very worried.'[8] It may have been this worry which led him to wrap up his elder's text in layer upon layer of narrative devices.

It could be said that the neighbouring and closely related 'Legend of the Grand Inquisitor' is also cocooned. But at least that has a single narrator, who is also its 'author', while the novel's official narrator plays no part in its presentation. By contrast, Zosima's discourse is introduced by this narrator; it comprises Alyosha Karamazov's written, revised and retrospective account of what Zosima may have said on more than one occasion; and it in turn introduces Zosima's retrospective account of conversations with Markel, the young man in the woods, or the Mysterious Visitor. Thus introduced, the Mysterious Visitor dwells on his own distant past. The authenticity and effectiveness of each layer are reduced the further each is removed from Zosima's cell and the time of his impending death. Given the nineteenth-century attitude to the revelatory character of 'last words', this distancing could well have been avoided. In all respects there is a curious, untypical and untoward dissipation of intensity involved. It is almost as if the ultimate narrator, Dostoyevsky himself, is seeking to absolve himself from at least some responsibility for his elder's teaching, however much he claimed 'completely' to agree with it.[9]

Even to interrupt and so retard the narration was hardly typical of Dostoyevsky. Although one or another of his literary models may have suggested and sanctioned the device, Dostoyevsky must still have willed to use it for reasons of his own. One of these models may have been the monk Parfeny's travel tales, which Dostoyevsky both possessed and treasured (*Skazaniye o stranstvii i puteshestvii po Rossii, Moldavii, Turtsii i Svyatoy Zemli...* (Moscow, 1856)): certainly Zosima's style owed something to Parfeny, as Dostoyevsky openly acknowledged.[10] In the third volume of Parfeny's work the evenly paced narration is suddenly interrupted by a heading in Gothic type: this paves the way for a 'separate' discourse, thirty-four pages long, on a Siberian starets, Daniil.[11] The heading itself contains at least one phrase which is echoed in the heading of Alyosha's piece.[12] But it is the formal rather than the thematic parallel which deserves to be noted. Of equal interest is the break in the narrative of Hugo's *Les misérables* to which S. Linnér has drawn attention.[13] Hugo's device is all the more pertinent since it is employed to give prominence to the teachings of a saintly cleric: these are allotted two short chapters entitled 'Ce qu'il croyait' and 'Ce qu'il pensait'. It is well known that Dostoyevsky loved *Les misérables*. But whether or not Hugo influenced the form adopted for Zosima's teachings is ultimately of minor importance compared with the influence which he may have had on other aspects of the work. These remain to be discussed below.

Amvrosy's books and other sources

The separateness of Zosima's teachings is modified to some degree by the way in which they are anchored in the early pages of the novel, where the character of Zosima is established and a setting is provided for him. The setting, at least, gained considerably in authenticity since a significant proportion of the circumstantial and atmospheric detail is derived from Dostoyevsky's visit to the monastery at Optina Pustyn in the summer of 1877. The visit was brief (26–7 June), he had only three occasions to encounter the famous starets Amvrosy (two of them, admittedly, in semi-private), and it could hardly be said that he emerged from Optino as an expert on monasticism in general or on *startsy* in particular. But as always there were books to supplement his experience.[14] He acquired two general books on the monastery.[15] He could also draw on Parfeny's account of an earlier pilgrimage on which the itinerant monk was able to meet starets Leonid.[16] On Leonid himself he possessed the standard biography.[17] As important, at one time or another he obtained some of the spiritual writings which were published, popularized or (at the very least) approved by the community at Optino, among them sermons by Symeon the New Theologian,[18] a work on repentance by Mark the Ascetic,[19] and a commentary on Psalm 6 by Anastasios of Sinai.[20] It seems likely that many of these works, if not all, were gifts from starets Amvrosy, who always had copies of them available for his 'more honoured visitors'.[21] Most important of all may have been Dostoyevsky's acquisition of Isaac of Syria's Ascetic Discourses, elegantly translated into Russian from the Greek under the title *Slova podvizhnicheskiya.*[22] Mere possession of such works did not necessarily safeguard him against a distorted presentation of Orthodox monastic life or attitudes any more than his brief and exceptional visit to Optino. But at least he was in a position to draw on some primary sources of considerable dignity and importance when he felt impelled to do so.

The same may be said of Biblical texts. In view of Zosima's own insistence that Bible readings should play a greater part in the spiritual education of the Russian people (XIV, 266; VI, ii), it is not surprising that he himself incorporates at least some scriptural quotations and, more often, references into his discourse. He dwells for some time on the story of Job (XIV, 264–5; VI, ii), and mention is made of several other narratives from the Old Testament (XIV, 266–7; VI, ii). The New Testament is also used as a point of reference. The parable of Lazarus and the rich man plays a significant part in Zosima's discussion of hell (XIV, 292; VI, iii), and several of his sayings involve a paraphrase of New Testament texts.[23] Two sentences are quoted in the young Zosima's discussion with the Mysterious Visitor (XIV, 281; VI, ii); and one of these, indeed, provides the entire novel with its epigraph (XIV, 5). Even so, the list is surprisingly short. The text is hardly saturated with scriptural material, and Zosima cannot be said to depend on such material for his text's coordinates or even for its validation. It may be that at least some knowledge of the Christian scriptures could have been taken for granted even in such an educated audience as Dostoyevsky addressed. On the other hand he may have had his own reasons for being reticent when dealing with material like this.

Argument by image

Certainly, he did not intend to refute Ivan's atheistic propositions 'point by point', as he explained in a letter to Pobedonostsev of 24 August NS 1879: the answer had to be given 'indirectly' by means of 'an artistic picture'.[24] In this respect he was at one with his correspondent. Pobedonostsev himself had written to him in June that year to say that it was 'madness to ask: *prove* your faith to me. What should be said is: *show* me your faith.' And he had gone on to say that 'this faith is not to be made manifest in some abstract formula, but in the living image of a live man and of a live endeavour – in the image of God, which is that of Adam the man – and more than man, that is Christ the Son of God'.[25] Both correspondents would thus have agreed with Renan's judgement to the effect that Jesus himself 'put forward no rational demonstration to his disciples and demanded no intellectual concentration on their part. It was not his convictions that he preached, but his very self.'[26] Dostoyevsky was certainly intrigued by Renan[27] and (prompted by Renan) himself planned to have his prince (that is, Stavrogin) say in *The Devils* that Christ puts forward 'no teaching' as such: 'the main thing is Christ's image, from which any teaching devolves' (XI, 192). Hence the importance of harbouring this image, the responsibility (according to Zosima) both of the Russian monk and, by extension, of the Russian people (XIV, 284, 285; VI, iii).

But if Christ's teaching is not to be propounded point by point, the image needs to be all the more vivid and convincing. The utterly (and impressively) silent Christ of the Grand Inquisitor Legend (XIV, 239; V, v; cf. Mark 15:3–5) needs to be brought more clearly into focus through Zosima's discourse or, better, through his person. It was after all Dostoyevsky's cherished ambition to create the 'utterly' or 'positively beautiful man'.[28] But it can hardly be argued that Zosima is an effective *alter Christus*, still less Alyosha Karamazov; while the Russian monk in general (and, even more, the Russian people as a whole) are themselves altogether out of focus and in any case beyond the novelist's control.

Argument superseded by elation

If reason is not to the point, if the authority of scripture is not invoked, and a beautiful (that is, convincing) image difficult to sustain, the role of emotion as a path to cognition, insight or revelation may need to be enhanced. When Alyosha, in an early draft for *The Brothers Karamazov*, 'understood that knowledge and faith [were] different and opposed to one another', Dostoyevsky carefully supplemented the entry with a marginal note on the way in which Alyosha came to realize that there are 'other worlds' and also links with them: in the process he gave a tentative picture of how such understanding was achieved. In Dostoyevsky's words, 'he understood – at least, attained or even only felt' these things (XV, 201). But even though he 'only' felt, his perception was apparently authentic and profound. Dostoyevsky was to devote much care to the depiction of such feeling. And although he felt that Zosima's discourse, in particular, would be found 'absurd since too elated' by his reader, he clearly hoped that the reader himself would ultimately experience at least some of this elation and so be convinced.

The most obvious circumstantial expressions of such elation are three. The first is the all-important shedding of tears. The second involves the rather more mysterious kissing of the earth. The third, a subdivision of the first, involves a combination of the first and second: the watering of the earth with tears. In other words, a cult of the earth is served by the cultivation of tears: in Zosima's words, 'fall on the earth and kiss it, water it with your tears, and the earth will bear fruit from your tears, even though no one saw you or heard you in your isolation' (XIV, 291; VI, iii).

Starets Amvrosy of Optino possessed the gift of tears, though there is no indication that Dostoyevsky saw him demonstrate the fact during his brief visit to Optina Pustyn. Dostoyevsky rarely visited other monasteries, if ever, and thus had few opportunities to observe such tears. Nevertheless it should not be assumed that his concern for them is due merely to his being 'brought up on Karamzin'.[29]

Once more, Parfeny's travels may have provided him with stimulus, the more so since Parfeny speaks of tears at Optino itself.[30] Furthermore, the engraving which forms the frontispiece to Parfeny's fourth volume shows an Athonite monk (*iyeroskhimonakh* Arseny) actually shedding copious tears. But for a richer and more systematic treatment of the subject Dostoyevsky had only to turn to his copy of St Isaac of Syria's seventh-century classic, *Slova podvizhnicheskiya.*

Isaac of Syria and the cult of tears

Not only is its author mentioned in Dostoyevsky's notebooks for *The Brothers Karamazov* (XV, 203, 205): the work itself appears more than once on the actual pages of the finished novel. Admittedly, it is given a negative and even dismal context. The first owner of Isaac's text to be mentioned is Grigory Vasilyevich Kutuzov, who possessed a manuscript copy. He at least 'read it stubbornly over many years'. For all that 'he understood virtually nothing of it, though for this very reason maybe loved and valued this book more than any other' (XIV, 89; III, i). His adopted son, Smerdyakov, is eventually found to have a printed version of the same work on his bedside table. It is first mentioned as 'some fat book or other in a yellow cover': Smerdyakov 'was not reading it, he was apparently sitting down and doing nothing' (XV, 58; XI, viii). Only later is the book brought into play, and then merely as a hiding place for the booty derived from the murder of Fyodor Pavlovich Karamazov: 'Smerdyakov pressed the money down with it.' Smerdyakov's visitor, Ivan, 'managed mechanically to read the title': it is given to the reader in Ivan's simplified version as *Svyatago ottsa nashego Isaaka Sirina slova* (*The Discourses of our Holy Father Isaac of Syria*) (XV, 61; XI, viii), rather than *Tvoreniya izhe vo svyatykh ottsa nashego avvy Isaaka Siriyanina, podvizhnika i otshel'nika. . .Slova podvizhnicheskiya* (*Ascetic Discourses, a Work of our Father among the Saints Isaac of Syria, Ascetic and Recluse*). But however misused the book or garbled its title, there is no doubt as to its identity. And whereas its function here is to underline Smerdyakov's (and by extension Ivan's) lack of concern for the spiritual values embodied in it, there may be a more positive, albeit anonymous, role for it elsewhere in the novel.

Isaac of Syria has no doubt about the value of tears. They are the fruit of penitence and spiritual perception, the precondition for a revelation.[31] Zosima's advocacy of tears may be said to have its foundation in such teachings as these. But there are two important factors which prevent an identification of the two.

Isaac is careful to stress that tears have a limited place in monastic spirituality. They are the accompaniment of an infant's spiritual birth (p. 339), they lead him to spiritual maturation (p. 100), and 'they are a sure sign that the mind has left this world and has experienced that spiritual world' (p. 100). Yet at the same time the progress continues, for silence (*hesychia*) is beyond tears, and the ascetic's eyes 'may be likened to a spring of water for up to two years or more; and that is when he achieves a stilling of his thoughts, while after the stilling of his thoughts, insofar as human nature can partially encompass it, he enters on that rest of which St Paul has spoken (Hebrews 4:3). And after this peaceful rest the mind begins to contemplate mysteries' (pp. 339–40). Tears are thus no more than a stage in the progress to divinization, not a self-sufficient peak. Furthermore they are themselves the result of a process. There can be no decision to shed tears, only a decision to repent and to practise ascesis. Tears are the by-product of such a decision. By contrast, Zosima suggests that they themselves must be zealously pursued (XIV, 292; VI, iii). There is no suggestion that they should be treated as a passing phenomenon, or that their value is ultimately a limited one. Nor, unlike Isaac (pp. 100–1), does he attempt to differentiate between different stages or types of weeping.

Dostoyevsky–Zosima thus accepts an element of Isaac's vocabulary, while giving it a specific and a limited application. But with the injunction that tears be mingled with the ground, still more with the injunction that the earth be kissed, he moves far beyond Isaac and indeed beyond the whole tradition of which Isaac is a part.

This is not to say that exultation in the created order is itself treated with mistrust by Orthodox writers. On the contrary, such exultation may be particularly intense insofar as the Orthodox world since patristic times has preserved an understanding of Creation which involves no rigid separation between nature and grace. 'Man cannot create a space-interval between himself and God', as Paulos Gregorios has recently put it: 'God is the reality which sustains both man and nature, and it is through man himself and through nature that God presents himself to man. In this sense, it is foolish to see God and nature as alternative poles placed so that if man turns towards one he must turn his back on the other.'[32] Moreover, man is neither utterly nor irremediably fallen, and can act both as a microcosm and a mediator: consequently, as one

Cypriot saint has written, 'creation does not venerate the Maker directly and by itself...it is through me that the heavens declare the glory of God, through me the moon worships God, through me the waters and showers of rain, the dews and all creation, venerate God and give glory'.[33]

Isaac himself has a powerful passage which may have provided Dostoyevsky with an insight into this aspect of Orthodox tradition. The passage has been quoted by several writers, though simplistic conclusions about Isaac's writings and, more particularly, Dostoyevsky's dependence on them, have too often accompanied such quotations.[34] Nevertheless it requires (and deserves) to be quoted once again.

'What is purity?' asks Isaac by way of introduction, and responds, 'a heart which is mercifully disposed to all created nature'. A few lines later he poses the supplementary question, 'what is a merciful heart?' It is this which prompts his well-known answer:

> When a man's heart is aflame on behalf of all creation, of all people, of birds, of animals, of demons and of any creature. Whenever they are remembered or whenever they are seen a man's eyes will shed tears. His heart will grow tender (*umilyayetsya*) from the intense and great compassion which engulfs it; and it is incapable of bearing or hearing or seeing any harm whatsoever or [any] minor injury which may be suffered by creation. (p. 209)

Zosima's heart is indeed aflame in a comparable manner, as are his brother's and his disciple's (XIV, 263, 328; VI, ii, VII, iv). However Isaac is once more describing the symptoms of a spiritual state, and not its *raison d'être*. His description relates to a larger context, which modifies its impact. Within its context, moreover, it constitutes an exception rather than the rule. It required a determined and eclectic reader – a 'reader of genius'[35] – to remove it from this context and to use it as the kernel of what is beginning to reveal itself as a personal and altogether different system. Yet even this key passage provides no model for the actual veneration of the earth.

The veneration of the earth

Is there something in the Franciscan tradition which might do so? The question is not asked without good reason. 'Pater Seraphicus' is used more than once as a description of Zosima, and it is Alyosha himself who prompts the reader to ask why: '"Pater Seraphicus" – he took that name from somewhere or other – from where?' (XIV, 241; V, vi). It is a curiously positive term, for all its Latin (which makes it stand out starkly against a page of Cyrillic type), its Western provenance, and its introduction by Ivan: almost inevitably it refers to Francis of Assisi.[36] The surviving lists of Dostoyevsky's library holdings give no indication of an interest in St Francis, and it remains to be established whether he pursued any reading in this sphere. But at least it may be said that had he done so he would have found support for Zosima's attitude to nature. In particular he would have been struck by Francis' use of the term '*sora nostra mater Terra*' – 'our sister, mother Earth' – in his renowned *Canticle of brother Sun*;[37] indeed, the lyrical exultation of the canticle as a whole would have been congenial to him. The occasions on which Francis shed tears on mother Earth are few, but they may be significant. Thus one of the earliest Lives of the saint, the *Legenda Maior* by St Bonaventure, states that he once 'moistened the place with his tears'.[38] It is a phrase which is remarkably close (in Russian translation it could have been closer still) to Zosima's injunction, 'Soak the earth with the tears of your joy' (XIV, 292; VI, iii), as well as to Alyosha's subsequent action in 'watering' it with his tears (XIV, 328; VII, iv). Even in Francis however there is no question of kissing the earth as well.

The kissing of the earth was not a new subject for Dostoyevsky. Such kissing is present in his work at least since *Crime and Punishment* (VI, 405; VI, viii), and he was to return to it in *The Devils* (X, 116–17; I, iv, 5). In the first of these, Raskolnikov's kiss involves an act of repentance and reconciliation: Sonya has urged him to kiss the earth which he had defiled by his murders (VI, 322; V, iv). In the second, Marya Timofeyevna Lebyadkina speaks of an equally mysterious veneration of the earth: the earth is perceived by her at one and the same time as the type of the *Bogoroditsa* (Theotokos; Birthgiver of God), the great mother, and as Mother-damp-earth (X, 116; I, iv, 5):[39] to water the earth with one's tears brings joy in all things and leads naturally to the kissing of the earth.

Marya Timofeyevna's approach is closer to Zosima's than is Sonya's. Zosima's shedding of tears and kissing of the earth are also an expression of joy and *umileniye* ('tender emotion') at the integrity, beauty and sanctity of the cosmos. And yet it is Sonya's type of earth veneration, rather than Marya Timofeyevna's, for which a parallel is to be found in Russian sectarian or popular religious practices. Thus, confession to the earth was a widespread phenomenon from at least the time of the fourteenth-century Strigolnik heresy in Pskov and Novgorod. This could naturally involve a desire for reconciliation with the earth, which would have been harmed and defiled by man's sin. Since the earth was treated as sacred, oaths might be taken by it: in this connection the earth might be kissed or even ingested.[40]

However, this is far removed from Zosima's joyful kissing of the earth. Parallels for such behaviour are difficult to trace. For the present only one has come to my attention. An account of the 1860s describes the peregrinations of a certain pilgrim Darya or Daryushka. In the course of her travels she once 'kissed the earth in an impulse of joy and gratitude to God, who created this earth and walked upon it'.[41] The account was published during the 1860s in the St Petersburg periodical *Strannik*. Three issues of this periodical (for the years 1880 and 1881) are now known to have been in Dostoyevsky's library.[42] But it is not known whether Dostoyevsky read the relevant issue of two decades earlier. In any case it may be doubted whether Daryushka's one impulsive gesture could have been sufficient to provide the framework and justification for Zosima's system. Nor by itself does it provide evidence of a specifically Orthodox or Russian custom.

Zosima and the Church

The tears, prostrations and the kissing of the earth have one feature in common, their intense immediacy. Moreover their character is personal and individualistic rather than ecclesial. There is some desultory talk of the Church in the early chapters of the novel: Paisy makes a clear and positive statement on the Church's role in man's salvific progress (XIV, 27–9, 57; I, v, II, v) and Zosima himself speaks briefly of the Church as an agent of reconciliation in society. In one sentence he even mentions her sacraments (XIV, 60; II, v). But in general, and certainly in respect of the devotional practices advocated by him, the Church is not involved, recollected or (apparently) required. Nor do the discourses, which might be expected to contain the essence of Zosima's teachings, refer to sacraments or services, the normal manifestations of Orthodox church life. By way of an exception a single Holy Week service (the Liturgy of the Presanctified for Great Tuesday) is mentioned: but this is remembered as part of Zosima's childhood, and Zosima looks back to it with nostalgia, almost as if it no longer referred to the present. And even though Zosima's role as confessor is mentioned (XIV, 28,

301; I, v, VIII, i), the reader is not shown him practising as such. Zosima, moreover, is a priest, as is made plain by his title *iyeroskhimonakh* (XIV, 260, 295; VI, ii, VII i), his capacity to bless (XIV, 49, 72; II, iv, vii), and the funeral rites which are his due (XIV, 295, 304; VII, i). Yet there is no suggestion that he participates in any service, either at the monastery proper (which his health might prevent) or even – and in this he differs from Amvrosy[43] – at his more secluded scete. Nor does he experience any regret on this score.

It is therefore not altogether inappropriate that his own sacramental needs are ignored by his immediate entourage. Even though all his associates were well aware that his death was imminent (XIV, 257; VI, i) and Zosima himself spoke openly about it (XIV, 148, 257; IV, i, VI, i) no thought was given to the administration of confession, unction or communion. As if by way of compensation, Dostoyevsky had made special efforts to secure the necessary texts and advice concerning the laying-out of a newly deceased monk (XIV, 295; VII, i). The future Over Procurator of the Holy Synod, Pobedonostsev, ensured that his friend should be given the required support.[44] Yet Dostoyevsky was well aware that he also needed details of the rite for unction and communion: he reminded himself of the need in his notebooks (XV, 254). It is therefore the same Dostoyevsky who must be held responsible for not acting on this reminder and for his eventual failure to heed the pre-mortem needs of his Pater Seraphicus. Was he perhaps seeking to manipulate his dying so that the last sacraments would not overshadow or displace Zosima's final prostration, the final kissing of the earth (XIV, 294; VI, iii)? For it would not have been proper for Zosima to prostrate himself that day after communion and thus to diminish a communicant's God-given dignity.[45] Be that as it may, the death of Zosima, 'unhousel'd...unanel'd', is yet one more expression of his separateness from the sacred structures and prescriptions of his Church.

Zosima's recommended path to salvation therefore involves heightened intensity; and it concerns the individual rather than the group, the body or the Church. At the same time, it is a path which does not necessarily demand a lifelong discipline on the part of those that tread it. In this respect Zosima differs markedly from Isaac of Syria and the elders of Optina Pustyn. Admittedly, he makes some judicious remarks about the lasting effort required to sustain love (XIV, 290; VI, iii). He even mentions 'obedience, fasting, prayer' as the only way towards 'freedom and joy' (XIV, 285; VI, iii). Yet Zosima himself shows no sign of the spiritual struggle which led him to his present state, nor does he mention such a struggle even for didactic reasons.[46] By contrast, the traditionalist ascetic Ferapont is presented as a ridiculously whited sepulchre and his stance, in effect, is condemned (XIV, 151–5, 301–4; IV, i, VII, i). Zosima is less concerned for disciplined and barely perceptible progress than for immediate transformations.

'Life is paradise, the keys are in our keeping'

Such transformations are within the individual's reach. Zosima's brother is the first to suggest that they can virtually be willed: 'Life is paradise, and we are all in paradise, yet we do not want to know it, but if we did want to know it, paradise would begin tomorrow the whole world over' (XIV, 263; VI, ii). Zosima is to remember these words and to paraphrase them (XIV, 270, 272; VI, ii). The Mysterious Visitor is likewise to speak along these lines: 'Paradise, he said, is hidden in each of us, here it is hidden within me also, and I have only to wish it, and it will come about the very next day in actual fact and immediately for the whole of my life' (XIV, 275; VI, ii).

No argument is actually put forward against man's cooperation with God (*synergeia*) in seeking to attain this paradise. Yet neither is this Orthodox principle advanced or even mentioned. On the contrary, the assumption that man himself determines the inauguration of his paradise could effectively preclude any such cooperation. According to one of Dostoyevsky's notebook entries for the novel, 'Life is paradise, the keys are in our keeping' (XV, 243).

In making such a statement he was at one with an obscure scholar, some of whose writings had been submitted to him anonymously in December 1877. He was never to learn the name of their author, N. F. Fyodorov. But he read them 'as if they were my own',[47] and they were to inform his thinking in later chapters of the novel.[48] In respect to paradise however the evidence suggests a striking parallel, rather than an influence. Difficult as it is to establish the exact identity of the text at Dostoyevsky's disposal,[49] this is not likely to have contained the passage in which Fyodorov most explicitly asserts that 'the kingdom of God or paradise must be created only by men themselves'. Even so, it is of interest to note that Fyodorov's paradise will be the product not only of people's 'full perception' and their 'strength of will', but also of their 'depth of *feeling*'. Nevertheless, Fyodorov is at variance with Dostoyevsky in one respect: those who achieve this paradise do so not as individuals, but by deploying 'all the means [at the disposal] of all people in their togetherness'.[50]

For Dostoyevsky's separate individual, the attainment of paradise does not necessarily involve transfiguration. Dostoyevsky was evidently not ignorant of the Orthodox teaching on the ultimate divinization of man, on man's striving towards theosis (*obózheniye*). In one of his notebook entries for Zosima's discourse he makes specific reference to it. In the Orthodox world, and in particular since the fourteenth-century councils which upheld the teachings of Gregory Palamas, the light of Christ's Transfiguration on Mount Tabor had long been accepted as a model and an assurance of man's theosis. Hence the burden of Dostoyevsky's fourfold notebook entry: 'Your flesh will be transformed. (Light of Tabor.) Life is paradise, the keys are in our keeping' (XV, 245). Yet the established text does not retain the first two statements, and the concept of life as paradise is thus deprived of an important gloss and validation.

Paradise or heaven?

As it is, Zosima's paradise is predominantly a terrestrial condition. Zosima repeatedly uses the term *ray* for its designation. In the Russian translation of the Bible (favoured by Zosima) *ray* stands for the garden (LXX: *paradeisos*) of Eden, as well as for the paradise ('an intermediate state between death and resurrection' for the redeemed)[51] to which the Good Thief is promised entry (Luke 23:43). Occasionally it may also be used as a synonym for 'heaven': Zosima himself seems to use it in this sense when he applies it (as Luke does not) to the parable of Lazarus and the rich man. But this is not necessarily its primary or most appropriate connotation in the context of the novel (and Constance Garnett was ill-advised to opt for it *passim*). Fyodorov had spoken insistently of the necessity for 'paradise on earth';[52] in his support he could have cited Old Testament apocalyptic writings, in which 'the site of the reopened Paradise is almost without exception the earth or the New Jerusalem'.[53] Yet once this paradise becomes an earthly prospect, a Fyodorov or a Dostoyevsky may transfer its expected realization from the ultimate to the comparatively immediate future and significantly reduce its eschatological implications in the process. Even the exceptional use of the phrase 'kingdom of heaven' (or 'heavenly kingdom') by the Mysterious Visitor (XIV, 275; VI, ii) does not swing the balance in an other-worldly direction since such a kingdom in the New Testament is itself perceived largely as a present reality, as the sovereignty of God 'over the lives and actions of men here, with a view to their entrance into the perfect Kingdom of God in the hereafter'.[54] The orientation of the 'here' towards the 'hereafter' should distinguish this kingdom from merely utopian states: it is thus of some importance to gauge the strength of such orientation.

Love and mutual responsibility

The most important key to this *ray* is love. Had not Isaac of Syria stated that 'paradise [*ray*] is love of God'?[55] This finds its echo in Zosima. But the echo is muted. Zosima speaks less specifically of man's love for God, more of love for man (however sinful he may be) and – insistently and poignantly – of love for all Creation. 'Brothers, do not fear sin,' says Zosima, 'love man even in his sin, for this is the likeness of divine love and the peak of love on earth. Love all God's Creation, [Creation] as a whole and every grain of sand [within it]. Love each leaf, each of God's rays. Love the animals, love the vegetation, love anything that is. When you love everything, then shall you penetrate to God's mystery in things' (XIV, 289; VI, iii).

The immediate consequence, if not the concomitant of this love is a man's recognition of responsibility for the sins of his fellows. Both Markel and Zosima propound the formula (anticipated by Shatov in *The Devils* (X, 446; III, v, 3)) that 'anyone is culpable before all for everyone and for anything' (XIV, 262; VI, ii); or (more interestingly) 'for each [m.] and for all [f.]' – '*za vsyekh i za vsya*' (XIV, 290; VI, iii). The latter phrase carries overtones of a sacrificial acceptance of such responsibility: the eucharistic offering in the Liturgy of St John Chrysostom is made in almost identical terms, '*o vsyekh i za vsya*'. The same Liturgy – celebrated in Russian churches virtually throughout the year – would have familiarized Dostoyevsky with the communicant's prayer about 'sinners of whom I am first' (a phrase borrowed from 1 Timothy 1:15).[56] Dostoyevsky would have encountered the same message in Isaac of Syria. For Isaac had urged each reader of his work to consider himself 'responsible and culpable in respect of everything'.[57]

If a man loves his fellows and is indeed responsible for their sins he is impelled to seek their forgiveness. They for their part would also seek forgiveness for their sins. In the words of Zosima's dying brother, 'Even though I am sinful in respect of all, they will in turn forgive me, there's paradise for you. Am I not in paradise now?' (XIV, 263; VI, ii). Another key to paradise therefore is the mutual forgiveness of sins.

The problem of hell

Sin is not to be feared (XIV, 289; VI, iii): it is never beyond forgiveness. There is only one exception to this rule. In the words of Isaac, 'no sin is unforgivable – apart from unrepented sin'.[58] Isaac's axiom is to be elaborated in Zosima's text. Its first part is implied throughout; its second informs the final section of Zosima's discourse (XIV, 292–3; VI, iii). But if Isaac could be said to provide an epigraph, it is another (and in this case newly canonized) saint who may have provided at least some of the substance for this text: Tikhon Zadonsky, former Bishop of Voronezh.

Dostoyevsky had a longstanding interest in Tikhon. In 1870 he could already speak of having welcomed him enthusiastically into his heart 'long ago'.[59] He also welcomed him into his library. The recently discovered list of its contents refers to no less than *twenty-one* editions of a short work by Tikhon on repentance.[60] Such an avid collector of one work by this author is not likely to have ignored the remainder; and although he does not seem to have possessed the handsome second edition of Tikhon's collected works in fifteen volumes which appeared in 1860, it would be wrong to assume that he had no familiarity with it. Dostoyevsky went out of his way to acknowledge that parts of Zosima's discourse were based on 'certain homilies by Tikhon Zadonsky', and referred particularly to the section on sacred scripture.[61] But the final section also bears a marked resemblance to some of Tikhon's work.

Tikhon insists, with Isaac, that no sins are beyond forgiveness for the penitent: 'no matter how numerous, great or burdensome they may be, God possesses a still greater abundance of mercy'.[62] Tikhon, together with Zosima, also dwells on the fate of those who fail or refuse to repent. Thus both discuss the role of hell and both ponder the anguish of those who realize, too late, that they could and should have acted otherwise before their death. Each refers to the parable of Lazarus and the rich man by way of illustration.[63]

Yet if Tikhon may be said to provide Dostoyevsky with a model and a stimulus, this is not to say that the two writers are at one in all respects. Indeed, the differences between them are of as much interest as the similarities.

Tikhon speaks consistently of the sinner's deviation from God and of God's judgement in respect of this. By contrast, God is not mentioned at all in the main part of Zosima's discourse on hell (XIV, 292–3; VI, iii), except insofar as the Lazarus parable requires two mentions of 'the Lord'. The sinner has deviated not so much from God, as from love: hell is 'suffering caused by the fact that it is no longer possible to love'. Whereas the capacity to love was given as man's birthright at the time of Creation: 'I am and I love' is Zosima's non-Descartean gloss on Genesis. The emphasis is on man's psyche rather than on God's grace. The quotation 'God is love' (1 John 4:8) is conspicuous by its absence. Some references to God towards the very end of the passage hardly compensate for his absence hitherto; the less so since he is given a peculiarly negative context. The unrepentant 'cannot contemplate the living God without hate and demand that there should be no God of life, that God should destroy himself and all that He created'. Yet even they are said to 'curse [?only] themselves in cursing God and life': their target is an elusive one.

Only in the case of those who so condemn themselves does Zosima foresee the eternal torment which Tikhon presumes to be the lot of all the condemned without distinction. This is another significant difference between them. For tentatively, and with apologies for lack of clarity, Zosima postulates that many if not most condemned sinners are not utterly lost. The damned may yet come to a realization that the righteous still extend their love towards them. Simultaneously they will become ever more aware of their inability to reciprocate it. This in turn could generate humility. And it is this which eventually prompts 'a certain form of that active love which they spurned on earth and, as it were, some action in conformity with it' (XIV, 293; VI, iii). Zosima thus provides the foundation for Grushenka's more explicit (and certainly more picturesque) folk-legend of the onion, which is soon to follow (XIV, 318–19; VII, iii).

In yet one other respect does Zosima go his own way. Tikhon does not speak of suicides. Zosima not only considers them, but makes a point of questioning the rigidity of Orthodox practices in their regard. 'The Church in its outward expression seems to reject them' (XIV, 293; VI, iii): however, Zosima (like Makar in *The Raw Youth* (XIII, 310; III, iii, 2)) daily offers prayers on their behalf. The positive improvement even of their lot is therefore postulated. In the five sentences devoted to this subject, Zosima may be preparing the reader for the suicide of the charmless Smerdyakov.

Zosima's presentation of hell is consistent with his humanitarian and his humanistic train of thought, and he differs from Tikhon to a marked extent. Yet in his brief discussion of suicide he is curiously close to yet another spiritual authority, the subject of that biography which Dostoyevsky may have received at the hands of Amvrosy in 1877 and in any case possessed: the starets Leonid, in effect the founder of eldership (*starchestvo*) at Optina Pustyn. For information on Leonid, Dostoyevsky could draw not only on this work, but also on his familiar Parfeny, several of whose pages are devoted to starets Leonid.

It has already been noted that Leonid's eventual successor Amvrosy provided much of the circumstantial detail for the portrait of Zosima. But Leonid could have helped to fill it out. He too was cheerful, calm, direct and simple;[64] he too shed tears of joy.[65] Like Amvrosy (and Zosima) after him, he too would receive 'people of every walk of life' in his cell, 'gentry, merchants and simple folk' alike.[66] The cell itself was to be found 'half a verst from the monastery, in the midst of a wood',[67] not unlike Zosima's ('four hundred paces from the monastery, through a little wood', according to the instructions given to F. P. Karamazov (XIV, 33; II, i)). But none of this is as important as the correspondence between Leonid's attitude to suicides and Zosima's. Leonid's is expressed in a prayer which he composed for a disciple whose father had committed suicide. It began with the words, 'Take to task, O Lord, the fallen soul of my father and if it be possible, have mercy.'[68] The phrase 'if it be possible' kept the prayer within the bounds of propriety, as presumably did Zosima's private and silent practice of similar prayers. In any case, the censorship left both accounts in place. For once Dostoyevsky's deviation from accepted standards of Orthodoxy could be justified by reference to an authentic monastic source.

The Russian people and the salvation of the world

Prayer for suicides and for the denizens of hell is the natural expression of that mutual love and forgiveness which Zosima preaches. If these can help to overcome the problems of the world beyond, so much more obviously can they resolve the social problems of the here and now. Thus, the reconciliation of the rich and poor is to be brought about by shame on the part of the rich, matched by the humility and tenderness of the poor (XIV, 256; V, vii): psychological and spiritual, rather than political or economic factors are at issue. The source and the guarantee of such a reconciliation are something mysterious which is latent, waiting to be realized, in the common people of Russia and in those who are at one with them, the monks: the image (*obraz*) of Christ (XIV, 284, 285; VI, iii). The existence of this image is an article of faith. No definition of it is attempted. Yet it is the people's possession of the image which renders them sacred. In Zosima's words, 'This is a people that bears God' within itself: '*sei narod — bogonosets*' (XIV, 285; VI, iii).

Therefore, as he asserts, 'God will save Russia'; 'The Lord will save Russia, as He has repeatedly saved her before'; 'God will save His people, for Russia is great in her humility' (XIV, 286; VI, iii). No other nation is mentioned in this connection: no other nation, so it appears, has comparable potential. Other nations are merely in the background as future beneficiaries of Russia's own salvation.

Zosima can claim to possess a peculiar insight into this problem since it is the Russian monk (specifically *Russian*) who has succeeded in preserving this image of Christ 'gloriously and undistorted . . . in continuity with the ancient fathers, the apostles and martyrs'. This is the star which is now to 'shine forth from the East' (XIV, 284; VI, iii), the precious diamond which is to shine forth to the whole world (XIV, 287; VI, iii). Yet the 'God-bearing' nation as a whole is to play an all-important part in its diffusion. Salvation is to 'derive from the people, its humility and faith' (XIV, 286; VI, iii). Thus what seemed to begin as an assertion of the age-old tradition of Orthodoxy is unobtrusively transformed into an expression of nineteenth-century Russian nationalism, if not messianism. No longer is the Church the guardian of the truth, nor even (as the Slavophiles might have expressed it) the members of the Church, but the members of a particular nation. This is hardly to be distinguished from what the recent Constantinopolitan Church Council of 1872 had condemned as *phyletismos*, a teaching whereby nationalistic concepts distort and challenge the Church's universal mission.

Indeed, there is a danger not only of the Church but of God becoming a function of nationality. 'Whoever does not believe in God is not going to believe in God's people,' says Zosima (XIV, 267; VI, ii): his statement almost suggests that belief in God has its justification insofar as it has that particular outcome. Once more God is not presented as an absolute but rather (in Stavrogin's words) as 'a simple attribute of nationality' (X, 199; I, vii); and the reader may well be reminded of Shatov's hesitant credo, formulated in response to Stavrogin's questions in *The Devils*. Shatov had also asserted that the Russians were 'the only "God-bearing" people'. He was challenged as to his own beliefs in God. 'I believe in Russia,' he replied. 'I believe in her Orthodoxy...I believe in the body of Christ...I believe that the new [second] coming will take place in Russia...' ...'But in God? In God?' 'I...I shall believe in God' (X, 200–1; II, i, 7).

Is Zosima's credo significantly different? He could proclaim his belief in joy, love, mutual forgiveness, the beauty of Creation, the image of Christ as cherished and propagated by the Russian people, a terrestrial and immediately attainable paradise. If he had been challenged with the question, 'But in God?' he might have had no answer other than an evasive counter-question, 'Surely that amounts to God?' It is not altogether surprising that the Russian censorship at one time prohibited the separate publication of Zosima's discourse. It was felt that the circulation of such 'mystical-social teachings' among the lower classes would be harmful since they display 'only an apparent similarity to the teachings of Christ, while being essentially opposed to the doctrine of the Orthodox faith'. In the minutes of the censorship committee (3 December 1886), the passages dealing with 'paradise on earth' were quoted with evident scorn. Doubts about Zosima's orthodoxy (his teachings were compared with Tolstoy's) were clearly reinforced by an appreciation of Dostoyevsky's powers to convince. He was, after all, a 'gifted belletrist'.[69] Repeated appeals against the decision were of no avail.[70]

Alyosha 'wakeful and yet not awake'

But whatever the nature of Zosima's credo in the abstract, it is to receive its testing and (Dostoyevsky would have hoped) its vindication in Alyosha's experience immediately after the elder's death. Alyosha had left the monastery for a confrontation with Grushenka. He had returned towards the end of the day and was reintroduced to the vigil over Zosima's body by the Gospel reading which had begun immediately after the first requiem service (*panikhida*) and which was to continue throughout the coming night (XIV, 295; VII, i).

There is a new vigour in the exposition. The Zosima insert with its elaborate narrative devices, its deliberately stylized speech, its generous time-scale on the one hand and its pretensions to timelessness on the other, is replaced by a straightforward 'eyewitness' account of Alyosha's activities and conversations; this is eventually to merge into a 'first-hand' account of his inner experiences. This 'first-hand' account is to occupy the greater part of only one short chapter ('Cana of Galilee'), hardly three pages of print (XIV, 326–8; VII, iv). Nevertheless Dostoyevsky had no hesitation in describing it as 'the most significant in the whole book, and possibly in the novel as well'.[71]

As the title of the chapter suggests, it is the narrative of the marriage of Cana (John 2:1–11) which Alyosha hears when he arrives back at the cell. But he is on the verge of sleep after a tiring and disturbing day, and his mind easily wanders. The wedding feast merges imperceptibly into a messianic banquet for which other Gospel passages (such as Matthew 22:1–10) provide the framework and the raw material. These in turn provoke reminiscences of related homiletic material: Dostoyevsky borrows several phrases from a paschal homily attributed to St John Chrysostom (XIV, 327; VII, iv; cf. XV, 243, 263), thus fulfilling an intention (expressed as early as Eastertide 1876) 'to end with the sermon of Chrysostom, "If anyone come at the ninth hour"' (XV, 613).

Dostoyevsky was by no means inexperienced in the description of dreams. Even so, it may be that in the case of so significant a dream-vision as Alyosha's was to prove, he may have been glad once more of some guidance or support from Isaac of Syria. At least it may be noted that there are two passages in Isaac which could be used to place Alyosha's experience in the context of monastic spirituality.

Isaac speaks of two kinds of rapture which may overtake the monk. The first is experienced 'sometimes at the hour of prayer, sometimes during a reading', while the other may occur 'during the night, when you find yourself between sleep and wakefulness, somehow sleeping yet not asleep, wakeful yet not awake'. In either case, 'when this delight comes upon a person and vibrates throughout his body, then is the hour when he thinks that the kingdom of heaven itself is nothing other than this very same thing'.[72] At least something of Alyosha's condition is anticipated here.

Equally applicable is another passage in which Isaac suggests that 'vision' (which he distinguishes from 'revelation') can be experienced in a variety of ways, 'in sleep or else at times of waking, sometimes with all clarity, at other times as if in an apparition and somewhat unclearly; for which reason even the recipient of the vision often does not know himself whether he sees the vision in a waking or somnolent state'. Moreover, 'it is possible to hear a voice asking for assistance, sometimes to see someone clearly face to face, to engage in conversation, to ask questions and to receive replies'.[73] It is certainly not difficult to relate Alyosha's conversation with Zosima at the messianic banquet to such words as these.

Alyosha's rapture is divided into two parts. The first involves his vision of the marriage feast (XIV, 327; VII, iv), the second his experience of the cosmos in Zosima's garden (XIV, 328; VII, iv).

The reader's own expectations – supported by Isaac's comments – would prepare him for some lack of definition. Alyosha's dreams, visions and contemplations are effectively presented as they evolve, and there is no room for the kind of clarification (or attempt at clarification) which a retrospective narrative might prompt. Even so, an acceptance of a narrative device, a reader's willing suspension of disbelief, should not preclude subsequent examination of the vision's substance, a search for its core.

The messianic banquet

Alyosha's first visionary experience involves a fresh presentation of some of Zosima's principal concerns. Particular emphasis is given to joy and forgiveness. It appears that even Zosima himself, in common with many of his fellow guests at the banquet, has escaped from the possibility of damnation only by virtue of a single 'onion', the exceptional good deed which has counted in his favour. All the more reason, therefore, to make merry at the messianic feast.

Yet the feast is curiously presented. The messiah himself, the great host, is not to be seen at first hand. Nor is he to be named, except obliquely. In what may be a reference to such texts as Malachi 4:2 or Revelation 21:33, Zosima speaks of him as 'our Sun' (XIV, 327; VII, iv).[74] Zosima himself presumably sees him, since he asks Alyosha 'Do you see our Sun, do you see Him?'[75] But Alyosha avoids the challenge with a whispered, 'I am afraid. I do not dare to look.' Therefore neither can the reader look at the mysterious presence. Zosima provides a brief comment on some of his host's qualities but the single sentence devoted to this hardly compensates for the effective absence of the Jesus who was explicitly named and presented on the previous page within the framework of the Gospel reading and Alyosha's preliminary musings on it (XIV, 326; VII, iv). There is a degree of evasiveness here, and censorship restrictions (which Dostoyevsky shows no sign of anticipating in his notebooks) can provide only a partial explanation for it.

Alyosha in Zosima's garden

But there is more evasiveness to come. For what does Alyosha experience when he leaves the elder's cell?

> His soul, replete with rapture, thirsted for freedom, space, expanse. Above him was inversed the heavenly dome, generous and unfathomable, full of silent glowing stars. From zenith to horizon stretched the Milky Way, as yet indistinct and out of focus...The luxuriant autumn flowers in the beds had gone to sleep until morning. The silence of the earth seemed to merge with that of the heavens, the mystery of the earth with that of the stars...Alyosha stood, watched and suddenly threw himself to the earth as if he had been cut down.

It is at this moment that Zosima's counsels are followed to the letter. Alyosha kisses the earth and waters it (or to follow the Russian literally, her) with his tears:

> He had no idea why he embraced her, he made no attempt to assess why he was so irresistibly impelled to kiss her, to kiss the whole of her, but kiss her he did, weeping, sobbing and watering her with his tears, and he vowed in his elation to love her, to love her for ever. 'Water the earth with your tears of joy and love those tears of yours' resounded in his soul.

Not only the earth, but the entire cosmos is brought closer through such tears.

> What was he weeping for? Oh, he wept in his rapture even for these very stars, which shone out to him from the abyss; and 'he was not ashamed of such ecstasy'. It seemed as if threads from all those countless worlds of God had simultaneously come together in his soul, and it was all a-tremble, 'coming into contact with [these] other worlds'. He wanted to forgive everyone and for everything and to seek forgiveness, no, not for himself but for all, for everything and for everyone, while 'there are also others interceding for me' came another echo from within his soul.

Alyosha was left under no illusion that he was under the sway of some superior force.

> With every passing minute he could feel clearly and as it were tangibly that something as firm and as immutable as that heavenly vault was entering his soul. Some kind of idea had

> somehow come to dominate his mind, and from this moment, moreover, for his whole life, and for ever. He fell to the ground a weak youth, but he rose as a warrior, fortified for the rest of his life, and he sensed this immediately, that very moment of his rapture. Never was Alyosha able to forget that moment later, not for so long as he lived, never. 'Someone visited my soul that hour,' he would say later, with firm conviction in his words. (XIV, 328; VII, iv)

And so, at one fell swoop, Dostoyevsky brings together the kissing of the earth, joy, tears and mutual forgiveness. The mutual forgiveness, moreover, is given a cosmic dimension. It is prompted, justified and sustained by that cosmic harmony of which Alyosha has received such palpable intimations.

It is undoubtedly a high-water mark in the novel, as Dostoyevsky himself suggested. At the very least it is a watershed in the life of the character whom Dostoyevsky's narrator designated as 'my hero' (XIV, 5; Author's preface). For we witness his initiation into mysteries which leave him marked for life.

Yet what these mysteries mean is left frustratingly unclear. No vaguer terms could have been chosen to describe them. 'Some kind of idea' comes to dominate Alyosha's mind 'somehow'. It is 'something firm and immutable' which enters his soul. Only in retrospect does Alyosha come to correct the impression given by these imprecise and markedly impersonal phrases: it is only then that 'someone' is said to have visited his soul. But the fact that this supplementary and retrospective account needs to be fortified by reference to his 'firm convictions' can provoke as much scepticism as it allays. In any case 'someone' hardly does duty as one of the divine names. The same must be said *a fortiori* about 'something'.

The image (*obraz*) which Dostoyevsky had hoped to present has become hopelessly diluted and probably distorted. Certainly Alyosha's experience could never be described as a theophany. If anything it is a cosmophany. From another point of view it may be seen as the expression of cosmolatory. A parallel for it is thus not to be sought in Isaac of Syria, Tikhon of Voronezh, Amvrosy of Optino or Francis of Assisi.

The garden of Bishop Bienvenu

But this is not to say that there is no clerical figure to be cited as a possible source or stimulus for Dostoyevsky. The most obvious such cleric however was not the product of the Syrian desert nor of the Russian *pustyn'* (monastery). Like Zosima himself, he was a nineteenth-century novelist's creation. His author was that 'great poet, whose genius [as Dostoyevsky acknowledged at the beginning of that critical summer of 1879] has exercised so powerful an influence on me ever since my childhood', Victor Hugo.[76] His home is *Les misérables*, which Dostoyevsky re-read at least as recently as 1874,[77] and of which he possessed three complete editions.[78] His name is Monseigneur Bienvenu (more correctly, Charles-François Bienvenu Myriel), Bishop of Digne.

Dostoyevsky's own regard for this bishop is demonstrated in a letter of 1877, in which he takes pleasure in a friend's positive appreciation of him.[79] It seems likely that Dostoyevsky also demonstrated his regard for him in those pages of *The Brothers Karamazov* which have just been examined. For not only does Hugo's hero (Jean Valjean) experience an ecstatic vision of the bishop, his spiritual sponsor, and shed copious tears at the conclusion of it:[80] the bishop himself has many characteristics which are also to be found in Zosima. Moreover, and most important, he is familiar with an experience which closely resembles that of Alyosha in the garden.

Monseigneur Bienvenu 'had an excess of love' (p. 76). The essence of his teaching was '*Love one another.*' Indeed, he declared this to be 'complete': 'he wished for nothing more, and this was the whole of his doctrine' (pp. 81–2). His beliefs in other matters were less clear, certainly less explicit (p. 76). But he possessed a childlike gaiety, and 'it seemed as if joy emanated from the whole of his personality' (p. 78). Nevertheless, stories of his youth suggested that – like Zosima (XIV, 269–70; VI, ii) – he had once been a passionate and possibly a violent man (p. 77). This could not have been suspected at his present age, sixty-five, an age which he shares with Zosima (XIV, 37; II, ii), and also, at the time of Dostoyevsky's visit to Optino, with another of Zosima's putative models, Amvrosy. In view of what was said above, Hugo's comparison of Bienvenu with Francis of Assisi is of some interest, although it is not developed by him (p. 77).

Some of Bienvenu's attitudes and experiences are shared by Alyosha Karamazov. Particularly striking is the way in which Hugo's bishop relates to the night sky. He would engage in a kind of ritual before sleep which involved a visit to his carefully tended garden and contemplation 'in the presence of the great spectacles [provided] by the night sky': 'He would be there alone with himself, collected, peaceful, full of adoration, comparing the serenity of his own heart with the serenity of the ether, moved in the shadows by the visible splendours of the constellations and the invisible splendours of God, opening his soul to the thoughts which descended from the Unknown.'

Unlike Alyosha, therefore, the bishop goes beyond the stars to thoughts (at least) of their creator:

> He mused on the grandeur and the presence of God; on the eternity to come, that strange mystery; on past eternity, that stranger mystery still; on all the infinities which were yet to be discovered by his eyes in all directions; and without seeking to comprehend the incomprehensible, he observed it. He did not study God; rather was he overwhelmed by him. (p. 79)

Yet even here, the Creator is to be apprehended mainly, if not only, through his works. Bienvenu divided his leisure time between 'gardening by day and contemplation by night': 'was this narrow enclosure [his garden], with the skies for its ceiling, not enough to be able to adore God alternately in his most charming and in his most sublime creation?' (p. 79). Consequently here also a certain depersonalization of the divinity is likely to occur which links Bienvenu's experience most closely with Alyosha's. For that 'something' which entered Alyosha's soul during his ecstatic moments in the monastic garden finds its parallel, perhaps its explanation, in the following words:

> In moments like these, offering up his heart at the hour when the nocturnal flowers offer up their scent, illumined like a lamp in the midst of the star-spangled night, welling over in ecstasy, amidst the universal radiance of Creation, he himself probably could not have said what was taking place in his mind; he felt something escape from him and something descend into him. Mysterious exchanges between the depths of the soul and the depths of the universe. (p. 79)

Are Alyosha's 'exchanges' substantially to be distinguished from the bishop's? The parallel ought not to be ignored. At the very least it provides yet one more reminder that Alyosha's experience is not necessarily nor yet obviously the fruit or the foundation of a Christian Orthodox commitment. His tears, prostrations, kissing of the earth and communing with the cosmos may still intrigue, impress or even move the reader with their innocent intensity. But despite the Christian cosmetics which Dostoyevsky has partially applied, they speak of little more than nature mysticism.

The prophet and his unbelief

The would-be prophet had attained his 'hosanna', his faith, 'through a great *furnace of doubt*'.[81] Yet the doubt had not been left behind. It informs the arguments of Ivan, it gives Zosima's counterweight, that Western monk, the Grand Inquisitor, his haunting and his lasting power. Dostoyevsky thus had good reason to emulate the possessed boy's father in the Gospels and to pray, 'Lord, I believe; help thou mine unbelief' (Mark 9:24).

In the case of Zosima and Alyosha, who could have been, respectively, the proponent and the champion of belief, the unbelief is not so far to seek as might have been expected. And in the case of either, but especially Alyosha, the reader is ultimately confronted with what A. B. Gibson has succinctly termed 'the combination of the sincerest piety with the apparent absence of its object'.[82]

Notes

1. F. M. Dostoyevsky, *Pis'ma*, ed. A. S. Dolinin (4 vols., Moscow/Leningrad, 1928–59), vol. 4, p. 171.
2. F. M. Dostoyevsky, *Polnoye sobraniye sochineniy*, vol. 11 (St Petersburg, 1895), pp. 300, 387.
3. K. V. Mochul'sky, *Velikiye russkiye pisateli* (Paris, 1939), p. 123; *id.*, *Dostoyevsky: Zhizn' i tvorchestvo* (Paris, 1947), p. 343 (translated by M. Minihan as *Dostoevsky: His Life and Work* (Princeton, 1967), p. 421); D. V. Grishin *Dnevnik pisatelya F. M. Dostoyevskogo* (Melbourne, 1966), p. 164; M. V. Jones, *Dostoyevsky: The Novel of Discord* (London, 1976), p. 195; A. Walicki, *A History of Russian Thought from the Enlightenment to Marxism* (Oxford, 1980), pp. 345–7.
4. K. N. Leont'ev, *Vostok, Rossiya i Slavyanstvo* (Moscow, 1885–6), vol. 2, pp. 280–309.
5. Dostoyevsky, *Pis'ma,* vol. 4, pp. 169–70.
6. M. M. Bakhtin, *Problemy poetiki Dostoyevskogo* (Moscow, 1963), p. 334; transl. by R. W. Rotsel as *Problems of Dostoevsky's Poetics* (Ann Arbor, 1973), p. 211.
7. Dostoyevsky, *Pis'ma*, vol. 4, pp. 53–4.
8. *Ibid.*, vol. 4, pp. 109–10.
9. *Ibid.*, vol. 4, p. 91 (Letter to Lyubimov of 7 August NS 1879).
10. *Ibid.*, vol. 4, p. 92.
11. Parfeny, *Skazaniye*, 2nd edn (Moscow, 1856), vol. 3, pp. 154–88.
12. 'Skazaniye o pochivshem o Boze startse Daniile . . . ': 'Iz zhitiya v Boze prestavivshegosya . . . startsa Zosimy . . .'.
13. Sven Linnér, *Starets Zosima in The Brothers Karamazov* (Stockholm, 1975), pp. 124–5.

14. L. P. Grossman's publication of Dostoyevsky's library holdings (Grossman, *Biblioteka Dostoyevskogo* (Odessa, 1919), pp. 125–67 and Grossman, *Seminariy po Dostoyevskomu* (Moscow/Petrograd, 1922), pp. 20–53) has recently been supplemented by L. P. Desyatkina and G. M. Fridlender, 'Biblioteka Dostoyevskogo (Novyye materialy)', in *Dostoyevsky: Materialy i issledovaniya* (Leningrad, 1980), vol. 4, pp. 253–71. The titles in the notes which follow (15, 17, 19–22) are derived from both these sources.
15. *Kozel'skaya Vvedenskaya Optina pustyn'* ([?] Moscow, 1873) and *Istoricheskoye opisaniye Kozel'skoy Vvedenskoy Optinoy pustyni* (Moscow, 1876).
16. Parfeny, *Skazaniye*, vol. 1, p. 175f.
17. *Zhizneopisaniye Optinskago startsa iyeromonakha Leonida (v skhime L'va)* (Moscow, 1876).
18. Title unknown (L. P. Grossman, *Seminariy*, p. 44); possibly *Dvenadtsat' slov prepodobnago Simeona Novago Bogoslova*, since this was published by Optina Pustyn.
19. Mark Podvizhnik, *Slovo o pokayanii* (Kozel'sk: Vvedenskaya Optina pustyn', 1867).
20. *Beseda na 6-yi psalom sv. Anastasiya Sinaita* (1870 and 1873, the latter of which was published at Optina Pustyn).
21. Arkhimandrit Agapit, *Zhizneopisaniye v Boze pochivshago optinskago startsa iyeroskhimonakha Amvrosiya* (Moscow, 1900).
22. Dostoyevsky possessed the translation published at Sergiyev Posad in 1854 (Grossman, *Seminariy*, p. 45). I have used the same translation, but in the second edition: *Tvoreniya izhe vo svyatykh ottsa nashego avvy Isaaka Siriyanina, podvizhnika i otshel'nika, byvshego yepiskopom khristolyubivago grada Ninevii: Slova podvizhnicheskiya* (Sergiyev Posad, 1893).
23. For example, *PSS*, XIV, 275; VI, ii (Luke 17:21); *PSS*, XIV, 291; VI, iii (Matthew 7:1); *PSS*, XIV, 287–8; VI, iii (Philemon [1]:16).
24. Dostoyevsky, *Pis'ma*, vol. 4, p. 109.
25. *Literaturnoye nasledstvo*, 15 (1934), 138.
26. E. Renan, *Zhizn' Iisusa* (St Petersburg, 1900), p. 58.
27. E. I. Kiyko, 'Dostoyevsky i Renan', in *Dostoyevsky: Materialy i issledovaniya* (Leningrad, 1980), vol. 4, pp. 106–22.
28. Dostoyevsky, *Pis'ma*, vol. 2, pp. 61, 67.
29. *Ibid.*, vol. 2, p. 300.
30. E.g. Parfeny, *Skazaniye*, vol. 1, pp. 264, 277.
31. Isaak, *Slova podvizhnicheskiya*, pp. 105, 223. Subsequent references are given in the text.
32. Paulos Gregorios, *The Human Presence: An Orthodox View of Nature* (Geneva, 1978), p. 84.
33. Leontios of Cyprus (6th–7th century), quoted in Kallistos Ware, *The Orthodox Way* (London/Oxford, 1979), p. 70.
34. E.g. R. V. Pletnyov, 'Zemlya', in A. L. Bem (ed.), *O Dostoyevskom: Sbornik statey*, vol. 1 (Prague, 1929), p. 161.
35. The phrase ('Dostoyevsky – genial'nyy chitatel'') provides the title for

Bem's article in A. L. Bem (ed.), *O Dostoyevskom: Sbornik statey*, vol. 2 (Prague, 1933), pp. 7–24.

36. For alternative readings of the term as a reference to the final scene of *Faust* (II, v) see the works cited in *PSS*, XV, 563. To these might be added N. Vil'mont, *Velikiye sputniki* (Moscow, 1966), pp. 273–5.
37. Vittora Branca, 'Il *Cantico di frate Sole*: studio della fonti e testo critico', *Archivum franciscanum historicum*, 41, fasc. i–iv (1948), 85.
38. *Legenda Maior*, X.4: 'loca spargebat lacrymis'. Text in *Analecta franciscana*, 10, fasc. v (1941), 603.
39. For earlier such associations of maternal types see S. Smirnov, *Drevne-russkiy dukhovnik* [. . .] (Moscow, 1914), vol. 1, pp. 265 (and n. 1), 274.
40. Smirnov, *Drevne-russkiy dukhovnik*, vol. 1, p. 274.
41. Quoted (without precise indication of source) by F. I. Udelov, 'Dostoyevsky i Optina pustyn'', *Vestnik russkogo studencheskogo khristianskogo dvizheniya*, 99 (1971), 13.
42. *Dostoyevsky: Materialy i issledovaniya*, vol. 4, p. 265.
43. Agapit, *Zhizneopisaniye*, vol. 1, pp. 86–8.
44. *Literaturnoye nasledstvo*, 15 (1934), 135.
45. On this Orthodox attitude see Arkhimandrit Kipriyan [Kern], *Yevkharistiya* (Paris, 1947), p. 328.
46. Zosima must therefore be distinguished from the exceptional monk, mentioned by Isaac, whose single prayer, ceaselessly repeated for over forty years, 'replaced for him the service day and night' (p. 234).
47. Dostoyevsky, *Pis'ma*, vol. 4, p. 9.
48. A. K. Gornostayev, *Ray na zemle; k ideologii tvorchestva F. M. Dostoyevskogo: F. M. Dostoyevsky i N. F. Fyodorov* (Harbin, 1929), pp. 37–87.
49. Gornostayev (*Ray na zemle*, p. 41) believes that the text corresponds to the (subsequently revised) pages given in N. F. Fyodorov, *Filosofiya obshchago dela* (Verny, 1906), vol. 1, pp. 64ff (presumably pp. 64–127).
50. Quoted in Gornostayev, *Ray na zemle*, p. 44. Italics mine.
51. G. Friedrich (ed.), *Theological Dictionary of the New Testament* (Grand Rapids, 1973), vol. 5, p. 769 (J. Jeremias).
52. Quoted in Gornostayev, *Ray na zemle*, p. 84. Gornostayev's own title reflects Fyodorov's concern.
53. Friedrich, *Theological Dictionary*, vol. 5, p. 767 (J. Jeremias).
54. Bernard Orchard *et al.* (eds), *A Catholic Commentary on Holy Scripture* (London, 1953), p. 939 (R. Ginns).
55. Isaak, *Slova podvizhnicheskiya*, p. 391.
56. I use 'first' as a literal translation for the Slavonic *pervyy*. Authorized Version has 'chief', Revised Standard Version 'foremost'.
57. Isaak, *Slova podvizhnicheskiya*, p. 53.
58. *Ibid.*, pp. 16–17.
59. Dostoyevsky, *Pis'ma*, vol. 2, p. 264.
60. *Dostoyevsky: Materialy i issledovaniya*, vol. 4, p. 265. Tikhon's work *Pokayaniye* (various eds, 1840–78) formed part of his *O istinnom khristianstve* (Tikhon, *Sochineniya* [Moscow, 1860], vol. 6, pp. 1–42).
61. Dostoyevsky, *Pis'ma*, vol. 4, p. 92.

62. Tikhon, *Sochineniya*, vol. 1, p. 141.
63. Tikhon, *Sochineniya*, vol. 3, p. 232 and ('O pokayanii'), vol. 6, p. 13; cf. Dostoyevsky, *PSS*, XIV, 292–3; VI, iii.
64. *Zhizneopisaniye optinskago startsa iyeromonakha Leonida (v skhime L'va)* (Moscow, 1876), pp. 57, 77.
65. Parfeny, *Skazaniye*, vol. 1, p. 277.
66. *Ibid.*, vol. 1, p. 276.
67. *Ibid.*, vol. 1, p. 280.
68. Quoted by F. I. Udelov, 'Dostoyevsky i Optina pustyn'', in *Vestnik russkogo studencheskogo khristianskogo dvizheniya*, 99 (1971), 10.
69. V. Lebedev (ed.), 'Otryvok iz romana "Brat'ya Karamazovy" pered sudom tsenzury', *Russkaya literatura*, no. 2 (1970), 123–5.
70. Only in the early years of the twentieth century was the censorship to relent. M. A. Novoselov issued two separate brochures containing sections of Zosima's discourse (=*PSS*, XIV, 263–8; VI, ii and 288–91; VI, iii). See F. I. Fudel', 'U sten Tserkvi', *Nadezhda: Khristiyanskoye chteniye*, 2 (Frankfurt-am-Main, 1979), 281.
71. Dostoyevsky, *Pis'ma*, vol. 4, p. 114.
72. Isaak, *Slova podvizhnicheskiya*, p. 196.
73. *Ibid.*, p. 103.
74. The editors of *PSS*, XIV (1976) demoted the capital S to a minuscule since it was presumed to refer to God (who himself does not merit a capital in normal Soviet practice). I have restored the capital in accordance with *Polnoye sobraniye sochineniy* (St Petersburg, 1885–6), vol. 6, p. 247. Dostoyevsky's MS has not survived (*PSS*, XV, 397–8).
75. The pronoun *Yego* could also be translated 'It'; but the next paragraph declares that this Sun has 'become like us out of love', and this reference to the Incarnation argues for *Yego* as a masculine pronoun. The capital letter (omitted in *PSS*, XIV, but present in *Polnoye sobraniye sochineniy* (1885–6), vol. 6, p. 247) supports such a reading.
76. Dostoyevsky, *Pis'ma*, vol. 4, p. 55.
77. A. G. Dostoyevskaya, *Vospominaniya*, ed. L. P. Grossman (Moscow/Leningrad, 1925), p. 185.
78. *Dostoyevsky: Materialy i issledovaniya*, vol. 4, p. 268.
79. Dostoyevsky, *Pis'ma*, vol. 4, p. 592.
80. V. Hugo, *Les misérables*, vol. 1, in his *Oeuvres complètes*, ed. J. Cornuz (Paris, 1966), vol. 2, p. 157. Subsequent references are given in the text.
81. Notebook entry, *Biografiya, pis'ma i zametki iz zapisnoy knizhki F. M. Dostoyevskago* (St Petersburg, 1883), [pt 2], p. 375.
82. A. B. Gibson, *The Religion of Dostoyevsky* (London, 1973), p. 196.

7

The philosophical dimension: self and freedom

STEWART R. SUTHERLAND

I

The elucidation of the notion of freedom seems to be a task without end. The enthusiasm which philosophers show for this particular issue waxes and wanes, but never seems to die: even the question of what styles of argument are appropriate provokes deep divisions. Indeed one could accurately chart the beach-heads of the intellectual equivalent of the English Channel, by considering the different strategies adopted by Anglo-Saxon and French philosophers grappling with this issue. The role of the novel in such discussion seems quite secure in French intellectual life, but it is still regarded with some suspicion in the citadels of English-speaking philosophy. The difference is not simply that Sartre was both novelist and philosopher, because of course one of the most perceptive of English-speaking philosophers is Iris Murdoch. The difference has much more to do with what is accepted by English-speaking philosophers as a typically philosophical argument. This is not to suggest that there is a single identifiable paradigm, for as we shall see there are uncertainties even here. Nonetheless the intellectual botanizer would have little difficulty in the English-speaking world in separating works of fiction from works of undoubted philosophical pedigree. The division of labour implicit in all this brings both strengths and weaknesses. Anglo-Saxon standards of philosophical rigour and consistency are indeed high: at times however they are also narrow and falsely constricting.

This paper will be a discussion of some aspects of Dostoyevsky's treatment of the notion of freedom. I shall try to establish by specific comparison that his concerns and his insights are not far from those which have been and are central in English-speaking philosophy. Further, I shall argue that students of Dostoyevsky as well as students of philosophy would benefit from an appreciation of this. The philosophical issues are not Dostoyevsky's sole concern, but they are important and require *philosophical* elucidation: conversely, the filling out of narrative and character which is still central to the definition of the novel is one very important way of showing the limitations in certain types of philosophical enquiry. The main focus of the following discussion will be upon *Notes from Underground* (1864) and *The Brothers Karamazov* (1880).

II

The clarification of the notion of freedom is a task that can take many forms. My initial argument is that there are striking similarities between the points which emerge from Dostoyevsky's exploration of the psyche of the splenetic, repellent narrator of the *Notes*, and from a much more formal and analytic treatment of the matter in a group of papers in the philosophy of mind published in Britain a century or more later, that is to say in our own time. It is however part of the novelist's brief to clarify more fully the limitations implicit in such philosophical explorations.

It is doubtless ultimately foolish, but nonetheless moderately instructive, to attempt to excise from *Notes from Underground* what is implied about the concept of freedom. To attempt to do so will inevitably be to invite and receive criticism. As it is, commentators evoke different emphases and atmospheres in their respective accounts. For example, the following remarks, from Mochulsky and Wasiolek respectively, are moving in quite contrary directions:

MOCHULSKY: Investigation of the irrational blind will, being cast about in void self-formation, reveals the tragedy of personality and freedom.[1]

WASIOLEK: The world view that takes mature form in *Notes from Underground* and that will be refined in dramatic form in the great novels that follow is neither confused, nor contradictory, nor paradoxical. At its base lies the dialectic in which good may be chosen to be evil and evil chosen to be good.[2]

Wasiolek's remarks are positive and suggest, if not exactly a linear progress on this matter from the *Notes* through the great novels, then at least the laying of a foundation which Dostoyevsky would not subsequently have to reassess. It is implied that here, in definitive form, Dostoyevsky has stated and accepted, in a manner that will not be further questioned by him, the picture of man as essentially creating himself and his values through the choices which he freely makes.[3]

Implicit in such a statement is a confidence both about freedom and about Dostoyevsky's unswerving attachment to it, which must be questioned on both counts. On the one hand there is a self-confidence about freedom as the key to human life which is almost Sartrian, and over which Mochulsky casts a shadow in his perceptive reference to the in-built 'tragedy of personality and freedom'. It is worth noting how Sartre explicates his apparently negative 'I am condemned to be free', in the immediately following sentence: 'This means that no limits to my freedom can be found except freedom itself or, if you prefer, that we are not free to cease being free.'[4] On the other hand, as I shall argue in due course, Dostoyevsky did come to put a question mark against any form of ultimate optimism which centres on the notion of salvation through freedom. Nonetheless there is clear support for Wasiolek's view of the importance of that account of freedom which achieved its earliest firm statement in *Notes from Underground*, and it is to a more detailed elaboration of this that we must now give our attention.

My argument will be that the central *philosophical* focus in the discussion of freedom in the *Notes* is negative: in the end the primary philosophical point at issue is the refutation of determinism. I propose demonstrating this in two ways – on the one hand by detailed reference to the text of the *Notes*, and on the other by indicating the close parallel to be drawn between Dostoyevsky's treatment of the subject and the formal argument on this topic offered by an important article in the issue of the philosophical journal *Mind* for 1960.[5]

The narrator of the novel is obsessed both with the theory and with the practice of self-affirmation. He dreads but admits the possibility that even in his faults and offences, 'I have been, as it were, guilty without guilt, according to the laws of nature' (V, 103; I, ii). It seems that actually to *do* something, even something mean, lies always the other side of the stone wall: 'What stone wall? Why, of course, the laws of nature, the conclusions of the natural sciences, mathematics' (V, 105; I, iii). His dilemma is the dilemma of a man who perpetually runs up against the stone wall but who refuses 'to accept that wall merely because I have encountered a stone wall and have insufficient strength [to knock it down]' (V, 105–6; I, iii).

Dostoyevsky's fear here is not simply the fear that we are merely part of the physical world or what Kant called the world of 'phenomena'. His worry, prompted by Chernyshevsky's *What is to be Done?*, is more than that. He fears that there might be 'a formula which shall exactly express our wills and whims'; for

> if there shall ever be discovered . . . a genuine mathematical formula, then perhaps man will immediately cease to will, indeed perhaps he will cease to exist altogether. Who, after all, wants to exercise his will in accordance with tables? Not only that, he would be immediately transformed from a human being into an organ-barrel sprig or something of the kind. (V, 114; I, viii)

Further than this however (a point whose peculiar significance for this paper will emerge shortly) is that the Underground Man perpetually lives in the shadow of an anxiety lest he should be found wholly predictable, whether to himself or others. He resolves not to arrive before the others at the dinner party for Zverkov, but on the day he admits that he knew in advance that 'I *should* be the first to arrive.' His worry here is more that 'he cannot help it', for he fears even more both the opinion that others do have of him, and the very fact that they can so easily 'sum him up'. As Bakhtin writes:

> The 'underground man' thinks most about what others think or might think about him and strives to keep one step ahead of every other consciousness, everyone else's thoughts about him, every other point of view toward him. At all essential points in his confession he strives to anticipate possible definitions and assessments of him by others.[6]

Thus Dostoyevsky's philosophical protest is against the picture of man conformed to natural law, determined in his activity, for whom reason and nature coincide, in that there is always a calculable right and rational course of action which serves best his own pre-determined need. Such a man is in the end wholly predictable and perspicuous to others, whether he acts 'rationally' or otherwise. Of course, this negative protest against the anthropology and ethics of 'calculemus' runs throughout his later writing and to that extent Wasiolek is correct: foundations are laid here. The foundations however are negative: he *rejects* that view. In its place he offers the picture of a man who introduces himself with the words, 'I am ill; I am full of spleen and repellent', and for whom the preoccupation of his life was for a time to wander the Nevsky Prospekt in the hope of confronting a particular army officer whom he might jostle. The eventual outcome of this was that our hero, after several failed missions

> came to a sudden decision, screwed up my eyes and – our shoulders came into violent collision! Not an inch did I budge, but continued on my way on a completely equal footing! He didn't even look round, and pretended he had not noticed me; but he was only pretending, I am sure of it. To this day I am sure of it. (V, 132; II, i)

Can Dostoyevsky really be trying to tell us something fundamental about human nature here? Surprisingly he can, but at this stage his point is rather more limited than Wasiolek allows. This is hardly a panegyric to free self-creating action. It is the mean and venomous outpourings of a little man who, if he were less vicious in temperament, we should simply classify as 'bloody-minded'. Can bloody-mindedness be a definitive human property? In the very strict sense in which I am now going to specify it, the answer is 'yes', and to see this is to grasp more clearly the philosophical point at stake.

III

There is a marked similarity between the view which Dostoyevsky via his underground voice is contesting, and the view which Donald MacKay defines with a view to rejection, in his paper 'On the logical indeterminacy of a free choice'. His summary of the foundation in argument of the stone wall of 'the laws of nature, of the deductions of learning and the source of mathematics', is as follows:

> If my physical brain-processes were wholly physically determined, and if my decisions could be inferred uniquely from my brain-processes, then a fully informed observer of my brain-processes could know the outcome of my choices with certainty before I made them, and my impression of freedom in making these choices would therefore be an illusion, due to mere ignorance of the true state of affairs.[7]

This is the worry of the Underground Man stated in the precise accents of twentieth-century analytic philosophy. It even includes the fear that someone else might be able to predict accurately what next we shall do. Dostoyevsky's suggestion seems to be that we might just outwit such an observer provided the springs of our action are in the end not part of a public, observable calculus.

Any philosopher worth his salt however must question such a suggestion: does it not approximate to wishful thinking? This is, as we see, MacKay's question also – a question which has even more pressing insistence in the light of the increasing knowledge of the nature of the human brain. The conclusion of MacKay's argument is that the human agent is not deluded in his belief in human capacity to make free choices, and the implications of his argument bear a marked similarity to those of Dostoyevsky's fiction.

At the centre of MacKay's argument is the acceptance that from the observer's viewpoint an agent's behaviour may be highly, apparently even wholly, predictable. Nothing in Dostoyevsky's novel denies this. Equally however MacKay shares with Dostoyevsky the refusal to suggest with the Romantics, or philosophical inner sense theorists, that nonetheless there is one additional inner subjective factor of which only the agent is aware. The Underground Man certainly makes no such claims, and this is *one* of the factors which separate him from the heroes of Romantic sensibility. Quite strikingly he seldom seems to know quite what he will do next. In the last dramatic scene of his encounter with Liza, as he pursues her into the street, to the question 'Where could she have got to?', he adds the much more significant 'And why was I running after her at all?' The self-confessed 'non-hero' of the novel does not offer us any form of privileged access to demonstrate from inner intuition that he is free – that the stone walls of the laws of nature do not completely enclose him.

The essence of Dostoyevsky's response to determinism illustrates precisely one of the crucial emphases of MacKay's paper. Any prediction offered by the observer is open to falsification by the action of the agent. Now it is not merely that as it so happens some agents can anticipate the predictions which observers make about them sufficiently well to bloody-mindedly falsify them. This as a matter of fact may be true, but it is of course open to even more quick-witted observers to build the 'bloody-mindedness factor' into their prediction. However, it is at this point that it may begin to dawn on us that we are not dealing here with a matter of pure psychological fact about who can outwit whom.

There is in the example an element which points to the need of the observer to keep his prediction secret – at least from the agent. This is not a contingent point, it is a matter of the logic of the situation. The observer's prediction, if we go as far as possible down the path of determinism, may be that of the super-observer who in principle has a complete knowledge of the agent's brain-states at T_x. His prediction, based on this, is that at T_{x+1} the agent will do Z. Now the important point is that although the situation may appear to be exactly parallel to the case of an observer predicting changes in an inorganic substance between T_x and T_{x+1}, there is a subtle yet devastating difference. In the latter case, the prediction is true for all language-users, and can be made public. In the former case neither of these logical consequences follows.

The second point provides the clue here: the observer cannot make the prediction public because by so doing he invalidates the assumption upon which it is made, viz. the possession of all relevant information. The very act of publishing it – *to the agent* – renders its basis out of date. This is true because of the difference between human beings and inorganic matter. Human beings respond not only to physical stimuli, they respond to information. The point made by bloody-mindedness is precisely this. Just as Zverkov and his friends presumed that if they were sufficiently rude to our non-hero he would quit the dinner party, so he sensed their belief and acted on or rather reacted to it by remaining.

Nonetheless it might be suggested that MacKay and Dostoyevsky here won a pyrrhic victory in the battle against determinism: for surely it is a simple matter for the wise observer to build this into his prediction, and real students of human nature would have found other ways of persuading an unwanted guest to leave. Nonetheless the logical point still stands: if it is determinism that is in the dock, the vital point is that always the 'real' prediction must be kept secret, or again the data in which that real (unstated) prediction is made will be out of date.

This brings out the other major point of difference between predictions about inorganic matter and predictions about human beings. Predictions are made by language-users. A prediction about the change in the behaviour of water being heated to 100° centigrade is either true or false for *all* language-users. If true, it is, in a phrase from MacKay's Eddington Lecture, 'binding on (valid and definitive for) everyone'. The logical difference is that an apparently similar prediction about human behaviour is not 'binding on everyone', because it is not binding on the agent. In that sense Dostoyevsky is right to find evidence for the rejection of the relevance of the seeming 'stone wall of the laws of nature' where he does. Equally the force of the remarks quoted earlier can now be seen thrown even more clearly into philosophical relief:

> if there shall ever be discovered...a genuine mathematical formula, then perhaps man will immediately cease to will,

> indeed perhaps he will cease to exist altogether. Who, after all, wants to exercise his will in accordance with tables? Not only that, he would be immediately transformed from a human being into an organ-barrel sprig or something of the kind. (V, 114; I, viii)

Of course, as we now see plainly, Dostoyevsky is not postulating a possible state of affairs which might be brought about by growth in the precision of our predictive capacities: he is telling us what the logical difference is between predictions about inorganic matter and predictions about human behaviour – between men and organ-barrel sprigs.

How easy and perhaps tempting it might have appeared to Dostoyevsky to tell us a story about inner certainties and intuitions of freedom hidden from the public gaze of the observer. But he avoided the temptations and instead rested his case wholly on the difference seen in man's capacity for perhaps wilful, perhaps impulsive, but in the end *free* choice. In this sense his argument, like that of MacKay, is essentially negative in character – showing us that whatever is true of human action, full-blooded determinism cannot provide an adequate account of it.

In summary, I have been arguing that the sort of account given by Wasiolek of Dostoyevsky's treatment of the idea of freedom in *Notes from Underground* is rather overdrawn. The forebodings contained in the remarks quoted from Mochulsky have not yet been discussed, but as a prolegomenon to doing so, it has been essential to see the negative features of the points made by Dostoyevsky. Primarily he has been offering a rejection of determinism which, as comparison with Donald MacKay's argument has shown, has considerable implicit sophistication. Despite the subtlety however it is premature at this stage of Dostoyevsky's development to see a 'world view that takes mature form' (Wasiolek), rather than the impassioned rejection of an alternative world view. I find Bakhtin's summary here much more precise and, incidentally, virtually a restatement of some of the central elements of MacKay's argument:

> He is aware of his objective definition, neutral both to foreign consciousness and to his own self-consciousness, and he takes into account the viewpoint of a 'third party'. But he also knows that all of these definitions, both biased and objective, rest in his hands and cannot finalize him, precisely because he himself perceives them; he can go beyond their limits and make them invalid. He knows that he has the *final word*, and

> he seeks, come what may, to retain for himself this final word about himself, the word of his self-consciousness, in order through it to become what he is not. His self-consciousness lives on its unfinalizedness, its openendedness and indeterminacy.[8]

Dostoyevsky has however given hints to be developed in subsequent novels of a rather fuller account of human freedom, and of its indispensability to our understanding of human beings, and it is to these hints that we now turn.

IV

Bakhtin can again help direct our enquiry: 'Dostoyevsky's hero is not an objectified image, but rather an autonomous word, a *pure voice*; we do not see him, we hear him.'[9] In this work we are not given the picture of a human being but rather an analysis of one aspect of humanity. The limitation implicit in this is quite apparently matched by limitations in the conception of freedom which it allows.

There are marked analogies between these limitations and those under which much philosophical discussion of freedom labours. There is a clear tendency in much philosophical writing to discuss freedom as if it were a quality of individual acts of will, without paying much attention to what it might then mean to say that *human beings* may act freely. The philosophical emphasis is one of the targets of Nietzsche's aphoristic attack on received philosophical wisdom about the will:

> Philosophers are accustomed to speak of the will as if it were the best-known thing in the world; indeed Schopenhauer has given us to understand that the will alone is really known to us, absolutely and completely known, without subtraction or addition...Willing seems to me to be above all something *complicated*, something that is a unit only as a word.[10]

These limitations are present in much philosophy written since the time of Nietzsche. They might also seem to be present in Dostoyevsky's *Notes from Underground*: the difference is that whereas in the case of much contemporary – particularly Anglo-Saxon – philosophy, there is little overt acknowledgement of the limitations of this type of treatment of human freedom, there is, I suggest, ample evidence that Dostoyevsky was well aware of the artificiality of the discussion of freedom in the *Notes*. Bakhtin's comment on the 'indeterminacy' of that novel is entirely apposite:

> And this is not merely a characterological trait of the 'underground man's' self-consciousness; it is the dominant of his construction by the author. The author indeed leaves the final word to his hero. And precisely it, or, more exactly, the tendency toward it, is necessary to the author's design.[11]

The point here is that in his rejection of determinism Dostoyevsky complements what I have argued to be a subtle philosophical point by a deliberately artificial isolation of the human being and his will into 'an autonomous word, a pure voice'. This is undoubtedly necessary to make the point which so resembles that of MacKay's paper, but it is a mistake of the first order to forget that the 'hero' of the novel is in fact an artificial slice of humanity. Similarly it is a mistake which philosophers have often made, to fail to realize the essentially selective and fragmented account of human action which their arguments often unwittingly imply.

One exception to this generalization is the quite remarkable British Academy Lecture by Sir Peter Strawson, 'Freedom and Resentment'. Strawson modestly refers to much of what he has to say as consisting of 'commonplaces'. In his discussion of different possible constructions of determinism he urges upon us (particularly perhaps if we are philosophers) 'the central commonplace' of

> the very great importance that we attach to the attitudes and intentions towards us of other human beings, and the great extent to which our personal feelings and reactions depend upon, or involve, our belief about these attitudes and intentions. I can give no simple description of the field of phenomena at the centre of which stands this commonplace truth; for the field is too complex. Much imaginative literature is devoted to exploring its complexities; and we have a large vocabulary for the purpose.[12]

Strawson's remarks have wide significance for this paper.

First and foremost there is at least an acknowledgement of the strength of imaginative literature in this context – the opportunity which the novelist has to do justice to the complexity of human will and action. Dostoyevsky's exploration of a literary construction which deliberately edits out some of this complexity is indirect tribute to the same point. The second crucial issue to which Strawson draws attention is the importance of reactive attitudes such as anger, compassion, resentment, for our discussion of freedom.

Of course the Underground Man, as we have seen, is a quintessential example of this. His life is polarized upon what he (albeit mistakenly) believes to be the attitudes of others to him. There is an interesting point of both comparison and contrast between him and Dostoyevsky's next great 'non-hero', Raskolnikov. Both characters embody explorations of the nature of human freedom, and both characters are 'isolated'. In each case one sign of that isolation is ultimately a lack of self-knowledge. It is not however the lack of self-knowledge in itself which is indicative of the isolation: rather it is that the nature of the isolation is logically and psychologically related to the reasons for the lack of self-knowledge.

Both the Underground Man and Raskolnikov show in their different cases that human beings can act in unexpected and startling ways. As we have seen, the Underground Man even amazes himself from time to time – most strikingly in his running after Liza at the end of the book. Raskolnikov's uncertainty about himself and his reason for committing murder comes out most clearly in the long discussion with Sonya in which he confesses his deed and attempts to explain it to her. At first he seems to have many explanations – too many – theft, helping his mother, temptation by Satan, emulating Napoleon and so on; then he reformulates his view: 'You are right, Sonya, that is not it at all. Totally different causes were at work here!' (VI, 320; V, iv). Very significantly the next sentence provides a connection to our main theme: 'I haven't talked to anyone for ages, Sonya...' Even so he is not content and shortly connects these two points: 'I wished, Sonya, to kill without casuistic argument, to kill for myself, for myself alone' (VI, 321–2; V, iv). Insofar as he reaches a conclusion, Raskolnikov stresses exactly what we find in the *Notes* – self-affirmation. But of course this in itself does not give self-knowledge: it leaves Raskolnikov, Sonya and the reader quite as puzzled as before. The philosophical form of the puzzle is about the nature of freedom, and of free self-affirmation.

There is a sense however in which we have made little progress. We have simply restated the problem. Dostoyevsky rejects determinism, and we may agree with him, and with MacKay when the latter points to 'the logical indeterminacy of a free choice'. Nonetheless we remain puzzled as to how we should move from this negative point to a positive understanding of, say, Raskolnikov. It is this point of puzzlement that we must examine in more detail – the isolation of the central characters of these two novels.

The Underground Man's isolation takes form from two essential [illegible] the one hand he desperately wishes to belong to [illegible] the other he is incapable of doing so because, in his [illegible]ssion with the attitudes of others to him, he system-[illegible]reads these attitudes and misdirects his own responses. [illegible]se of Raskolnikov the isolation is different. Whatever the [illegible]gical or social causes given as the origins of this isolation, the [illegible]come is logically quite distinct. His isolation is defined eventually in the act of gratuitous murder – perhaps the only act (alongside gratuitous lying) which, if we stress the word 'gratuitous', symbolically destroys the structure of society. Capricious actions of the mean and petty Underground Man can be tolerated: society is not essentially weakened by them. Capricious murder 'for myself' is however in a different category. The measure of the significance of this is that we regard it as *prima facie* evidence of mental illness. To set at naught *all* respect for human life is to set oneself apart from fellow human beings in the most radical way possible.[13]

The freedom, then, of these two men is a freedom which to some extent takes them out of human society. It is the freedom of isolation, and it is the only type of freedom which can be uncovered if we allow the contours of our discussion of freedom to become over-simplified – by focussing, for example, upon chimerical pure, simple acts of will. Nor is any improvement likely to be found in the currently more fashionable philosophical approach to the concept of action through pursuit of so-called 'basic actions'.[14]

The limitations of this approach to freedom are to be seen in two important related facts. First, the two Dostoyevskian 'heroes' do not understand themselves; nor, as the exploration of Raskolnikov's story makes plain, is he understood even by those who are closest to him. The reason for this dual lack of understanding is one and the same and is the consequence of the second crucial feature which limits severely this approach to the examination of human freedom: the isolation in question is quite radical. It deprives Raskolnikov and the Underground Man as well as all who encounter them of the necessary intellectual resources to give and receive explanations of their behaviour. Explanations and understandings are deposited within society. What counts as an explanation of, and what is a possible form of understanding oneself or others has its contours within social intercourse. Strawson draws related consequences from this point when he argues that the 'existence of the general framework of attitudes itself is something we are given with the fact of human society'.[15] To disrupt one's relationship to that general framework or, in extreme cases such as Raskolnikov and his murder, to cut oneself off from it is to be radical in one's isolaiton from one's fellow human beings; and this, whether undertaken deliberately or by accident, does in the end deprive one of the means of self-understanding.

The connection which I see between these points and the earlier quotation from Strawson is as follows: the isolation of each of these two Dostoyevskian heroes is to be understood in terms of either a distortion of (*Notes from Underground*) or a virtual absence of (*Crime and Punishment*) all the human relationships summarized in and derived from the reactive attitudes of which Strawson writes. Strawson's argument is that the nature of human society and human relationships is such that 'a sustained objectivity of inter-personal attitude, and the human isolation which that would entail, does not seem to be something of which human beings would be capable, even if some general truth were a theoretical ground for it'.[16] In his own way Dostoyevsky stresses this point no less than Strawson, but there are some differences which must be indicated if Strawson's position is to be fairly presented.

What they have in common here is a general strategy to reject determinism and to remind us both that in this context reactive attitudes are extremely important, and that there are some very puzzling features in the suggestion that on theoretical grounds we might treat all human beings 'objectively' in all circumstances. The tactics however differ. Strawson considers in fairly general terms whether it is possible to construct a picture of human society in which such a possibility is sketched out. His answer is in the negative. Dostoyevsky on the other hand presents us with two very specific pictures. The first is the selective artificial representation of a man who in his capriciousness shows the logical inadequacy of determinism but whose distorted relationships with others leave him isolated and inadequate as a representation of human freedom. The second picture (Raskolnikov) is of a man who has so isolated himself from human society that in the opening pages of the novel he has little sense of the attitudes and feelings of others to him, and at the same time is not himself the subject of such reactive attitudes. Little wonder then that, on overhearing Alyona Ivanovna's half-sister Lizaveta agree to call on some friends at seven o'clock the next day, Raskolnikov 'felt that now all freedom of rational thought and free will were gone, and that suddenly everything was irrevocably decided' (IV, 52; I, v).

In his isolation Raskolnikov does only see the old woman as an object and in so doing has begun to lose the sense of himself as other than an object, or in the language of the *Notes* 'an organ-barrel sprig'.

V

In this final section of the paper I want to carry forward to *The Brothers Karamazov* Dostoyevsky's treatment of the notion of isolation and freedom. My argument so far has been that Dostoyevsky's exploration of freedom in the two earlier major works discussed has focussed on two main points: the first is a negative one, the rejection of determinism; the second is the inadequacy of an account of human freedom which rests solely on this negative basis. There are two further related points to be drawn from *The Brothers Karamazov* which will add significantly to our enquiry.

In the 'Admonitions of the elder Zosima', which constitute the third chapter of the sixth book of *The Brothers Karamazov*, Zosima is reported as offering two related comments on isolation. In one such comment he connects a preoccupation with the satisfaction of desires, a false sense of freedom and one form of isolation:

> 'You have needs and so satisfy them, for you have the same rights as the most powerful and rich. Don't be afraid of satisfying them and even multiply your needs.' That is the modern doctrine of the world. In that they see freedom. And what follows from this right of multiplication of needs? In the rich, *isolation* and spiritual suicide. (XIV, 284; VI, iii)

Here isolation is regarded as a penalty of a certain form of life and is contrasted with 'the solitude of the monk': 'But we shall see which will be the most zealous in the cause of brotherly love. For it is not we, but they, who are in isolation, though they don't see that' (XIV, 285; VI, iii). The isolation in question grows from the growth of particular attitudes and the loss of others: acquisition and exploitation replace compassion and care, and so isolation grows.

In a sense this form of isolation is but prolegomena to the period in which the isolation 'which prevails everywhere' will develop even more fully and eventually reach its limit (cf. XIV, 275ff.; VI, ii). The root of this radical isolation is not simply the multiplication of demands for the satisfaction of individual desires: rather its foundations are in precisely the truncated and distorted views of human freedom to be found in *Notes from Underground* and in *Crime and Punishment*:

> Everywhere in these days the human mind in its m
> begun not to understand that true security is to b
> social solidarity rather than in isolated individual
> this terrible isolation must inevitably have an end,
> suddenly understand how unnaturally they are sep
> one another. (XIV, 276; VI, ii)

What is most significant about this for an account of Dostoyevsky's views of freedom is its explicit rejection of the adequacy of individualistic accounts of freedom.

Now the sophistication of this point should, I hope, be apparent from the references to Strawson's lecture. Dostoyevsky is not denying the importance of the individual *tout court*, nor is he rejecting the point made in relation to the logical indeterminacy of a free choice. He is however showing clearly that to treat human action, or acts of self-affirmation, in such discrete isolated units is fraught with danger. The dangers can only be clearly perceived by recognizing 'social solidarity'. This is not to substitute social for physical determinism: rather it is to give central place to Strawson's point that the notion of human action which is based on an 'objective' view of human beings, and which ignores the web of social and reactive attitudes to which we belong, verges on incoherence. The point here is not one of psychological but of logical impossibility. In this I go a little further than Strawson's lecture, for I do not want to argue, as I believe Dostoyevsky does, that to remove altogether reactive relationships to fellow human beings is to empty the notion of a free human action of all content. Whatever such a proposal would leave, it would not in any sense be recognizable as human activity. This is, I believe, the philosophical force of the preoccupation with human solidarity which we find in Dostoyevsky's later writings. Clearly there are many other roots to this, not least in Slavonic and Orthodox sensibilities, but there is also the statement of a philosophical point about the conditions necessary for an adequate account of human freedom – the condition that this will not be found by concentration on individual, isolating acts of will.

The second main relevant issue raised in *The Brothers Karamazov* is *prima facie* even more puzzling. A further major question mark is set against attaching unconditional value to the notion of freedom.[17] It would be wrong to overemphasize this, but I believe that we do have here good grounds for finding less than unalloyed enthusiasm for freedom in the later Dostoyevsky. It is hard to deny force to the questions which the Inquisitor puts to Christ about freedom. He argues: 'nothing is more seductive for man than his freedom of conscience, but nothing torments him more' (XIV, 232; V, v). Whatever view of the Inquisitor we are finally persuaded to adopt, there is more than a hint at times of a perhaps dead compassion, survived by a sense of the pain and anguish which 'the gift of freedom' brings.

Dostoyevsky speaks through all his characters at times and this is one example of the 'polyphonic' novel at work. Freedom, the rejection of determinism, is not necessarily to be accepted without hesitation. It must be seen warts and all. Perhaps it is what is finally true of the human condition, but if so the consequences are grave as well as important. Even if we do manage to avoid the danger of isolation, Mochulsky's warning of 'the tragedy of personality and freedom' is perhaps a more adequate portal to the exploration of Dostoyevsky's thought than Wasiolek's evident enthusiasm for 'the world view that takes mature form in *Notes from Underground*'.

Notes

1. K. Mochulsky, *Dostoevsky: His Life and Work*, trans. M. Minihan (Princeton, 1967), p. 255.
2. E. Wasiolek, *Dostoevsky: The Major Fiction* (Cambridge, Mass., 1964), p. 57.
3. Cf. *ibid.*, p. 56. 'Dostoevsky's moral world is dialectical: man is poised with every choice he makes between self and God. Those two poles are absolute and unqualified, and man *makes* his nature by choosing his acts to serve one or the other. The values his acts have are born with the choices he makes.'
4. J.-P. Sartre, *Being and Nothingness* (New York, 1966), p. 567.
5. D. M. MacKay, 'On the logical indeterminacy of a free choice', *Mind*, 69 (1960), 31–40. Critical discussion of this paper is to be found in J. R. Lucas, *The Freedom of the Will* (Oxford, 1970) and A. M. Munn, *Free-Will and Determinism* (London, 1960).
6. M. Bakhtin, *Problems of Dostoevsky's Poetics*, trans. R. W. Rotsel (Ann Arbor, 1973), p. 42.
7. MacKay, *Mind*, 69 (1960), 31.
8. Bakhtin, *Problems*, p. 43.
9. *Ibid.*, p. 43.
10. F. Nietzsche, *Beyond Good and Evil*, trans. Walter Kaufmann (New York, 1966), section 19.
11. Bakhtin, *Problems*, p. 43.
12. P. F. Strawson, *Freedom and Resentment, and Other Essays* (London, 1974), p. 5.
13. I have discussed related aspects of this point in 'Language and interpre-

tation in *Crime and Punishment*', *Philosophy and Literature*, 3 (1978), 223–36.

14. See, for example, A. C. Danto, 'Basic actions', in A. R. White (ed.), *The Philosophy of Action* (London, 1968), pp. 43–58.
15. Strawson, *Freedom and Resentment*, p. 23.
16. *Ibid.*, pp. 11–12.
17. I have discussed this more fully in my *Atheism and the Rejection of God: Contemporary Philosophy and 'The Brothers Karamazov'* (Oxford, 1977), ch. 5.

8

Formalist and structuralist approaches to Dostoyevsky

CHRISTOPHER R. PIKE

In the middle of the 1920s Boris Eykhenbaum, defending the theoretical principles elaborated by Russian formalism, referred tolerantly to 'the naive and touching "aestheticism" by which our older critics and historians of literature discovered the "neglect of form" in Tjutcev's poetry and simply "poor form" in writers like Nekrasov or Dostoevskij'.[1] Indeed, it is perhaps a truism of Dostoyevsky scholarship that, while the nineteenth century valued his novels for their arresting themes and striking characters, it did not regard those same works as significant contributions to the development of the genre. And, while it stood in awe of Dostoyevsky as a polemist and thinker, it showed scant respect for his qualities as a craftsman or an artist. Vladimir Seduro comments: 'At the beginning of the twentieth century almost no scholarly study had been made of Dostoyevski's literary provenance and style, his genres, plots, language, syntax, epithets, similes, and other formal elements.'[2] All this was to change within thirty years, with the rise of the formalist school and the emergence of Bakhtin's highly original assessment of Dostoyevsky's work. Nevertheless, much of the achievement of Shklovsky, Tynyanov, Vinogradov, Bakhtin and others rests on the re-vision, in terms of form and structure, of the tensions, oppositions, paradoxes and dualities perceived by earlier critics in Dostoyevsky's 'content'.

It cannot be claimed that the formalists (excluding Bakhtin) devoted themselves extensively to the study of Dostoyevsky. There are remarkably few individual studies of the author in formalist writings and their contribution to Dostoyevsky scholarship consists principally of Viktor Shklovsky's work on plots and plot techniques, Yuriy Tynyanov's exploration of parody and Viktor Vinogradov's formalistic stylistic analyses.[3] However, there are many scattered references by the formalists to Dostoyevsky and it seems unquestionable that they regard him not only as 'a great Russian author', but also as a novelist of unique, if enigmatic achievement, to whose works their principles and theories would ultimately have to be related. At the same time, the complexity, the controversialism and the dimensions of Dostoyevsky's work seem to have been too much for an emergent and radically new school of thought, which preferred to restrict its early endeavours to works of more accessible structure.

Nevertheless, the studies by Shklovsky, Tynyanov and Vinogradov manifest common features underlying their different emphases, which both unite them within formalism and relate them directly to Bakhtin's later work. On the basis of its fundamental premisses of the specificity of literature and the consequent opposition of 'poetic' to 'practical' language, formalism displayed two principal directions in its approach to prose literature. The first was an interest in the form of the literary work (its construction, its motifs, devices and techniques) and the second, the syntax of literature as a system (its norms and canons, its evolution).[4] The oppositional principles of much of the formalists' theoretical vision ('poetic' and 'practical' language, literature and life, 'plot' and 'fable') found peculiar reflection both in the tendencies of their study of Dostoyevsky and in the later, expanded dualities of Bakhtin's 'polyphony' and 'carnival'.

Shklovsky's interest in Dostoyevsky is based principally on the resemblances between Dostoyevsky's novels and 'boulevard' or sensational literature. The irreverent Shklovsky, a revolutionary in art (if not in politics), delighted in the alternate canonization and decanonization of low-style and high-style devices and motifs throughout the evolution of literature. 'Dostoyevsky elevates the devices of the boulevard novel into a literary norm,' he wrote. 'Each new school of literature is a revolution, something like the emergence of a new class.'[5] In his collection of articles, *On the Theory of Prose*, he demonstrates (principally in relation to *Crime and Punishment*) how Dostoyevsky's boulevard heritage affects the plot structure of his novels. Shklovsky's illustration of staircase (*stupenchatoye*) construction, retardation and framing devices within his general theory of the functioning of art through impedance of perception reveals Dostoyevsky's application of devices of mystery, suspense and deception, appropriate to novels of action and event, in novels ostensibly of ideas and issues.[6]

While Shklovsky's investigation of plot devices is a productive explanation of certain aspects of the disjuncture experienced by readers and critics between the 'form' and the 'content' of Dostoyevsky's works (and is thus part of Shklovsky's campaign to wean them from these redundant categories), his most fruitful statements about Dostoyevsky are probably his comments on the significance of oxymoron in literature. It is worth quoting Shklovsky in some detail:

> The title of one of Dostoyevsky's stories, 'The Honest Thief', is undoubtedly an oxymoron, but the *content* of this story is also an oxymoron, one which has been *unfolded into a plot*.
>
> Thus we approach the concept of oxymoron in plot. Aristotle says (and I am not quoting him like Holy Scripture) ...'but when suffering appears among friends, for example, if a brother kills a brother, a son a father, a mother a son, or a son a mother, or intends to kill, or does something else like that, that is the subject which the poet should seek'.
>
> Here the oxymoronic quality is based on *the opposition between kinship and enmity*.
>
> Many plots are based on oxymoron, for example, a tailor kills a giant, David kills Goliath, frogs kill an elephant and so on. The plot here is playing the role of justification, motivation and, at the same time, development of the oxymoron. Dostoyevsky's 'justification of life', such as Marmeladov's prophecy about drunkards at the final judgement...
>
> The effect is increased by another device. In this instance, the contrasts are based not only on the alternation of themes, but also on *the disjuncture between thought or experience and their setting*. There are two basic types of literary setting (*peyzazh*): setting which coincides with the basic action, and setting which contrasts with it.[7]

As so often, Shklovsky makes his point hurriedly and loosely but, also typically, there is a great deal of substance to it, perhaps more than he realizes. Oxymoron, the combination of apparent opposites to make a point, is a remarkably apposite figure to apply to Dostoyevsky's work. The antithetical duality of the oxymoron exists not for the sake of opposition or paradox, but to produce a positive meaning; alongside, or beyond the two explicit poles of the oxymoron there exists a third, implicit or hidden member of the construction, which acts as a resolution. To view duality in Dostoyevsky as an oxymoronic form, created to achieve something beyond itself, may be helpful to those who are uneasy with the apparently undirected and unproductive 'polyphony' of the novels, as perceived by Bakhtin. The enigma, the 'problem' within Dostoyevsky's poetics is the hidden third element, the 'point' of the oxymoron, the resolution to the conflict which Dostoyevsky so often fails to achieve explicitly (e.g. the flawed 'salvation' that is to follow the 'crime' and 'punishment' of Raskolnikov) and which is perhaps not realizable on the same axis as the novel itself.

Tynyanov's essay pursues the mechanics of literary evolution in a demonstration of Dostoyevsky's interaction with Gogol through parody. To the formalists, parody and stylization were among the most important techniques by which new literature was fashioned from old. In Tynyanov's argument, the way in which Dostoyevsky defines and redefines his literary direction through the multi-faceted parody, in *The Village of Stepanchikovo*, of Gogol's *Correspondence with Friends*, exemplifies the 'dialectic' of literature. At the same time, parody is a further manifestation of that duality in the operation of literature upon which formalism tended to dwell, and which was particularly evident in the work of Dostoyevsky:

> Perhaps this subtle tissue of stylization–parody suspended over a tragic, developed plot constitutes the unique quality of the grotesque in Dostoyevsky.
>
> Parody exists to the extent that the second, parodied plane shows through the work; the narrower, the more defined and the more limited this second plane, the more all the details of the work present a dual aspect (*dvoynoy ottenok*) and are perceived with a double vision (*pod dvoynym uglom*), the stronger the element of parody.[8]

Tynyanov also pursues the contrastive and invertive duality of Dostoyevsky's world in other aspects, most effectively, from the point of view of later criticism, in what he says of character and dialogue. He quotes Dostoyevsky's statement on the writer's need to reveal unusual traits in ordinary people: 'ordinariness which has no desire at all to remain what it is, but desires at any cost to become original and independent'. Tynyanov continues:

> These traits are created by contrasts; Dostoyevsky's characters are, above all, contrastive. The contrasts are revealed in the speeches of the actors; the end of these speeches is inevitably a contrast to their beginning, a contrast not only in the unexpected transition to another theme (a unique application in Dostoyevsky's conversations of 'the destruction of illusion'),

> but in intonation as well: the heroes' speeches, which begin peacefully, end in furious outburst, and vice versa.[9]

In this, and in later comment on contrast and dialogue in the epistolary form of *Poor Folk*, Tynyanov strongly prefigures the notions of internal and external dialogue described by Bakhtin. Moreover, in his comments about plot, he anticipates the significance of inversion in Bakhtin's interpretation and sketches a relationship between plot and character which is essential to the balance of polyphony:

> In *Crime and Punishment* the contrast between plot and characters is artistically organized: into the framework of a criminal plot are inserted characters who are in contrast with it: the murderer, the prostitute and the detective in the plot scheme are replaced by a revolutionary, a saint and a sage. In *The Idiot* the plot unfolds by means of contrast, coinciding with the contrastive revelation of the characters; the high point of plot tension represents at the same time the highest revelation of characters.[10]

Finally, moving on from this Bakhtinian exposition of an idea very close to Shklovsky's concept of the oxymoronic plot, Tynyanov comes near to Bakhtin's notions of 'carnival' in his remarks on 'masks': 'The outward appearances of Svidrigaylov, Stavrogin and Lambert are emphasized masks. Here perhaps we have another contrast: a verbal *mask* covering a contrasting *character*.'[11] The image of Dostoyevsky's characters as participants in a deceptive masquerade is found again in Viktor Vinogradov's studies, particularly in relation to the role of the narrator.

Vinogradov was no formalist, believing firmly that stylistics and the stylistician should know their place, and that no study of 'form' should attempt to be a total vision of literature. Nevertheless, his studies of Gogol and Dostoyevsky, carried out in the early 1920s, not only received the formalists' blessing, but were closely in line with their interests. They also represent some of the finest stylistic analyses of nineteenth-century Russian literature.

Vinogradov's major work, *The Evolution of Russian Naturalism*, shares the Shklovskian dual approach to prose, the study of the system of the text being described as the 'functional–immanent' point of view and that of the system of literature as 'retrospective–projectional'. Vinogradov pursues the inseparable interrelationship of these two viewpoints in theory and history of literature respectively.[12] Vinogradov takes issue with Tynyanov's case for parody but his view of literary evolution as exemplified in Dostoyevsky's *The Double* is remarkably close to that of Shklovsky and Tynyanov:

> In *The Double* Dostoyevsky employed a device of plot construction which is characteristic of his poetics, consisting of the stylistic transposition of known literary constructions (often taken even from a deposed school of literature). This resulted in the uniquely two-planed nature (*dvuplannost'*) of his plot semantics, in which the silhouettes of old forms, strangely transformed, seemed to glimmer through the new devices of composition...In fact, this is not a feature peculiar to Dostoyevsky's way of writing: it is one of the principles of literary struggle and reformation. There is no necessity for a parodic tendency. Neither is there any stylization. There is a certain 'metaphorization' of the integral verbal composition or of its parts. The plot thematics are perceived in terms of a dual literary existence.[13]

The most significant element in Vinogradov's conception of 'duality' in Dostoyevsky is undoubtedly his attention to the performance of the narrator in *The Double*. Not only does he critically examine the formalist theories of *skaz* (narrative style characterized by the personal tone of the narrator), but he presages the attention of later structuralism to narrative viewpoint, a factor which will be held by some to be fundamental to literary structure. Most importantly, Vinogradov's penetrating stylistic study of the author–narrator–hero relationship reveals the structure of narration, speech and dialogue in action, essential to Bakhtin's dialogic approach.

In his attention to the word, Vinogradov is drawn to the Gogolian/Tynyanovian concept of the word as *mask* and the resulting semantic disjuncture between the word and its 'real' content. Thus he refers to the way in which 'the exposition in *The Double* is refracted through the mask of "the modest narrator of the escapades" of the mad Mr Golyadkin'.[14] Vinogradov penetrates the complexity of the narrator's activity and the highly original remodelling of the narrator–hero–reader relationship undertaken by him:

> In *The Double* the narrator himself behaves not so much as a parodist, as an ironical stylizer. Examples of such bared uniformity between one of the forms of narrative style and the language of 'the double' are quite numerous...The examples given, demonstrating the combination of the self-definitions of

> Mr Golyadkin and the petty verbal traits of the detached observer, give sufficient emphasis to the notion that the 'Petersburg poem', in many parts at least, takes the form of a story about Golyadkin by his 'double', i.e. 'the man with his language and concepts'. It is in the application of this innovative device in the construction of 'the image of the author' that the reason for the failure of *The Double* is to be found.[15]

The scholars studied so far evince a similar 'double' approach to literature as work and as system. They exhibit, moreover, a chicken-and-egg interdependence between the dualities implicit in their own theories and those which they discover in Dostoyevsky's works. It is therefore not surprising that the pervasive dualism of their findings, especially the antithetical evolution of literature, the oxymoronic plot, the notion of mask and divided word, and the ambivalence of narrator and character voice should ultimately result in a 'whole' view of Dostoyevsky, that of Mikhail Bakhtin.

Bakhtin's general poetics has exerted considerable influence on French and Soviet structuralism and semiotics and is of increasing interest to Anglo-American scholars today. His work on Dostoyevsky specifically has been the most productive critical stimulus in scholarship so far.[16]

Bakhtin's conception of Dostoyevsky's work is usually discussed in terms of language (word, dialogue, polyphony) and genre (menippea, novel, carnival). It should not be forgotten however that to Bakhtin the source of Dostoyevsky's innovative activity lies in his revolutionary concept of the literary character as an independent consciousness. It is no accident that three out of the four chapters in the first part of Bakhtin's original study (1929) are overwhelmingly concerned with the hero, namely the chapters on the hero, the idea (as represented, or lived by the hero) and the functions of adventure plot in Dostoyevsky (functions largely connected with the hero). Subsequently, Bakhtin was well aware that the major objection to his views lay in his apparent neglect of the function of the author, consequent upon his character-focus.[17] Significantly, the major developments in the second edition (1963) are moves away from excessive character-focus: the expansion, remodelling and renaming of the second chapter, from 'The hero in Dostoyevsky' to 'The hero and the position of the author in relation to the hero in Dostoyevsky's work'; and the complete rewriting in terms of 'carnival' of the now central historical–poetic fourth chapter on Dostoyevsky's place within literary tradition, with the title change from 'The functions of adventure plot in Dostoyevsky's works' to 'The genre and plot-compositional characteristics of Dostoyevsky's works'.

In its final form, Bakhtin's study advances a vision of Dostoyevsky which begins with a definition of the Dostoyevskian hero 'not as a manifestation of reality, possessing definite, fixed socio-typical and individually characterological features' (*Problemy*, 1963, p. 62), but as '*a particular point of view on the world and on himself*, as the position of meaning and of evaluation of a man in relation to himself and to surrounding reality' (pp. 62–3). The hero's independent consciousness of self and others frees him from the authorial domination to which characters in previous 'monological' (one-voiced) novels had been subjected. Whereas the monological hero 'cannot cease to be himself, i.e. go beyond the boundaries of his character, his typicality, his temperament' (p. 69), Dostoyevsky frees his hero into a dialogical existence: 'Everything that the monological author used to keep for his own use in the creation of the ultimate unity of the work and its depicted world, Dostoyevsky gives away to his hero, turning all of it into a facet of his self-consciousness' (p. 69). But the contents of the hero's consciousness are no more fixed, closed and categorized than those of Dostoyevsky the author. The elements of consciousness exist only in a perpetual attempt at self-definition, through articulation and response: 'Dostoyevsky's hero is not an object-image, but a sovereign word, *a pure voice*; we do not see him, we hear him...the entire artistic construction of Dostoyevsky's novel is oriented towards the revelation and clarification of that hero's word' (p. 71). The emancipated intercourse of these voices creates the semantic dialogue of the novel, the enactment of the 'great dialogue' which is the novel's highest concern, the point at which the novel abuts the 'unclosed whole' of life. The role of the author is now different: 'And so, the new artistic position of the author in relation to the hero in Dostoyevsky's polyphonic novel is a *seriously realized dialogical position which is fully pursued*...To the author the hero is not a "he", not an "I", but a total "you", i.e. a different, other fully justified "I" ("you are")' (pp. 84–5). Although Bakhtin is prepared to admit that Dostoyevsky may retain 'a necessary minimum of pragmatic, purely *informative* superior knowledge' (p. 99), he insists upon the new equality of polyphonic relationship between author and hero.

Bakhtin next considers 'the idea', which, in the eyes of many previous and subsequent critics, has been said to be almost identical with the hero in Dostoyevsky. Here the emphasis is on the dynamic mutability of the idea in the chain-reaction world of polyphony, a mutability directly associated with the nature of the hero. The hero is not only a conscious individual, but an ideologue: 'Therefore the [hero's] word about the world merges with his confessional word about himself. To Dostoyevsky, truth about the world is inseparable from the truth of the personality' (p. 103). At either end of the polyphonic dialogue the consciousnesses use their voices to articulate themselves through ideas, but within monology the 'other's idea' (*chuzhaya ideya*) cannot be depicted as such – 'It is either assimilated, or polemically rejected, or it ceases to be an idea' (p. 112). Dostoyevsky however allowed the 'other's idea' to retain its full significance: 'the idea is interindividual and intersubjective, its sphere of existence is not the individual consciousness, but the dialogical intercourse *between* consciousnesses' (p. 116). Towards the end of this chapter, Bakhtin again returns, slightly uneasily, to the problem of dominance, here not that of the author, but that of the ideal idea-image, lodged in an image-word. Dostoyevsky's world is one of 'mutually illuminating consciousnesses', among which he seeks 'the highest, most authoritative statement (*ustanovka*)'. Acceptance of the ideal of Christ or the perfect man would be to Dostoyevsky 'not faithfulness to his own convictions... but faithfulness to the authoritative image of man' (p. 130). Such an image, notes Bakhtin, was never realized in his work.

In the fourth chapter the original treatment of the adventure plot serves only as an introduction to the lengthy discussion of the carnivalesque tradition of literature and Dostoyevsky's place within it, a dimension of Bakhtin's approach which developed only after the first edition, during and after his work on Rabelais. The mutability of the picaresque-style hero is emphasized: 'The adventure plot...is just like clothing which drapes the hero, clothing which he can change as often as he likes' (p. 139). Attention, however, soon moves to the much wider problem of carnival as the traditional manifestation of the inversion, duality and polyphony evident in Dostoyevsky's work:

> Carnival is a spectacle without a stage and without a division into performers and spectators. In a carnival all are active participants and all are brought into communion with the carnival act. People don't watch carnival and, strictly speaking, they don't even enact it, they *live* in it, they live according to its laws, as long as those laws remain in force, they live a carnival

> life. Carnival life is life pulled out of its *usual* rut, it is to some extent 'life turned inside out', 'life upside down' ('*monde à l'envers*'). (pp. 163–4)

This description bears on Dostoyevsky's world with particular force. It recalls not only the overt scandal scenes, but the general sense of hectic, populace-wide involvement, the upsetting of traditional values and authorities throughout the novels. At the same time, the anarchic removal of the boundary between participants and spectators reflects Bakhtin's own apparent 'transgression' of the boundary between art and life in his attribution of ideological sovereignty to literary characters. And finally, the notion of 'carnivalesque literature' is not without its links to earlier formalist thought. As Aage Hansen-Löve has pointed out, the changes in perspective which result from inversion make carnivalization a form of 'making strange' (*ostraneniye*).[18] Carnivalesque inversion itself is the socio-cultural background of the canonization–decanonization operative in formalist theory. Perhaps most significantly, carnivalization is an oxymoronic principle: a contradiction (inversion of the norm) is established for the sake of a resolution to be achieved. In social terms, the end, the third element, is normal life again, but better, with the easing of accumulated social tensions and the reconfirmation of accepted hierarchies. What is the resolution in the carnivalization of literature? To Bakhtin, carnivalization constituted 'an unusually flexible form of artistic vision, a kind of heuristic principle which permitted the discovery of the new and previously unseen' (p. 224), in Dostoyevsky's case, the extensiveness of human experience. Through the relativization effected by carnival

> everyone and everything must know each other and know about each other, they must come into contact, they must meet face to face and *begin to talk* to one another. Everything must be mutually reflected and mutually illuminated dialogically. Therefore, everything that is separated and at a distance must be collected into a single 'point' of space and time. (p. 239)

The most important event which will take place at this space–time point (to the setting of which, on threshold or stairway, in crowded room or open square, Bakhtin also devotes attention) is the enunciation of the word. Appropriately, the extensive fifth chapter (originally the second part of the 1929 edition, then subtitled 'An experiment in stylistics') is devoted to the word in its different situations and functions. The word is Bakhtin's fundamental unit of analysis, appropriate both to Dostoyevsky and to the new 'metalinguistics' as the metamorphic, polyvalent bearer of the hero's consciousness:

> The word is not a thing, but the eternally mobile, eternally mutable medium of dialogical intercourse. It is never limited to one consciousness or one voice. The life of the word is in its transition from mouth to mouth, from one context to another, from one generation to another. Throughout, the word never forgets its path and can never finally free itself from the power of those concrete contexts which it has entered. (p. 270)

One is struck, at the last, by the consistent emphasis on *mutability*, originally in Dostoyevsky's literature of personal evolution in a world of instability, then in formalist notions of the changing values of literature and the variegation of appearance and reality, and now in Bakhtin's delineation of the consciously evolving hero, the dynamism of the idea, the disruption of carnival and the atomically unstable word.

Bakhtin's academic work as a whole is characterized by a dual emphasis on the novel and the word. Throughout, there are references to Dostoyevsky which confirm the critical influence on Bakhtin's theories of his work in the 1920s on the word, dialogue and polyphony in relation to Dostoyevsky and his subsequent elaboration of 'carnival' theory on Rabelais and Dostoyevsky. The significance of the word and dialogue is reflected particularly in the essays 'The word in the novel' of 1934–5, 'From the prehistory of the novel word' (both in *Voprosy*) and 'The problem of speech genres' of 1952–3 (in *Estetika*). Most of Bakhtin's other works are devoted to investigation of the exceptional status of the novel in its historical–poetic evolution, its elaboration of realism and its re-visioning of the world.

One of Bakhtin's earliest works, 'The author and hero in aesthetic activity' of the early to mid-1920s (*Estetika*, pp. 7–180), reveals his original focus on the new status of the hero in Dostoyevsky. He assigns all Dostoyevsky's principal characters (and, interestingly enough, some of Tolstoy's) to the category of novel in which the hero 'takes over' the author: 'the author cannot locate a convincing and stable evaluative point of reference outside the hero' (p. 18). He discusses the self-consciousness of Dostoyevsky's heroes as a variation of traditional Romantic self-referential confession (p. 128) and, above all, perceives in the self-assertion of the hero a crisis of authorship, in which 'the very position of outsideness is shaken up and appears insubstantial, the author's right to be outside life and to control it is contested' (p. 176). In 'The word in the novel' Bakhtin addresses himself to the dialogical functioning of the word and language (or 'languages'). His concept of the plurality of discourses or languages operative within literature, and of their transformation through interaction into objects of representation, is nowadays termed 'intertextuality'. He accords Dostoyevsky's work 'an exceptional and unique position' for its emphasis on interaction with the 'other's' word and stresses the incompletion of this activity: 'the utterances of Dostoyevsky's heroes are an arena of perpetual struggle with the other's word in all spheres of life and ideological creation' (*Voprosy*, p. 161).

In one of his most stimulating historical-comparative pieces, 'Forms of time and the chronotope in the novel' 1937–8 (*Voprosy*, pp. 234–407),[19] Bakhtin prefigures his remarks on the time–space 'point' of carnival (see above) by comparing Dostoyevsky to Dante in his attempt to cut across the boundaries of time, to 'reveal the world in a cross-section of simultaneity and coexistence' (p. 308). In the 'Concluding remarks', apparently written in 1973, Bakhtin returns to Dostoyevsky as an instance of the chronotope of the threshold, a point which almost annihilates space as a habitable medium and reduces time to a moment, the fateful moment of transition (p. 397). This is undoubtedly one of Bakhtin's most exciting perceptions about Dostoyevsky, one which is also treated in *Problemy poetiki*. In 'The problem of the text in linguistics, philology and other humanitarian sciences' (*Estetika*, pp. 281–307) written in 1959–61, shortly before the appearance of the second edition of the Dostoyevsky study, Bakhtin is again much concerned with the image of the character and that of the author, and especially their dialogical equality 'on one plane'. And in some of his last notes (*Estetika*, pp. 336–60) Bakhtin, returning again and again to Dostoyevsky, polyphony, dialogue and the word, divides the image of the author into a primary (uncreated) author and a secondary (an image of the author created by the primary author). Most strikingly, his delineation of these forms employs the Latin divisions of nature used in early mediaeval religious philosophy, reflecting Bakhtin's profoundly Christian conception of the nature of artistic creation (p. 353). Finally, no account of Bakhtin would be complete without reference to his follower and colleague, V. N. Voloshinov, whose book on language, written in collaboration with Bakhtin, discusses Dostoyevsky's employment of 'other's' (or 'reported') speech and free indirect style as linguistic manifestations of a dualistic, stratified reality.[20]

The influence of Dostoyevsky on Bakhtin's poetics cannot be mistaken. It is a lasting achievement of Dostoyevsky to have affected, through Bakhtin, the major development of structuralism and semiotics. Dostoyevsky's polyphony (despite Bakhtin's undoubted later attempts to re-establish some authority of the author) retained its validity and evolved into the central concept of 'heteroglossia' (*raznorechiye*) and the modern interpretation of intertextuality.[21] Dostoyevsky's use of scandal, mockery and 'de-crowning', together with the raw material of Rabelais, prompted the extended evolution of 'carnival' theory and, in particular, the study of 'laughter' in culture.[22] But Bakhtin's most important inheritance from Dostoyevsky is undoubtedly the concept of dialogue, the third element which circumflects the word–novel axis of Bakhtin's poetics. The polystrate of dialogue, reaching from the speech of literature through its thematics and structure and far beyond into concepts of reality and being, is the distinguishing feature of Bakhtin's pluralism.

Bakhtin's ideas have, of course, provoked considerable objections both within theoretical discourse and within Dostoyevsky scholarship. The most important theoretical disagreements arise over the question of the organizing/uniting principle in a polyphonic text, the boundary between literature and life in polyphonic vision and the assertion of the primacy of the novel as a polyphonic form.[23] These issues are not strictly relevant here, but the first two encapsulate the principal objections to Bakhtin raised by students of Dostoyevsky. Several later scholars have been concerned at the apparent ideological pluralism of polyphony. They find an uneasy contrast between the dominant, obsessional, 'convinced' image of Dostoyevsky the man and journalist and the liberal, tolerant, open-minded image of Dostoyevsky the polyphonic novelist. Isaiah Berlin, for example, argues that Gogol and Dostoyevsky are 'well-integrated personalities, with a coherent outlook and a single vision', compared with a deeply divided Tolstoy.[24] Malcolm Jones, referring to those who argue for a monistic Dostoyevsky, suggests that 'the truth is that Dostoyevsky manifests urges in both directions, and this truth is of the essence in understanding his work and its appeal to diverse minds'.[25] It would presumably be the final duality of polyphony for the polyphonic author to be in dialogue with himself.

The Soviet reaction to Bakhtin's work since 1929 is complex and is best followed through the account of it given in Vladimir Seduro's two books on the criticism of Dostoyevsky in Russia.[26] Lunacharsky's review of Bakhtin's study in 1929 and his article of 1931 were practically the only favourable references to his work for many years.[27] Otherwise, Bakhtin's work was unfavourably reviewed as formalistic, or simply forgotten on his disappearance to Kazakhstan. Seduro detects traces of Bakhtin's ideas in an article by Vasily Desnitsky in 1947 which refers to Dostoyevsky's 'placing of the author's "I" among the characters' (*Dostoyevski*, p. 258) and an address by Valery Kirpotin in the same year, which describes Dostoyevsky's world as 'a multiplicity of objectively existent psychologies affecting each other' (p. 269). In his second book, which discusses developments between the mid-1950s and the early 1970s, Seduro describes an era of increasing knowledge and acceptance of Bakhtin, in which even disagreement with him took the form of reasoned argument, rather than ideological rejection. He assesses A. V. Chicherin's engagement (conscious or unconscious?) with Bakhtin's view of language in Dostoyevsky (*Dostoevski's Image*, pp. 136–8) and gives a fascinating account of the pressures of the campaign for the publication of *Problemy poetiki* and its reception. He goes on to detail the wide-ranging general acceptance since 1962 of the theory of polyphony, with the major (and influential) exceptions of G. M. Fridlender, who insists upon the monological authority of the author, and Ya. O. Zundelovich, who claimed to detect, in an impressive study, a Dostoyevsky divided between reactionary thinker and realist artist (pp. 307–49).[28] Seduro's valuable accounts of the Bakhtinian heritage in the Soviet Union, however, do not include consideration of the later movements of Soviet structuralism and semiotics, which will be discussed below.

Despite the reservations described above, the polyphonic view of Dostoyevsky has been widely accepted in the West and is evident, more or less explicitly, in the great majority of modern studies of Dostoyevsky. This tendency is reinforced by the developing reputation and influence of the poetics which Bakhtin developed largely on the basis of this work. Nowhere has this been more strongly felt than in France. Dostoyevsky himself was an object of admiration to the 'New Novelists' (Nathalie Sarraute, Alain Robbe-Grillet, Michel Butor and others) who came to prominence in the 1950s. They appreciated Dostoyevsky as a precursor, for the modernity of his fragmented reality, the disintegration of traditional categories and authorities and the 'new' psychology of his characters. Nathalie Sarraute acknowledges the influence of his psychological portrayals (akin to her '*tropismes*') in *L'Ère du soupçon* (Paris, 1956),[29] while Michel Butor's essay on Dostoyevsky views gambling as a complex metaphor employed by Dostoyevsky as a form of self-exorcism in his writing of *The Gambler.*[30]

The 'New Novel' was closely associated with the development of new trends in criticism, which were to result in the 1960s in the multiplicity of French structuralisms. In 1961, René Girard, a critic on the fringes of this movement, described Dostoyevsky in terms which parallel earlier discussion in this essay.[31] In a study devoted to exposing the hidden third element of mediation and motivation in the 'triangularity of desire' operating between novel characters, Girard talks of 'the fundamental Dostoyevskian procedure' as being to 'bring about confrontations which exhaust all possible relationships between the different characters in the novel' (*Deceit*, p. 246). Like Butor, he is drawn to the image of the card game, this time to describe the role of the author:

> In Proust the game proceeds slowly; the novelist constantly interrupts the players to remind them of previous hands and to anticipate those to come. In Dostoyevsky, on the contrary, the cards are laid down very rapidly and the novelist lets the game proceed from beginning to end without interfering. The reader must be able to remember everything himself. (p. 246)

He goes on to celebrate Dostoyevsky as 'the creator of characters who are *freer* than those of other novelists', and talks of the opposition of Dostoyevsky to 'psychological' novelists, 'who imprison their characters in a maze of laws' (p. 247). But, according to Girard, the laws have not disappeared: they are to be found in the suppression of permanence and the gradual removal of the last appearances of stability and continuity (p. 247). Despite the insistence on a covert authorial regulation of the Dostoyevskian novel, there is a remarkable affinity between these lines and the 'imperfective' Dostoyevsky of Bakhtin.

However, within French structuralism and semiotics it is Julia Kristeva who has most evidently espoused Bakhtin. Like Sarraute and Girard, she is drawn to Dostoyevsky by his transgressive fracture of traditional identity and authority and to Bakhtin by his discovery, if not perception, of the ideological revolution in Dostoyevsky's dialogism.[32] In her earlier essay, Kristeva locates the emergence of the polyphonic novel at a cultural fracture-point, with more radical development since: 'while dialogue in Rabelais, Swift and Dostoievski remains at a representative, fictitious level, our century's polyphonic novel becomes "unreadable" (Joyce) and interior to language (Proust, Kafka)' ('Word', p. 71). Relishing the breaking of barriers and the infinite horizons of dialogue, she continues, with an emphasis which reflects the impermanent Dostoyevskian world:

> Bakhtin's term *dialogism* as a semic complex thus implies the double, language and another logic. Using that as point of departure, we can outline a new approach to poetic texts. Literary semiotics can accept the word 'dialogism'; the logic of *distance* and *relationship* between the different units of a sentence or narrative structure, indicating a *becoming* – in opposition to the level of continuity and substance, both of which obey the logic of being and are thus monological. (pp. 71–2)

In such a context, laughter in Dostoyevsky is an oxymoron: 'The laughter of the carnival is not simply parodic; it is no more comic than tragic; it is both at once, one might say that it is *serious*' (p. 80).

In her second, substantial and perceptive essay, Kristeva re-illustrates the modernity of polyphony: 'a plurality of languages, a confrontation of types of discourse and ideologies, with no conclusion and no synthesis – without 'monologic' or any axial point. Fantasy, horror, the dream-world, the sexual, all speak in this dialogic, this non-finite and unresolvable polyphony' ('The ruin of a poetics', p. 111). Bakhtin, in Kristeva's view, was one of the first to perceive that linguistics as such could not cope with the parameters of the word in the novel, where signification is indissociable from the speaking subject (pp. 108–9). The destabilization of identity ('the fragmentation of the "I"' or 'the breach of the "me"' which Kristeva derives from Bakhtin's concept of the mercurial hero) leads to a fundamental change in the representation of consciousness and ideology (Bakhtin's mutable 'idea'): 'they function only as material to be given a form. It is in this sense that a polyphonic text has only a single ideology: the *formative* ideology, which carries the form' (p. 114). Bakhtin's poetics, like Dostoyevsky's novels, breaches the boundaries of literature in its envisioning of subject and other, ideology and meaning. Thus Dostoyevsky's novels cease to be just 'novels' and become something more. But Bakhtin's poetics, losing its object as literature, falls into noble ruin, revealing beyond a continent for which other devices of exploration will need to be devised.

Whatever the limitations of her theoretical extrapolations, Kristeva's response to Bakhtin sheds valuable light on the nature of Dostoyevsky's modernity and the unique status of his novels. It is significant that her published work on Bakhtin relates to his treatment of Dostoyevsky for, as Ann Shukman points out, it is precisely the ideas of dialogue and polyphony which are essential to French structuralism's concept of 'texte pluriel'.[33] Shukman goes on to remark that, by contrast, the Moscow–Tartu school of Soviet semiotics values Bakhtin for his study of carnival and his work with Voloshinov on semiotics.[34]

In the light of this distinction of emphasis, it is perhaps not surprising that Soviet semiotics has as yet contributed only a small amount to the study of Dostoyevsky. Perhaps, indeed, they rest content with Bakhtin's conclusions about the author. However, Boris Uspensky's study of point of view is strongly influenced by Bakhtin and draws many of its examples of the different levels of point of view constituent of artistic structure from Dostoyevsky's work.[35] Uspensky's study has been critically received in the West and it shares a feature of Bakhtin's approach in making no clear definition of the categories of narration.[36] Interestingly enough, the resulting emphasis on 'authorial' activity in Uspensky's study produces some illustrations of narrative technique which seem very much at odds with 'polyphony', as in his assessment of the presentation of Ivan Karamazov.[37]

The Saransk volume (see note 34) contains two essays on Dostoyevsky.[38] Toporov's essay, explicitly pursuing the concepts of polyphony and carnival in the broader context of mythopoeia, begins by considering the universal mythopoeic pattern of conflict between the 'visible' cosmos and 'invisible' chaos, a conflict which takes the form of 'trial by single combat' (*ispytaniye-poyedinok*) during which the opposing forces themselves become ambivalent (Toporov, pp. 333–4). Toporov proceeds to illustrate, on the basis of *Crime and Punishment*, the syndromes of shift and disjuncture which characterize this remodelling of novelistic space. The perspective of unhealthiness shifts to that of tranquillity, the unexpected becomes a constantly realized possibility, time shifts are minimized ('suddenly', etc.) and the time–space continuum that is St Petersburg is divided into semiotic territories ranged between the middle (interior) and the peripheral (exterior) and connected by a path of graduated oppositions which are actualized in the spatial movements of the hero. Toporov proceeds to list at length the linguistic contours (of vocabulary, imagery and symbolism) which characterize sacral and desacralized loci within this mythorama.

Toporov's notion of Dostoyevsky as a mythopoet is not new. Vyacheslav Ivanov, who is Bakhtin's closest predecessor in his perception of polyphony, wrote in 1911 of Dostoyevsky as a creator of myths.[39] Moreover, many of the items of his analysis are well recognized: the use of 'suddenly' and 'strange', the relationship between *uzkiy*, *uzhas* and *ugol* ('narrow', 'terror' and 'corner'), the unsettling fluidity of proper names and the use of numerals 'to determine the dimensions of the world'. The selection and interpretation of these items are reminiscent of essays by Bitsilli and Matlaw.[40] Nor is Toporov entirely convincing in the *élan* of his attempt to relate Dostoyevsky directly to such material as ancient Vedic texts. The American anthropologist Dell Hymes comments: 'The interpretation of Dostoyevsky may make good sense. But it depends for its conviction on what one finds in Dostoyevsky. And I would want to see evidence before concluding that Dostoyevsky writes as he does because "trains of archaic, mythopoeic thought" have surfaced and been adapted.'[41] Nevertheless, given that the range of concept and comparison is so vast that Toporov cannot possibly justify it in an essay, his proposals do offer an intriguing extra dimension to carnival and suggest yet another aspect of explanation of Dostoyevsky's curiously modern and yet unmodern perception of reality. Potentially allied to this endeavour is Gachev's exposition of Dostoyevsky's representation of the material of reality (nature, air, life and the elements). Both essays are typical of the dominant Soviet semiotic interest in the time–space relationship (Bakhtin's 'chronotope') in Dostoyevsky.[42]

The most significant tendency imparted by formalist, structuralist and semiotic theorists, from Shklovsky to Toporov, to the contemporary study of Dostoyevsky is undoubtedly the acute awareness of the interdependence between 'form' and 'content' in his works and the appreciation of the complexity of that interrelated structure. In the light of Bakhtin's study and of Bakhtinian work in particular, there is no longer any justification for writing of Dostoyevsky's novels as amorphous manifestations of ideology.

The dominant focus of structuralist and post-structuralist work on Dostoyevsky's poetics continues to be the 'duality' which has been inherent in Dostoyevsky and in study of him since the beginning. In the context of the work reviewed here, 'duality' registers itself in the oxymoronic principles of titles and names, motifs, plots, themes and concepts; in the parodic, interactive construction of his novels and their constituent texts; in the paranormality of Dostoyevsky's carnivalesque realism; and most importantly, in the multivocal 'dialogue' which constitutes the polyphony at the heart of current debates.

The time is now past both for unquestioning acceptance of polyphony and for a monistic rejection of it. Most students of Dostoyevsky now accept the value and the relevance of Bakhtin's approach, but are concerned to concretize the details of an overview of Dostoyevsky which, in the width of its reference and the innovatory quality of its proposals, frequently remained without definition. At the centre of this current effort is the investigation of narration and voice in Dostoyevsky's novels. Such a tendency is the natural result of two conditions. The first is the investigation of the principles and mechanisms of narrative literature which are part of the general reorientation in postwar theoretical conception from literature as mimesis to literature as semblance. The second is the persistent lack of clarity and disquiet about the position and function of the 'author' within polyphony, as described earlier.

Polyphony has often been interpreted as a structure of relationships within which the author is passive and non-interventionist, or gives equal value to all viewpoints expressed. Certain critics, therefore, have taken issue with polyphony by demonstrating instances of intervention by the author in the text. Bakhtin, however, meets this challenge head on, as one of the earliest items in his revealing notes for the second edition of *Problemy*:

> Our point of view does not in any way affirm some kind of passivity on the part of the author, who merely produces a montage of other points of view, other truths, while completely renouncing his own point of view, his own truth. The question is not about this, but about a new, special interrelationship between his own and the other truth. The author is profoundly *active*, but his activity is especially *dialogic* in nature. Activity in relation to a dead thing, voiceless material which can be moulded and formed as desired is one thing, but activity *in relation to another living and fully justified consciousness* is quite another...Dostoyevsky often interrupts, but never stifles an other voice, never finishes it 'for himself', that is, speaking from another consciousness, his own...This is activity of a higher order. It overcomes not the resistance of inert material, but the resistance of an other consciousness, an other truth. (*Estetika*, p. 310)

Here, it would appear, Bakhtin admits the struggle for control by the author's voice, which seeks to 'overcome'. The distinction of activity by the polyphonic author would seem to lie not at all in any submission to characters, but in the range of conflict with them to which he, unlike a homophonic author, is prepared to expose himself. Todorov comments that in polyphony it is the structure of the relationship between characters and author which is different, not its content.[43] Indeed, Bakhtin goes on to say that Fridlender, in demonstrating the interventions made by the author in *The Idiot*,[44] is in most instances illustrating dialogical activity and thus supporting his (Bakhtin's) conclusions (p. 310).

Despite the sense of conviction in Bakhtin's argument, it remains difficult for many to conceive of how Dostoyevsky can be said to expose his consciousness completely to those of his characters and yet retain control of the work. Much of the problem here lies in the indefinition of Bakhtin's varying use of the terms 'author' and 'narrator' for 'pure' authorial activity, anonymous narrators, personified chroniclers and other categories of narration. Thus it is the 'authorial' voices in Dostoyevsky's writings which are the object of much study today, often in an attempt to clarify issues in the polyphony debate. Some of the leading work in this field has been done by the German scholar Wolf Schmid.[45]

Accepting neither the complete freedom of polyphony as advanced by Bakhtin, nor the domination of the work by Dostoyevsky the thinker (as opposed to Dostoyevsky the artist) as suggested by Zundelovich, Schmid evinces a double interest in narrative structure and reception aesthetics by concentrating instead on the construction and organization of texts and meanings within Dostoyevsky's works. Through a detailed characteristic-analysis of narrative text and character text ('Die Interferenz', p. 105) Schmid establishes the structural functions of 'textual interference', the effect achieved when character text permeates what is ostensibly narrative text. Textual interference performs two informative–aesthetic functions. By its complication of information, the contrast between text-characteristics and text-content, it necessitates the 'active cooperation' of the reader to define the point of view expressed. And, by focussing this ambivalence within key words and phrases shared by narrator and character, textual interference creates 'semantic polyvalency' ('Die Interferenz', pp. 111–12), in which meanings are divided, as in the narrator's interpretation of Velchaninov's 'illness' as 'a bad conscience' in *The Eternal Husband* (*Der Textaufbau*, p. 32).

What Schmid presents is a demonstration of the complexity of 'making strange' which results from textual interference. The confusion of reader-information which impedes the 'concretization of the represented world', together with semantic polyvalency (which recalls the formalists' and Bakhtin's conception of the word as a 'mask'), draws the attention of the reader to the structure of the work itself:

> the aesthetically organized work of literature does not fulfil its task by merely communicating facts, a piece of theoretical knowledge, a moral truth or a practical postulate; it is aimed rather at placing in the foreground of perception the proceedings of communication which have been complicated in one way or another. ('Die Interferenz', p. 113)

The effect of the focussing of attention on 'the proceedings of communication' is to make narration as the representation of facts a major theme of the work and to suggest as a principal, and preeminently modern function of Dostoyevsky's literature the exposure of the contingency of man's understandings.[46]

Schmid's work, which includes diachronic as well as synchronic treatment of the aesthetic reception of 'polyvalency', is the leading element in an impressive German contribution to the study of narrative structure and dialogue in Dostoyevsky.[47] Whereas Schmid sees the freedom of polyphony as being curtailed by the narrative's deliberate overemphasis of the literary process, Jacques Catteau, in a substantial study of Dostoyevsky's creativity, sees the convention of the literary work (its need for an ending) as placing a limitation on the polyphony which he otherwise accepts in large measure.[48] Writers in the English language tend to take issue with Bakhtin rather less, but show a comparable interest in narrative structure and dialogue. Recent work includes the late Jan Meijer's study of narration in *The Brothers Karamazov*, James Woodward's essay on transferred speech in *The Eternal Husband*, A. G. F. van Holk's text-grammatical analysis of *The Village of Stepanchikovo* and L. M. O'Toole's structural analysis of 'A Gentle Spirit'.[49]

Contemporary research on narrative and dialogue in Dostoyevsky is to be valued far more for its own conclusions than as 'evidence' in a trial of polyphony, the arguments about which may ultimately be reducible to linguistic wrangles about Bakhtin's notoriously promiscuous terms and statements. What does matter is the impetus given to students of Dostoyevsky by the entire descent of theory from formalism onwards, an impetus to reassess, in terms quite specific to Dostoyevsky, his view of the world, his representation of it in literature and his representation of literature (or its processes) as a model of the human relationship to the world. Certainly, no one can rest content with polyphony. Bakhtin's very cult of incompletion ensured that his exposition of it would demand even more than it would give. It does not seem irrelevant that the only major element of the work of literature which is not given synchronic (immanent) treatment in *Problemy poetiki Dostoyevskogo* is plot, which constitutes instead the diachronic element of the book. And it seems probable that a detailed study of the interrelationship within the text between plot and polyphony, in the form of chronotope and dialogue, could provide the key to the balance which is undoubtedly maintained in Dostoyevsky's novels, but which polyphony alone cannot explain.

But more essential to Dostoyevsky's works is the relationship between communication and meaning which structuralist criticism reveals. Vladiv comments: 'Bakhtin's very definition of the polyphonic novel seems to move on the edge of the theme of meaning and communication as the main topic of Dostoevskii's artistic preoccupation.'[50] Michael Holquist takes a similar view of Dostoyevsky in regard to his attitude towards 'Man':

> the metaphysical concern for the end of Man is realized in the most formal attributes of the structure of his novels, the narrative shape. And this is so because he was among the first to recognize that the question of what a man might be could not be separated from the question of what might constitute an authentic history. Each question is, in its own way, a dilemma of narrative.[51]

Narrative itself is sensed as a dilemma in Dostoyevsky. As noted earlier, he and Bakhtin have a sense of the godlike power of ordering, telling and interpreting: the 'divine' act of narration, like the knowledge of good and evil, is a double-edged instrument in human hands. Narration, communication, is an archaeology, the primary discourse of the world: like archaeology, it both re-creates and destroys the reality of which it seeks to give knowledge. Dostoyevsky's apprehension of narrative's significance is reflected in the remarkable correspondence between *histoire* and *discours* which obtains in his most advanced works:[52] the suspicions of complicity in the narration of *The Double*; the compulsive narration of events from an insubstantial world as part of the ethical debate over influence in *The Idiot*; the self-defining story of the narrator in 'A Gentle Spirit'; and the superb irony of the chronicler's painstaking attention to *facts* in *The Brothers Karamazov*, when a central event of the plot (Dmitry's conviction), and the principal theme of the novel, consists in the demonstration of a moral reality which transcends facts.

The action of Dostoyevsky's narrative and dialogue in continually removing literal 'truths' from the reader is paralleled by the activity of the novel in relation to the canon, as elaborated by Bakhtin. It is a view taken, as Holquist puts it, 'through the optic of the Dostoevskian example'. Bakhtin radicalizes for the novel the formalist concept of alternate canonization and decanonization in the history of literature, to the point at which the novel almost escapes classification as literature:

> 'novel' is the name Bakhtin gives to whatever force is at work within a given literary system to reveal the limits, the artificial constraints of that system. Literary systems are comprised of canons, and 'novelization' is fundamentally anticanonical. It will not permit generic monologue. Always it will insist on the dialogue between what a given system will admit as literature and those texts that are otherwise excluded from such a definition of literature.[53]

This description of the 'extra-literariness' of the (polyphonic) novel, echoed in Kristeva's description of polyphony as 'the principle of all upheavals', gives a sense of the extraordinary relationship between the structure of the novel and the structure of life in Dostoyevsky. In this context, the structure common to both is that of dialogue, which in Bakhtin's view 'permeates everything which has sense and meaning' (*Problemy poetiki*, p. 56). Looked at in this way, Dostoyevsky's endeavour may well be seen as the productively incomplete attempt to bring the axis of literature to a point of intersection with the axis of life, a point which might constitute the 'third element' of the resolution of duality.

Notes

1. Boris M. Ejxenbaum [Eykhenbaum], 'The theory of the formal method', *Readings in Russian Poetics*, ed. Ladislav Matejka and Krystyna Pomorska (Cambridge, Mass., 1971), p. 18.
2. Vladimir Seduro, *Dostoyevski in Russian Literary Criticism 1846–1956* (New York, 1969), p. 78.
3. Viktor Shklovsky, 'Syuzhet u Dostoyevskogo', *Letopis' doma literatorov*, 4 (1921), 4–5; also the references in his *O teorii prozy* (Moscow, 1929). The latter was reprinted Leipzig, 1977, to which edition reference is made here. Yuriy Tynyanov, *Dostoyevsky i Gogol': K teorii parodii*

(Petrograd, 1921), included in his *Arkhaisty i novatory* (Leningrad, 1929), reprinted Munich, 1967, to which edition reference is made here. Viktor Vinogradov, 'K morfologii natural'nogo stilya (Opyt lingvisticheskogo analiza peterburgskoy poemy "Dvoynik")' and 'Shkola sentimental'nogo naturalizma (Roman Dostoyevskogo "Bednyye lyudi" na fone literaturnoy evolyutsii 40-kh godov)' in his *Evolyutsiya russkogo naturalizma* (Leningrad, 1929), included in V. V. Vinogradov, *Poetika russkoy literatury* (Moscow, 1976), which is used for reference here. I am excluding from consideration as a formalist work Viktor Shklovsky's *Za i protiv: Zametki o Dostoyevskom* (Moscow, 1957). Although Victor Erlich sees it as 'a partial comeback' to formalism (in his *Russian Formalism: History–Doctrine* (The Hague, 1969), p. 142), I tend rather to agree with Julia Kristeva's description of it as 'a disappointing mixture of biography and impressionistic criticism' (see Kristeva, 'The ruin of a poetics', in Stephen Bann and John E. Bowlt (eds), *Russian Formalism* (Edinburgh, 1973) p. 118n). Bakhtin however is perceptive enough to draw out of it material of value (Mikhail Bakhtin, *Problemy poetiki Dostoyevskogo* (Moscow, 1963), pp. 53–7; translated as *Problems of Dostoevsky's Poetics* (see note 16), pp. 32–4).

4. For accounts of formalist theories of prose and literary evolution, see: Erlich, *Russian Formalism*, especially chs. X, XIII and XIV; Jurij Striedter, 'Zur formalistischen Theorie der Prosa und der literarischen Evolution', in *Texte der Russischen Formalisten* (Munich, 1969), vol. 1, pp. IX–LXXXIII; Aage A. Hansen-Löve, *Der Russische Formalismus* (Vienna, 1978), esp. pp. 238–303, 369–96.
5. Shklovsky, *O teorii prozy*, p. 227.
6. *Ibid.*, pp. 24–90, 125–76. See also the related categories of analysis ('running ahead', 'warning', 'slowing down' and the 'enigmatic' hero) in M. G. Davidovich, 'Problema zanimatel'nosti v romanakh Dostoyevskogo', in N. L. Brodsky (ed.), *Tvorcheskiy put' Dostoyevskogo* (Leningrad, 1924), pp. 104–30.
7. Shklovsky, *O teorii prozy*, pp. 236–7.
8. Tynyanov, *Dostoyevsky i Gogol'*, p. 433.
9. *Ibid.*, p. 426.
10. *Ibid.*, pp. 427–8.
11. *Ibid.*, p. 428.
12. Vinogradov, *Evolyutsiya*, pp. 141–2.
13. *Ibid.*, p. 104.
14. *Ibid.*, p. 106.
15. *Ibid.*, p. 129. Vinogradov was also ready to acknowledge the perceptions of earlier critics. He quotes Belinsky's observation in 1846 that the 'author' uses 'the language and concepts' of his hero in *The Double* (p. 126) and goes on to quote Annenkov's comments in 1849 on the foregrounding of narration in Dostoyevsky's early works (p. 166).
16. Bakhtin's work on Dostoyevsky was originally published as *Problemy tvorchestva Dostoyevskogo* (Leningrad, 1929) and republished, in considerably revised form, as *Problemy poetiki Dostoyevskogo* (Moscow, 1963). General essays on poetics and further material relevant to Dostoy-

evsky and other writers have been published in M. Bakhtin, *Voprosy literatury i estetiki* (Moscow, 1975) and *Estetika slovesnogo tvorchestva* (Moscow, 1979). Reference is to these editions as identified. The principal English translations are Mikhail Bakhtin, *Problems of Dostoevsky's Poetics*, trans. R. W. Rotsel (Ann Arbor, 1973) and *The Dialogic Imagination*, ed. M. Holquist (Austin/London, 1981), which contains the essays 'Epic and novel', 'From the prehistory of novelistic discourse', 'Forms of time and of the chronotope in the novel' and 'Discourse in the novel'. His other major work is M. M. Bakhtin, *Tvorchestvo Fransua Rable i narodnaya kul'tura Srednevekov'ya i Renessansa* (Moscow, 1965); this has been translated as *Rabelais and His World*, trans. H. Iswolsky (Cambridge, Mass., 1968). For a bibliography of works and secondary literature, see *The Dialogic Imagination*, pp. xxxiii–xxxiv.

17. His notes of 1961–2 for the reworking of his book show a concern to explicate the question of authorial position, a concern confirmed by reference to a letter of his to V. V. Kozhinov (Bakhtin, *Estetika*, pp. 309–12, 404).
18. Hansen-Löve, *Der Russische Formalismus*, pp. 456–62.
19. Excerpts from this essay appear as 'The forms of time and the chronotope in the novel', in *PTL: A Journal for Descriptive Poetics and Theory of Literature*, 3 (1978), 493–528, and it is translated in full in Bakhtin, *The Dialogic Imagination*.
20. See V. N. Voloshinov, *Marxism and the Philosophy of Language*, trans. L. Matejka and I. R. Titunik (New York, 1973), especially pt. III, chs. 2–3.
21. For a description of intertextuality, see Ann Jefferson, 'Intertextuality and the poetics of fiction', *Comparative Criticism*, 2 (1980), 235–50. Tzvetan Todorov comments: 'nous assistons ici à une singulière métamorphose: Dostoievski a cessé d'être l'*objet* de l'étude envisagée par Bakhtine pour passer du côté du *sujet* même . . . c'est Dostoievski, et non Bakhtine, qui a inventé l'intertextualité!' (T. Todorov, *Mikhaïl Bakhtine: Le principe dialogique* (Paris, 1981), p. 165).
22. George Steiner sees laughter as 'the supreme truth and the supreme custodian of human freedom' and concludes that laughter is 'the crux of Bakhtin's entire aesthetics' (Review of Bakhtin, *The Dialogic Imagination*, 'At the carnival of language', *Times Literary Supplement*, 17 July 1981, pp. 799–800). The leading Russian mediaevalist, D. S. Likhachev, who refers critically to Bakhtin, has written (with A. M. Panchenko) a cultural study of laughter-forms, *'Smekhovoy mir' drevney Rusi* (Leningrad, 1976).
23. See Ann Shukman, 'Between marxism and formalism: the stylistics of Mikhail Bakhtin', *Comparative Criticism*, 2 (1980), 225–6; Steiner, 'At the carnival', p. 800.
24. See Isaiah Berlin, 'The hedgehog and the fox', in his *Russian Thinkers*, ed. Henry Hardy and Aileen Kelly (London, 1978), p. 52.
25. Malcolm V. Jones, *Dostoyevsky: The Novel of Discord* (London, 1976), p. 38.

26. Vladimir Seduro, *Dostoyevski in Russian Literary Criticism 1846–1956* (New York, 1969) and *Dostoevski's Image in Russia Today* (Belmont, 1975).
27. A. V. Lunacharsky, 'O mnogogolosnosti Dostoyevskogo', *Novyy mir*, no. 10 (1929), 195–209 and 'Dostoyevsky kak myslitel' i khudozhnik', in F. M. Dostoyevsky, *Sochineniya* (Moscow/Leningrad, 1931).
28. G. M. Fridlender, *Realizm Dostoyevskogo* (Moscow/Leningrad, 1964). Ya. O. Zundelovich, *Romany Dostoyevskogo* (Tashkent, 1963).
29. See Gretchen Rous Besser, *Nathalie Sarraute* (New York, 1979), pp. 147–8, 160.
30. Michel Butor, 'Le joueur', in his *Répertoire* (Paris, 1960), vol. 1, pp. 120–9.
31. René Girard, *Deceit, Desire and the Novel: Self and Other in Literary Structure*, trans. Yvonne Freccero (Baltimore/London, 1969).
32. Julia Kristeva: 'Bakhtine, le mot, le dialogue et le roman', originally published in *Critique*, 239 (1967), pp. 438–65, republished in her *Semeiotike: Recherches pour une sémanalyse* (Paris, 1969). Reference here is to its translation as 'Word, dialogue and novel', in J. Kristeva, *Desire in Language* (Oxford, 1980), pp. 64–91; 'Une poétique ruinée', in Mikhaïl Bakhtine, *La Poétique de Dostoievski* (Paris, 1970), pp. 5–27. Translated as 'The ruin of a poetics', in Bann and Bowlt (eds), *Russian Formalism* (see note 3), pp. 102–19. Reference here is to this translation.
33. Ann Shukman, *Literature and Semiotics: A Study of the Writings of Yu. M. Lotman* (Amsterdam/New York, 1977), p. 4.
34. The indebtedness of the Moscow–Tartu school to Bakhtin is quite evident in the assistance given to Bakhtin by leading members of the group (see Bakhtin, *The Dialogic Imagination*, pp. xxv–xxvi) and the semiotic emphasis of papers in the Festschrift volume *Problemy poetiki i istorii literatury . . . k 75-letiyu . . . M. Bakhtina* (Saransk, 1973).
35. B. A. Uspensky, *Poetika kompozitsii: struktura khudozhestvennogo teksta i tipologiya kompozitsionnoy formy* (Moscow, 1970). Translated as *A Poetics of Composition*, trans. V. Zavarin and S. Witting (Berkeley, 1973).
36. Shukman, *Literature and Semiotics*, p. 172.
37. Uspensky, *Poetika*, p. 125. A recent article by another Soviet semiotician discusses the author–narrator–character relationship in the particular context of alienation: I. P. Smirnov, 'Otchuzhdeniye-v-otchuzhdenii (O "Zapiskakh iz mertvogo doma")', *Wiener Slawistischer Almanach*, 7 (1981), 37–48.
38. V. N. Toporov, 'Poetika Dostoyevskogo i arkhaichnyye skhemy mifologicheskogo myshleniya', pp. 91–109, and G. D. Gachev, 'Kosmos Dostoyevskogo', pp. 110–24. Toporov's article has been translated as 'On Dostoevsky's poetics and archaic patterns of mythological thought', *New Literary History*, 9 (1978), 333–52. Reference is to this translation.
39. Seduro, *Dostoyevski*, pp. 57–8.
40. P. M. Bitsilli, 'K voprosu o vnutrenney forme romana Dostoyevskogo', in P. M. Bitsilli *et al.*, *O Dostoyevskom: stat'i* (Providence, 1966),

pp. 1–71; R. Matlaw, 'Recurrent imagery in Dostoyevsky', *Harvard Slavic Studies*, 3 (1957), 201–25.

41. Dell Hymes, 'Comments on *Soviet Semiotics and Criticism*', *New Literary History*, 9 (1978), p. 409.
42. All the works on Dostoyevsky referred to in Karl Eimermacher and Serge Shishkoff's *Subject Bibliography of Soviet Semiotics: The Moscow–Tartu School* (Ann Arbor, 1977) deal with time and space in the novels. Most accessible to Western readers is T. V. Tsiv'yan, 'O strukture vremeni i prostranstva v romane Dostoyevskogo *Podrostok*', *Russian Literature*, 4 (1976), 203–55, which interprets the organization of time and space in terms of musicality (cf. polyphony) and dream. Toporov has also written a substantial piece on Dostoyevsky's story 'Gospodin Prokharchin' which has not yet been published. D. S. Likhachev has written on 'chronicle time' in Dostoyevsky, but in terms of a polyphony subjugated to the author. See his *Poetika drevnerusskoy literatury* (Leningrad, 1967), pp. 319–34.
43. Todorov, *Mikhaïl Bakhtine*, p. 164.
44. G. M. Fridlender, 'Roman *Idiot*', in *Tvorchestvo F. M. Dostoyevskogo* (Moscow, 1959), pp. 173–214.
45. Wolf Schmid, *Der Textaufbau in den Erzählungen Dostoevskijs* (Munich, 1973), a work which demands to be translated into English. Articles by Schmid on Dostoyevsky include: 'Zur Erzähltechnik und Bewusstseinsdarstellung in Dostoevskijs *Večnyj muž*', *Die Welt der Slaven*, 13 (1968), 294–306; 'Die Interferenz von Erzählertext und Personentext als Faktor in Bedeutungsaufbau des Doppelgängers', *Russian Literature*, no. 4 (1972), 100–13; 'Zur Semantik und Aesthetik des dialogischen Erzählmonologs bei Dostoevskij', *Canadian–American Slavic Studies*, 8 (1974), 381–97; 'Probleme einer diachronischen Rezeptionsästhetik dargelegt am Beispiel Dostoevskijs', *Russian Literature*, 4 (1976), 47–66.
46. See Slobodanka Vladiv, 'The use of circumstantial evidence in Dostoevskii's works', *Canadian–American Slavic Studies*, 12 (1978), 354. See also the pragmatic comparative study of the 'literariness' of the narrator of *The Brothers Karamazov* in Hans Wefers, 'Der literarische Erzähler als Faktor textueller Kommunikation und Konstruktion', *Wiener Slawistischer Almanach*, 3 (1979), 75–92.
47. There is an extensive list of German contributions in the bibliography to Slobodanka Vladiv's *The Narrative Principles in Dostoevskij's 'Besy': A Structural Analysis* (Bern, 1979), itself a post-Bakhtinian work of considerable originality. The major works are those of Horst-Jürgen Gerigk, *Versuch über Dostoevskijs 'Jüngling'* (Munich, 1965) and Johannes Holthusen, *Prinzipien der Komposition und des Erzählens bei Dostojevskij* (Cologne/Opladen, 1969). Brigitte Schultze has also produced a Bakhtinian study of dialogue as the central structural element in *Der Dialog in F. M. Dostoevskijs 'Idiot'* (Munich, 1974).
48. Jacques Catteau, *La Création littéraire chez Dostoievski* (Paris, 1978), pp. 373, 430–3.
49. Jan M. Meijer, 'The author of *Brat'ja Karamazovy*', in J. van der Eng

and J. M. Meijer, *The Brothers Karamazov by F. M. Dostoevskij* (The Hague, 1971), pp. 7–46 (this volume also contains essays on time and suspense); James B. Woodward, ' "Transferred speech" in Dostoevskii's *Vechnyi muzh*', *Canadian–American Slavic Studies*, 8 (1974), 398–407; A. G. F. van Holk, 'Verbal aggression and offended honour in Dostoevskij's *Selo Stepančikovo i ego obitateli*', *Russian Literature*, 4 (1976), 67–107; L. M. O'Toole, 'Structure and style in the short story: Dostoevskij's *A Gentle Spirit*', *Tijdschrift voor Slavische Taal en Letterkunde*, 1 (1972), 81–116 and in O'Toole, *Structure, Style and Interpretation in the Russian Short Story* (New Haven, 1982). For a structural analysis which employs the same categories as those of O'Toole, see my 'Dostoevsky's *The Dream of a Ridiculous Man*: seeing is believing', in J. M. Andrew (ed.), *The Structural Analysis of Russian Narrative Fiction* (Avebury Press), in press. Two other recent articles investigate gesture and tonality in the dialogic text: David K. Danow, 'Semiotics of gesture in Dostoevskian dialogue', *Russian Literature*, 8 (1980), 41–75; Victor Terras, 'Dissonances and false notes in a literary text', in Andrej Kodjak *et al.* (eds.), *The Structural Analysis of Narrative Texts* (Columbus, 1980), pp. 82–95.

50. Vladiv, 'Circumstantial evidence', p. 354n.
51. Michael Holquist, *Dostoevsky and the Novel* (Princeton, 1977), p. 194.
52. See O'Toole, 'Structure and style', pp. 86–7.
53. Bakhtin, ed. Holquist, *The Dialogic Imagination*, p. xxxi.

Dostoyevsky studies in Great Britain: a bibliographical survey

GARTH M. TERRY

The original aim of this bibliographical survey was to mark the centenary of Dostoyevsky's death by recording all work on Dostoyevsky by British scholars. This posed several immediate problems however, which proved to be insurmountable. The difficulty in tracing material sent abroad by British scholars for publication, and the difficulty in identifying those British scholars who had emigrated to Australia, Canada, the United States and elsewhere, were the two determining factors. It was decided therefore to limit the scope of the bibliography to work on Dostoyevsky which had been published in Great Britain. This would ensure that the vast majority of British work was covered but would exclude the aforementioned material published abroad. On the other hand, work by foreign authors published in Great Britain would come within the bibliography's scope, although this proved to be, as it turned out, only a small amount.

Dostoyevsky's influence on modern literature is considered to be enormous. E. H. Carr wrote in his excellent biography of Dostoyevsky in 1931 that 'Dostoevsky has influenced nearly all the important novelists who have arisen in England, France and Germany during the past twenty years' (*Dostoevsky, 1821–1881: A New Biography*, London, Allen & Unwin, 1931, p. 323). There have been numerous studies, both short and long, on Dostoyevsky's relation to, and influence on, such authors as Balzac, Camus, Dickens, Gide, Goethe, Lawrence, Schiller and Woolf. The list seems endless. In the 1930s there were three dissertations dealing with Dostoyevsky and England – W. Neuschäffer's published dissertation *Dostojewskij's Einfluss auf den englischen Roman* (Heidelberg, Carl Winters Universitätsbuchhandlung, 1935, 110 pp.), R. E. Passmore's *Dostoevsky in English, 1881–1934* (Columbia University, 1936), and H. Muchnic's published dissertation *Dostoevsky's English Reputation, 1881–1936* (Northampton, Mass., Smith

College, 1939, 219 pp.). More recently there was N. R. Sinyard's thesis *Responses to Dostoevsky in England* (University of Manchester, 1969).

Although most of Dostoyevsky's novels were written in the 1860s and 1870s, England lagged far behind the rest of Europe in knowing and appreciating him. In Germany, for instance, *Poor Folk* appeared in translation as early as 1850, *The House of the Dead* in 1864, and by 1890 nearly all of Dostoyevsky had been translated. An almost identical situation existed in France. It was only after 1880 however that Dostoyevsky appeared in England and it was not until the appearance of Constance Garnett's translations of Dostoyevsky's novels in the second decade of this century that he became widely read here. Dostoyevsky's two great contemporaries, Turgenev and Tolstoy, on the other hand, appeared in English translation as early as 1885 and 1862 respectively.

The first translation of Dostoyevsky to appear in English was Marie von Thilo's rather free rendering of his Siberian 'memoirs' – *Burned Alive; or, Ten Years of Penal Servitude in Siberia* (London, Longman, 1881, 361 pp.). Further translations appeared in the late eighties by Frederick Whishaw – *Crime and Punishment* (1886), *Injury and Insult* (1886), *The Idiot* (1887), *The Friend of the Family, and The Gambler* (1887), and *The Uncle's Dream, and The Permanent Husband* (1888). *The Brothers Karamazov* did not appear in English until 1912 when it was published as the first volume of twelve in Constance Garnett's translation of Dostoyevsky's works. Garnett's version of Dostoyevsky's works produced between 1912 and 1920 was the first adequate translation in English and remains to this day probably the most honest, close and natural one. It was responsible for opening the way in this country to a real appreciation of and interest in Dostoyevsky.

The first reference to Dostoyevsky in the English press, albeit a passing one, appeared in *The Athenaeum* on 25 December 1875, to be followed by further references in *The Contemporary Review* and *The Quarterly Review* in 1880. The first English article wholly devoted to Dostoyevsky was published under the title 'The Russian Novelist Dostojewsky' in *The Academy* (XXVIII, 1885, 395). It was in the form of a letter by H. S. Wilson. Two years later J. Lomas's article entitled simply 'Dostoevsky' appeared in the London *MacMillan's Magazine* (LV, 1887, 187–98). This constituted the first full-length article on Dostoyevsky. Other articles soon followed. It was in 1912 that the first monograph in English, a biographical study of Dostoyevsky, appeared – J. A. T. Lloyd's

A Great Russian Realist, Feodor Dostoieffsky (London, Stanley Paul & Co., 1912, 296 pp.).

It may be worth mentioning here three interesting Soviet articles which survey recent British scholarship on Dostoyevsky. They are M. M. Lur′e, 'Angliyskiye pisateli i kritiki o Dostoyevskom' in *Russkaya literatura i mirovoy literaturnyy protsess: sbornik* (Leningrad, Leningradskiy Gosudarstvennyy Pedagogicheskiy Institut, 1973, pp. 186–212); D. Zhantiyeva, 'Angliyskoye literaturovedeniye 50–60kh godov o Turgeneve, Tolstom i Dostoyevskom' in *Russkaya literatura i yeyo zarubezhnyye kritiki: sbornik statey*, chief ed. U. A. Gural′nik (Moscow, Khudozhestvennaya Literatura, 1974, pp. 198–242); and Yu. I. Sokhryakov and G. M. Kholodova, 'Problemy tvorchestva F. M. Dostoyevskogo v poslednikh angliyskikh i amerikanskikh monografiyakh' in *Russkaya literatura v otsenke sovremennoy zarubezhnoy kritiki*, ed. V. I. Kuleshov (Moscow, Izd. Moskovskogo Universiteta, 1981, pp. 189–221).

British scholarship on Dostoyevsky is thus exactly one hundred years old. It was the intention in this bibliography to record all material on Dostoyevsky's life and works published in this country from the appearance of von Thilo's translation in 1881 to this very day. It soon became apparent however that this was too large an undertaking for the present volume of essays and so the bibliography was reluctantly shortened to cover only postwar publications. There are a number of bibliographies available however which cover works on Dostoyevsky in the period up to 1944 and through which one can compile at least a basic list.

1881–1944

Critical and biographical material is adequately covered by the following two works – M. Beebe and C. Newton, 'Dostoevsky in English: a selected checklist of criticism and translations', *Modern Fiction Studies* (IV, 1958, 271–91) and G. M. Terry, *East European Languages and Literatures: A Subject and Name Index to Articles in English-Language Journals, 1900–1977* (Oxford, Clio Press, 1978, 275 pp.). Beebe's bibliography covers material over the period 1881 to 1958 and is arranged in two sections – the first lists general studies, both monographs and articles; the second consists of an index to studies of Dostoyevsky's individual works and includes translations, introductions and prefaces, relevant parts from material listed in section I, and special studies of individual works. My own work contains almost 550 articles (pp. 35–46) taken from English-language journals mainly of American and English origin. Articles are listed chronologically within two main sections, general articles and articles on individual works. Such a chronological arrangement allows one to survey the development of English-language scholarship over the years. Another useful bibliography may be found in H. Muchnic's book *Dostoevsky's English Reputation, 1881–1936* (pp. 194–209; see above).

Translations of Dostoyevsky's works into English are very adequately covered in a number of sources. Maurice B. Line's *A Bibliography of Russian Literature in English to 1900 (Excluding Periodicals)* (London, The Library Association, 1963, 74 pp.) contains English translations of Dostoyevsky's works in both the U.K. and the U.S.A. up to 1900. A very useful chronological list of the first appearances of translations is also provided. The bibliography by Beebe and Newton already mentioned covers translations for the period 1881 to 1958. R. C. Lewanski's work *The Literatures of the World in English Translation*, vol. II: *The Slavic Literatures* (New York, New York Public Library, 1971, 630 pp.) attempts to register all translations of Slavonic literatures from the very beginning to 1960. Entries for Dostoyevsky may be found on pp. 230–5 and include those translations contained in anthologies and journals.

1945–81

The following list contains material published on Dostoyevsky in Great Britain during the period 1945 to 1981. Material covered comprises monographs, journal and newspaper articles, translations, dissertations and reviews. The majority of entries are in English, of course, but some Russian titles are listed – for example, those in the Prideaux series of Russian Titles for the Specialist. They are transliterated according to the scheme used by *The Slavonic and East European Review*.

The list is arranged chronologically by year of publication. Exceptions to this arrangement are reviews and review articles of monographs published in this country. These are listed together with the work they review irrespective of when the reviews were written. Reviews of monographs published abroad, however, are listed under the name of the reviewer and under the year in which the review appeared. The publication date of each item has been omitted except in those cases where it differs from the year under which that item is listed.

Translations pose a problem since many of these, especially those by Constance Garnett first published at the beginning of this century, have been reprinted throughout the decades. In order not to overload this bibliography with reprints, therefore, I have listed such translations under the first year of their reprinting during the period covered by this bibliography, 1945–81, with added notes as to reprints and the original date of publication.

Although the bibliography is as comprehensive as possible, it should be stated here that very brief items relating to Dostoyevsky have not been included – *The Times*, for example, contains several such notices of two or three sentences only. Finally, a name index is to be found at the end of the bibliography together with an index to the works of Dostoyevsky published in this country either in the original or in translation.

Current work on Dostoyevsky may be found in the *Bulletin of the International Dostoevsky Society* and its successor *Dostoevsky Studies.* The International Dostoevsky Society was founded at the International Dostoevsky Symposium held in Bad Ems in September 1971 in celebration of the 150th anniversary of the author's birth. The *Bulletin* appeared annually and provided extensive bibliographical references, both current and retrospective, as well as other relevant information on Dostoyevsky studies in various countries. It ceased publication with no. 9, 1979, and has been replaced by the journal *Dostoevsky Studies*, which continues the bibliographical listings. Other sources of current information are the annually published *European Bibliography of Slavonic and East European Studies, The MLA International Bibliography of Books and Articles on the Modern Languages and Literatures* and *The Year's Work in Modern Language Studies.*

In this bibliography the place of publication is London unless otherwise stated. The following abbreviations have been used:

FMLS	*Forum for Modern Language Studies*
JES	*Journal of European Studies*
JRS	*Journal of Russian Studies*
L	*The Listener*
MLR	*Modern Language Review*
OSP	*Oxford Slavonic Papers*
RMS	*Renaissance and Modern Studies*
SEER	*The Slavonic and East European Review*
T	*The Times*
THES	*The Times Higher Education Supplement*
TLS	*The Times Literary Supplement*

1945

1. Dostoyevsky, F. M. *Dream of a Ridiculous Man. Another Man's Wife. A Meek Young Girl.* Trans. by B. Scott. Drummond, 92 pp.
2. Freud, S. 'Dostoevsky and parricide', *International Journal of Psycho-Analysis*, XXVI. 1–2, 1–8.
3. Lavrin, J. 'Dostoevsky', in his *An Introduction to the Russian Novel.* 3rd edn. Methuen, pp. 97–112.
   Originally pub. in 1942.

1946

4. Dostoyevsky, F. M. 'The Crocodile', in J. Lavrin, *Russian Humorous Stories.* Sylvan Press, 208 pp.
5. — 'An Honest Thief' and 'Bub-Boo', in *A First Series of Representative Russian Stories, Pushkin to Gorky.* Selected and ed.. . . by J. Lavrin. Westhouse, pp. 102–19, 121–37.
6. Harris, H. 'The epilepsy of Fyodor Dostoievski', *Journal of Mental Sciences*, April, 364–9.
7. Lloyd, J. A. T. *Fyodor Dostoevsky.* Eyre & Spottiswoode, 206 pp.
   Review in *TLS*, 20 September 1947, p. 478 ('The insufficient man').
8. Powys, J. C. 'Dostoievsky', in his *The Pleasures of Literature.* 2nd edn. Cassell, pp. 87–101.
   First edn pub. in 1938.
9. Roe, I. *The Breath of Corruption: An Interpretation of Dostoievsky.* Hutchinson, 110 pp.
10. Troyat, H. *Firebrand: The Life of Dostoievsky.* Trans. by N. Guterman. Heinemann, 438 pp.
11. Warner, R. 'Dostoievsky and the collapse of liberalism', in his *The Cult of Power: Essays.* John Lane, pp. 39–88.
    This chapter is reviewed in *TLS*, 19 October, p. 507 ('The wellspring').

1947

12. Hare, R. 'Tolstoy and Dostoevsky', in his *Russian Literature from Pushkin to the Present Day.* Methuen, pp. 104–42.
13. Lohr, F. *The Grand Inquisitor: Three Lectures.* London Forum Publications, 47 pp.
14. Mackiewicz, S. *Dostoyevsky.* Orbis, 203 pp.
    Review in *TLS*, 25 September 1948, p. 538.

15. Powys, J. C. *Dostoievsky*. John Lane, 208 pp.
    Review in *TLS*, 20 September, p. 478 ('The insufficient man').

1948

16. Dostoyevsky, F. M. *Crime and Punishment*. Trans. by C. Garnett. (Everyman's Library, 501). Dent, 493 pp.
    This trans., first pub. in 1914, has also been pub. by Heinemann in 1949 (488 pp.), by the Folio Society in 1957 (454 pp.), by Landsborough Publications in 1958 (448 pp.), and by Pan Books in 1979. Most have been reprinted since.
17. — *Dostoievsky's Crime and Punishment*. Dramatized by R. Ackland. Sampson Low, 111 pp.
18. — '*Notes from Underground*', in B. G. Guerney, *A Treasury of Russian Literature*. Bodley Head, pp. 437–537.
19. Lavrin, J. 'A note on Tolstoy and Dostoevsky', in his *From Pushkin to Mayakovsky*. Sylvan Press, pp. 146–56.
20. Lo Gatto, E. 'Genesis of Dostoevsky's *Uncle's Dream*', *SEER*, XXVI.67, 452–67.
21. Marchiori, J. Review of A. M. V. Guarnieri-Ortolani, *Saggio sulla fortuna di Dostoevskij in Italia* (University of Padua Publications, 24), Padova, CEDAM, 1947, in *SEER*, XXVI.67, 587–91.
22. Zander, L. A. *Dostoevsky*. SCM Press, 140 pp.

1949

23. Carr, E. H. *Dostoevsky, 1821–1881: A New Biography*. Allen & Unwin, 331 pp.
    First pub. in 1931. Reprinted in 1962. Review in *TLS*, 1 March 1963, pp. 145–6 ('The mystic rebel').
24. Dostoyevsky, F. M. *The Brothers Karamazov*. Trans. by C. Garnett. Heinemann, 832 pp.
    This trans. first pub. in 1912. Reprinted in 1957 by Dent in the series Everyman's Library, 802–3 (2 vols) and in the following year by Landsborough Publications (699 pp.).
25. — *The Friend of the Family*. Trans. by C. Garnett. New York/London, Macmillan/Heinemann, 358 pp.
    This trans. first pub. in 1920.
26. — *The Gambler*. Trans. by C. Garnett. Heinemann, 318 pp.
    This trans. first pub. in 1917.
27. Gide, A. P. G. *Dostoevsky*. Trans. from the French. Secker & Warburg, 176 pp.
    First pub. in 1925. Reprinted in 1952 and 1967.

28. Hemmings, F. W. J. 'The influence of the Russian novel on French thinkers and writers, with particular reference to Tolstoy and Dostoevsky'. Ph.D. thesis, Oxford University.
29. Katkov, G. 'Steerforth and Stavrogin on the sources of *The Possessed*', *SEER*, XXVII.69, 469–89.
30. Mirsky, D. S. *A History of Russian Literature, Comprising A History of Russian Literature and Contemporary Russian Literature*. Ed. and abridged by F. J. Whitfield. Routledge & Kegan Paul, 518 pp.
A History of Russian Literature and *Contemporary Russian Literature* were first pub. in 1927 and 1926 respectively. The chapters on Dostoyevsky are 'Dostoyevsky's early work' (pp. 172–6) and 'Dostoyevsky (after 1849)' (pp. 263–78).
31. Roe, I. 'Fyodor Dostoievsky: a Russian moment – 1849', *World Review*, December, 57–60.

1950

32. Curle, R. *Characters of Dostoevsky: Studies from Four Novels*. Heinemann, 224 pp.
Review in *TLS*, 21 July, pp. 445–6 ('The quest for Dostoevsky').
33. Dostoyevsky, F. M. *A Gentle Creature, and Other Stories*. Trans. with introd. by D. Magarshack. (Chiltern Library Series, 36). Lehmann, 272 pp.
Review in *TLS*, 21 July, pp. 445–6 ('The quest for Dostoevsky').
34. Fueloep-Miller, R. *Fyodor Dostoevsky: Insight, Faith and Prophecy*. Trans. by R. and C. Winston. (Twentieth Century Library Series). New York/London, Scribner, 137 pp.
35. Hemmings, F. W. J. 'Dostoevsky and the younger generation', in his *The Russian Novel in France, 1884–1914*. OUP, pp. 222–39.
36. — 'Dostoevsky in disguise: the 1888 version of *The Brothers Karamazov*', *French Studies*, IV.3, 227–38.
37. Simmons, E. J. *Dostoevsky: The Making of a Novelist*. Lehmann, 320 pp.
Review in *TLS*, 21 July, pp. 445–6 ('The quest for Dostoevsky').
38. Vakeel, H. J. 'Dostoevsky and humour', *Contemporary Review*, CLXXVII, 36–9.
39. Woodhouse, C. M. 'Dostoievsky as prophet', *Nineteenth Century*, March, 174–83.

40. Yermilov, V. V. 'Against the reactionary ideas in the work of Dostoievsky', *Modern Quarterly*, V.2, 136–51.

1951

41. Dostoyevsky, F. M. *Crime and Punishment.* Trans. with introd. by D. Magarshack. (Penguin Classics, 23). Harmondsworth, Penguin, 559 pp.
42. — *The Diary of a Writer.* Trans. and annotated by B. Brasol. 2 vols. Cassell, 1,097 pp.
    Review in *TLS*, 9 March, p. 150 ('A missionary voice').
43. Woodhouse, C. M. *Dostoievsky.* Barker, 112 pp.
    Review in *TLS,* 14 December, p. 806 ('World-changing novelist'). 2nd edn pub. in 1968.

1952

44. Hubben, W. 'Dostoevsky's Holy Russia', *Friend's Quarterly*, July, 182–7.
45. Ivanov, V. *Freedom and the Tragic Life: A Study in Dostoevsky.* Trans. from the Russian by N. Cameron. (Russian Writers and Thinkers Series). Harvill Press, 166 pp.
    Review by F. F. Seeley in *SEER*, XXXI.77, 1953, 603–4; in *TLS*, 3 October, p. 646.
46. Jones, G. V. 'Conscience, guilt and expiation: some notes on Dostoievsky', *Congregational Quarterly*, XXX.3, 245–52.
47. Wilson, E. 'Dostoevsky abroad', in his *The Shores of Light: A Literary Chronicle of the Twenties and Thirties.* Allen, pp. 408–14.

1953

48. Dostoyevsky, F. M. *Crime and Punishment.* Trans. by J. Coulson. OUP, 527 pp.
    Reprinted in 1973 by OUP in the series World's Classics, 619.
49. — *The Devils* (*The Possessed*). Trans. with introd. by D. Magarshack. (Penguin Classics, L35). Harmondsworth, Penguin, 669 pp.
50. — *The Idiot.* Trans. by E. M. Martin. (Everyman's Library Series, 682). Dent, 598 pp.
    This trans. first pub. in 1914.
51. — *Letters from the Underworld. The Gentle Maiden. The Landlady.* Trans. by C. Hogarth. (Everyman's Library Series, 654). Dent, 308 pp.

First pub. in 1913 under the title *Letters from the Underworld and Other Tales.* This edn was reprinted by Dent in 1957.

52. 'Vospominaniye o yunosti startsa Zosimy', in J. Coulson and N. Duddington, eds, *Russian Short Stories: XIXth Century.* Oxford, Clarendon Press, pp. 91–102.

1954

53. Brewster, D. 'Tolstoy, Dostoevsky and the "formless" novel', in her *East–West Passage: A Study in Literary Relationships.* Allen & Unwin, pp. 226–32.
54. Brookes, H. 'Children in the works of Dostoevsky'. M.A. thesis, Nottingham University.
55. Dostoyevsky, F. M. *The Idiot.* Trans. with introd. by D. Magarshack. (Penguin Classics, L54). Harmondsworth, Penguin, 661 pp.
    This edn also pub. by the Folio Society in 1971 (670 pp.).
56. Jones, G. V. '*Agape* and *Eros:* notes on Dostoievsky', *Expository Times*, LXVI.1, 3–7.
57. Lednicki, W. *Russia, Poland and the West: Essays in Literary and Cultural History.* Hutchinson, 419 pp.
    Contains the following chapters on Dostoyevsky: 'Europe in Dostoevsky's ideological novel' (pp. 133–79); 'Dostoevsky – the Man from Underground' (pp. 180–248); 'Dostoevsky and Belinsky' (pp. 249–61); 'Dostoevsky and Poland' (pp. 262–348).

1955

58. Dostoevsky, F. M. *Summer Impressions.* Trans. with introd. by K. Fitzlyon. Calder, 121 pp.
59. Futrell, M. H. 'Dickens and three Russian novelists: Gogol', Dostoevsky and Tolstoy'. Ph.D. thesis, School of Slavonic and East European Studies, London University.
60. Lawrence, D. H. 'The Grand Inquisitor', in his *Selected Literary Criticism.* Ed. by A. Beal. Heinemann, pp. 233–41.
61. Powys, J. C. 'Dostoievsky', in his *Visions and Revisions: A Book of Literary Devotions.* MacDonald, pp. 181–95.

1956

62. Dostoyevsky, F. M. *Memoirs from the House of Dead.* Trans. by J. Coulson. OUP, 294 pp.
    Reprinted by OUP in 1965 in the series World's Classics, 597 (361 pp.).

63. — *Poor Folk. The Gambler.* Trans. by C. Hogarth. (Everyman's Library, 711). Dent, 307 pp.
This edn first pub. in 1915. Reprinted in 1969 by Heron with an introd. by N. Andreyev.
64. 'Dostoevsky', *Soviet Culture,* III, March, 7–9.
65. Hare, R. 'Dostoevsky at home and abroad', *TLS*, 9 November, p. 672.
66. Moravia, A. 'The Marx–Dostoevsky duel, and other Russian notes', *Encounter,* VII.5, 3–12.
67. Phelps, G. *The Russian Novel in English Fiction.* Hutchinson's University Library, 206 pp.
Contains two chapters on Dostoyevsky: 'Gaboriau with psychological sauce?' (pp. 156–72); 'Absolute realism' (pp. 173–94).

1957

68. Dostoyevsky, F. M. *The Double: A Poem of St. Petersburg.* Trans. by G. Bird. Harvill Press, 254 pp.
69. 'Involvement [on *The Brothers Karamazov*]', *TLS*, 1 November, p. 657.
70. Kaufmann, W. A. 'Dostoevsky: *Notes from Underground*', in his *Existentialism from Dostoevsky to Sartre.* Thames & Hudson, pp. 52–82.
71. O'Connor, F. 'Dostoevsky and the unnatural triangle', in his *The Mirror in the Roadway: A Study of the Modern Novel.* Hamish Hamilton, pp. 199–222.
72. Seduro, V. *Dostoyevski in Russian Literary Criticism, 1846–1956.* New York/London, Columbia UP/OUP, 412 pp.
Review by F. F. Seeley in *SEER*, XXXVII.89, 1959, 522–4; by C. L. Wrenn in *MLR*, LIV.2, 1959, 293–5; in *TLS*, 29 August 1958, pp. 477–8 ('Dostoevsky and his critics').
73. Slonim, M. *Three Loves of Dostoevsky.* Redman, 318 pp.
74. Yarmolinsky, A. *Dostoevsky: His Life and Art.* 2nd edn. Arco, 434 pp.
First pub. in New York, 1934. Review in *L*, 21 February, pp. 315–16; in *TLS*, 22 February, p. 114 ('Unravelling Dostoevsky').

1958

75. Arban, D. 'Dostoevsky and the old man's murder', trans. by J. Stewart, *London Magazine*, V.10, 50–9.
76. Dostoyevsky, F. M. *The Brothers Karamazov.* Trans. with

introd. by D. Magarshack. 2 vols. (Penguin Classics, L78). Harmondsworth, Penguin.
Reprinted by the Folio Society in 1964 (845 pp.).

77. — *My Uncle's Dream*. Trans. by I. Litvinova. Moscow/London, Foreign Languages Publishing House/Sidgwick & Jackson, 405 pp. Contains 'My Uncle's Dream', 'Most Unfortunate' and *The Gambler*.
78. Mitchell, J. H. 'Some aspects of the problem of guilt with special reference to Kafka, Kierkegaard, and Dostoevsky'. Ph.D. thesis, Edinburgh University.
79. Slonim, M. 'Dostoevsky', in his *An Outline of Russian Literature*. (The Home University Library of Modern Knowledge, 236). OUP, pp. 139–54.
80. Woodhouse, C. M. 'The two Russians [the Russian character as revealed in Dostoyevsky's *The Possessed* and Goncharov's *Oblomov*]', *Essays by Divers Hands*, n.s. XXIX, 18–36.

1959

81. Dostoyevsky, F. M. *A Disgraceful Affair*. Trans. by N. Gottlieb. Merlin Press, 87 pp.
82. — 'The Grand Inquisitor' and 'A Gentle Spirit', in S. Graham, *Great Russian Stories*. Benn, 1,021 pp.
First pub. in 1929.
83. Hare, R. 'F. M. Dostoyevsky', in his *Portraits of Russian Personalities Between Reform and Revolution*. OUP, pp. 104–49.

1960

84. Baring, M. 'Dostoievsky', in his *Landmarks in Russian Literature*. (University Paperbacks, 7). Methuen, pp. 80–162.
85. Camus. A. *The Possessed: A Play in Three Parts*. Based on the novel by F. Dostoyevsky. Trans. by J. O'Brien. Hamish Hamilton, 159 pp.
86. Coulter, S. *The Devil Inside: A Novel of Dostoevsky's Life*. Cape, 384 pp.
87. Dostoyevsky, F. M. *The Dream of a Queer Fellow, and The Pushkin Speech*. Trans. by S. Koteliansky and J. Murry. (Unwin Books, 10). Allen & Unwin, 96 pp.
Originally pub. in 1916.
88. — *The Possessed*. Trans. by C. Garnett. Introd. by N. Andreyev. 2 vols. (Everyman's Library, 861–2). Dent.
This trans. first pub. in 1913.

89. — *Zapiski iz podpol'ya.* Bradda, 112 pp.
Text unstressed. Reissued by Bradda in 1963 in the series Russian Plain Texts (150 pp.) with a stressed text and introd. by F. M. Borras.
90. Kaspin, A. 'Dostoyevsky's Masloboyev and Ostrovsky's Dosuzhev: a parallel', *SEER*, XXXIX.92, 222–7.
91. Lord, R. 'Dostoevsky considered in relation to Apollon Grigor'ev, Vladimir Solov'yov, and N. F. Fyodorov'. M.A. thesis, School of Slavonic and East European Studies, London University.
92. Murry, J. M. 'Crime and Punishment', in his *J. Middleton Murry: Selected Criticism, 1916–1957.* Ed. by R. Rees. OUP, pp. 31–40.
93. Simmons, J. S. G. 'F. M. Dostoevsky and A. K. Tolstoy: two letters', *OSP*, IX, 64–72.
94. Steiner, G. *Tolstoy or Dostoevsky: An Essay in Contrast.* Faber & Faber, 355 pp.
Republished by Penguin in 1967 (332 pp.). Review by M. Futrell in *L*, 3 March, pp. 410–12; by H. Gifford in *Critical Quarterly*, II, 284–6; in *TLS*, 11 March, pp. 153–4 ('Grand Inquisition').
95. Yermilov, V. *Fyodor Dostoyevsky, 1821–1881.* Trans. by J. Katzer. Moscow/London, Foreign Languages Publishing House/Central Books, 294 pp.

1961

96. Dostoyevsky, F. M. *A Funny Man's Dream.* Trans. by O. Shartse. Moscow/London, Foreign Languages Publishing House/Central Books, 335 pp.
97. Fanger, D. L. 'Dostoevsky today: some recent critical studies', *Survey*, XXXVI, 13–19.
98. Louria, Y. '*Dédoublement* in Dostoevsky and Camus', *MLR*, LVI.1, 82–3.
99. Panichas, G. A. 'F. M. Dostoevsky and D. H. Lawrence: their vision of evil', *RMS*, V, 49–75.
100. Seeley, F. 'Dostoyevsky's women', *SEER*, XXXIX.93, 291–313.
101. 'Zurich sees two contrasting versions of Dostoevsky's *Crime and Punishment*', *T*, 20 June, p. 16.

1962

102. Dostoyevsky, F. M. *Dostoevsky: A Self-Portrait.* OUP, 279 pp.
Selection of Dostoyevsky's letters ed. and trans. by J. Coulson.

Review by M. Futrell in *L*, 29 November, p. 937; by F. F. Seeley in *SEER*, XLI.97, 1963, 544–7; in *TLS*, 1 March 1963, pp. 145–6 ('The mystic rebel').

103. — *The House of the Dead*. Trans. by H. S. Edwards. Introd. by N. Andreyev. (Everyman's Library, 533). Dent, 308 pp.
This trans. first pub. in 1911.

104. — *Letters...to His Family and Friends*. Trans. by E. C. Mayne. Introd. by A. Yarmolinsky. Owen, 344 pp.
Review by C. Wilson in *L*, 8 March, p. 437 ('In his own words'); in *TLS*, 23 March, p. 203 ('A tortured soul').

105. Hingley, R. *The Undiscovered Dostoyevsky*. Hamilton, 241 pp.
Review by M. Futrell in *L*, 27 September, p. 483; in *T*, 5 October, p. 17 ('Talk of – and laughter with – The Devils'); in *TLS*, 1 March 1963, pp. 145–6 ('The mystic rebel').

106. Lord, R. 'Dostoyevsky and N. F. Fyodorov', *SEER*, XL.95, 409–31.

107. Magarshack, D. *Dostoevsky*. Secker & Warburg, 512 pp.
Review by M. Futrell in *L*, 29 November, p. 937; in *TLS*, 1 March 1963, pp. 145–6 ('The mystic rebel').

108. Richards, D. 'Four utopias [discussion of Dostoyevsky, Zamyatin, Huxley and Orwell]', *SEER*, XL.94, 220–9.

109. Westbrook, P. D. *The Greatness of Man: An Essay on Dostoyevsky and Whitman*. New York/London, Yoseloff, 175 pp.

1963

110. Novak, M. 'The existentialism of Dostoievski', *Blackfriars*, XLIV, February, 63–9.

1964

111. Dostoyevsky, F. M. *Occasional Writings*. Selected, trans. and introduced by D. Magarshack. Vision, 335 pp.
Review by V. S. Pritchett in *New Statesman*, 22 January 1965, pp. 113–14.

112. Gifford, H. 'Dostoevsky: the dialectic of resistance', in his *The Novel in Russia from Pushkin to Pasternak*. Hutchinson, pp. 108–20.

113. Lord, R. 'Dostoyevsky and Vladimir Solov'yov', *SEER*, XLII.99, 415–26.

114. Thurneysen, E. *Dostoevsky: A Theological Study*. Trans. from the German by K. R. Crim. Epworth Press, 84 pp.

115. White, R. 'Evil and the novel: Dostoievsky and the value of the individual man', *Common Factor*, I, October, 47–8.

1965

116. Davie, D., ed. *Russian Literature and Modern English Fiction.* Chicago/London, Chicago UP, 244 pp.
Contains the following articles on Dostoyevsky: 'Turgenev, Dostoievsky and Tolstoy' (G. Saintsbury, 1907, pp. 23–30); 'Dostoievsky and Tolstoy' (D. S. Merezhkovsky, 1902, pp. 75–98); 'On Dostoievsky and Rozanov' (D. H. Lawrence, 1936, pp. 99–106).

117. Dostoyevsky, F. M. *Crime and Punishment. Prestupleniye i nakazaniye.* Introd. by M. H. Shotton. (Plain Literary Texts). Letchworth, Bradda, 546 pp.
Text in Russian, introd. in English.

118. — 'Son smeshnogo cheloveka', in G. Gibian and M. Samilov, eds, *Modern Russian Short Stories.* New York/London, Harper & Row, pp. 10–30

119. Fanger, D. *Dostoevsky and Romantic Realism: A Study of Dostoevsky in Relation to Balzac, Dickens and Gogol.* (Harvard Studies in Comparative Literature, 27). Cambridge, Mass./London, Harvard UP/OUP, 307 pp.
Reprinted in 1967. Review in *TLS*, 3 March 1966, p. 165 ('City of depths').

120. Giraud, R. *Deceit, Desire, and the Novel: Self and Other in Literary Structure.* Trans. by Y. Freccero. Baltimore/London, Johns Hopkins UP, 318 pp.
Contains the following two articles on Dostoyevsky: 'Technical problems in Proust and Dostoyevsky' (pp. 229–55); 'The Dostoyevskian Apocalypse' (pp. 256–89).

1966

121. Dostoyevsky, F. M. *The Gambler. Bobok. A Nasty Story.* Trans. with introd. by J. Coulson. (Penguin Classics, L179). Harmondsworth, Penguin, 238 pp.
New edn pub. in 1968.

122. — *Three Short Novels.* Trans. by A. R. MacAndrew. New York/London, Bantam, 462 pp.
Contains *Poor Folk, The Double* and *The Eternal Husband.* Reprinted in 1970.

123. Frank, J. 'The world of Raskolnikov', *Encounter*, XXVI.6, 30–5.

124. Jackson, R. L. *Dostoevsky's Quest for Form: A Study of His Philosophy of Art.* (Yale Russian and East European Studies, 1). New Haven/London, Yale UP, 274 pp.
Review by F. F. Seeley in *SEER*, XLVI.107, 1968, 503–5.
125. Johnson, C. A. 'Russian Gaskelliana [a comparison of *Mary Barton* and *Crime and Punishment*]', *Review of English Literature* [Leeds], VII.3, 39–51.
126. Lindstrom, T. S. 'The great truth-tellers: Tolstoy and Dostoyevsky', in his *A Concise History of Russian Literature.* Vol. 1. London UP, pp. 164–99.
127. Lord, R. 'Saint or blackguard? Robert Lord on Dostoevsky's *The Idiot*', *L*, 5 May, pp. 652–3.
128. Shteinberg, A. *Dostoievsky.* (Studies in Modern European Literature and Thought). Bowes, 126 pp.
Review in *TLS*, 2 June, p. 492 ('Dostoevsky as historian').

1967

129. Axthelm, P. M. 'Origins of the modern confessional novel: Dostoevsky', in his *The Modern Confessional Novel.* New Haven/London, Yale UP, pp. 13–53.
130. Dostoyevsky, F. M. *The Notebooks for 'Crime and Punishment'.* Ed. and trans. by E. Wasiolek. Chicago/London, Chicago UP, 246 pp.
Review by F. F. Seeley in *SEER*, XLVI.107, 1968, 503–5; in *TLS*, 11 January 1968, p. 34 ('Dostoevsky's proto-Raskolnikov'). See also no. 186.
131. — *The Notebooks for 'The Idiot'.* Ed. and with an introd. by E. Wasiolek. Trans. by K. Strelsky. Chicago/London, Chicago UP, 254 pp. See also no. 186.
132. Freeborn, R. Review of N. S. Trubetzkoy, *Dostoevskij als Künstler*, The Hague, Mouton, 1964, in *SEER*, XLV.104, 228–30.
133. Jones, M. V. 'Dostoyevsky and German idealist philosophy'. Ph.D. thesis, Nottingham University.
134. Lord, R. 'A reconsideration of Dostoyevsky's novel *The Idiot*', *SEER*, XLV.104, 30–46.
135. Masaryk, T. G. 'Dostoevsky', in his *The Spirit of Russia.* Vol. 3. Allen & Unwin, pp. 3–160.
Review by G. D. Humphreys in *JRS*, XVIII, 1969, 64–5.
136. Reeve, F. D. '*Crime and Punishment*', in his *The Russian Novel.* Muller, pp. 159–204.
Steiner, G. *Tolstoy or Dostoevsky*. See under 1960.

1968

137. Dilman, I. 'Dostoyevsky as philosopher: a short note', *Philosophy*, XLIII.164, 280–4.
138. Dostoyevsky, F. M. *Crime and Punishment.* Trans. by S. Monas. New York/London, New American Library/New English Library, 543 pp.
139. — '*The Devils*', in R. N. Stromberg, ed., *Realism, Naturalism, and Symbolism: Modes of Thought and Expression in Europe, 1848–1914.* Macmillan, pp. 48–67.
Extract from D. Magarshack's trans. pub. by Penguin in 1953.
140. — *The Notebooks for 'The Possessed'.* Ed. with an introd. by E. Wasiolek. Trans. by V. Terras. Chicago/London, Chicago UP, 431 pp.
For a review of this work, see no. 186.
141. — *Notes from Underground; White Nights; The Dream of a Ridiculous Man; and Selections from The House of the Dead.* New trans. . . .by R. MacAndrew. (Signet Classic, CT300). New York/London, New American Library/New English Library, 239 pp.
142. Goodheart, E. 'Dostoevsky and the hubris of the immoralist', in his *The Cult of the Ego: The Self in Modern Literature.* Chicago/London, Chicago UP, pp. 90–113.
143. Mihajlov, M. *Russian Themes.* Trans. by Marija Mihajlov. Macdonald, 373 pp.
Contains three chapters on Dostoyevsky: 'Dostoevsky's and Solzhenitsyn's *House of the Dead*' (pp. 78–118); 'Dostoevsky today' (pp. 119–69); 'Notes on Dostoevsky' (pp. 170–90).
144. Phelps, G. 'Gissing, Turgenev and Dostoyevsky', in P. Coustillas, ed., *Collected Articles on George Gissing.* Frank Cass, pp. 99–105.
145. Pritchett, V. S. Review of K. Mochulsky, *Dostoevsky: His Life and Work*, trans. with introd. by M. A. Minihan, Princeton, Princeton UP, 1967, in *New Statesman*, 6 September, pp. 287–8 ('Hunger for apocalypse').
146. Rowe, W. W. *Dostoevsky: Child and Man in His Works.* New York/London, New York UP/London UP, 242 pp.
147. Sonnenfeld, A. 'The Catholic novelist and the supernatural [Bernanos and Dostoyevsky]', *French Studies*, XXII.4, 307–19.

Woodhouse, C. M. *Dostoievsky.* See under 1951.

1969

148. Beaumont, E. 'The supernatural in Dostoyevsky and Bernanos: a reply to Professor Sonnenfeld', *French Studies*, XXIII.3, 264–71.
149. Dostoyevsky, F. M. *The Notebooks for 'A Raw Youth'*. Ed. with introd. by E. Wasiolek. Trans. by V. Terras. Chicago/ London, Chicago UP, 570 pp.
For a review of this work, see no. 186.
150. Gifford, H. Review of K. Mochulsky, *Dostoevsky: His Life and Work*, trans. with an introd. by M. A. Minihan, Princeton, Princeton UP, 1967, in *Essays in Criticism*, XIX, 325–30.
151. Jones, M. V. 'Dostoyevsky's conception of the idea', *RMS*, XIII, 106–31.
152. Lary, N. 'Dickens and Dostoevsky'. Ph.D. thesis, Sussex University.
153. Simmons, E. J. *Fedor Dostoevsky*. (Columbia Essays on Modern Writers, 40). New York/London, Columbia UP, 48 pp.
154. Sinyard, N. R. 'Responses to Dostoevsky in England'. M.A. thesis, Manchester University.

1970

155. Dostoyevsky, F. M. *The Brothers Karamazov*. Trans. by A. R. MacAndrew. Introd. by K. Mochulsky. Toronto/London, Bantam, 936 pp.
156. Freeborn, R. Review of T. Proctor, *Dostoevskij and the Belinskij School of Literary Criticism* (Slavistic Printings and Reprintings, 64), The Hague, Mouton, 1969; L. J. Kent, *The Subconscious in Gogol' and Dostoevskij* (Slavistic Printings and Reprintings, 75), The Hague, Mouton, 1969; V. Terras, *The Young Dostoevsky, 1846–1849* (Slavistic Printings and Reprintings, 69), The Hague, Mouton, 1969, in *SEER*, XLVIII.112, 443–4.
157. Friedman, M. S. *Problematic Rebel: Melville, Dostoievsky, Kafka, Camus*. Rev. edn. Chicago/London, Chicago UP, 523 pp. Previous edn pub. by Random House in 1963 under the title *Problematic Rebel: An Image of Modern Man*.
158. Lord, R. *Dostoevsky: Essays and Perspectives*. Chatto & Windus, 254 pp.
Review by M. V. Jones in *SEER*, XLIX.117, 1971, 616–18; by C. M. Woodhouse in *L*, 22 October, pp. 543–4.
159. Mungall, S. 'Dostoevsky and Camus'. M.A. thesis, Sussex University.

160. Pearce, R. 'Transformation: Dostoyevsky's *Idiot* and Kafka's "Metamorphosis"', in his *Stages of the Clown: Perspectives on Modern Fiction from Dostoyevsky to Beckett*. Carbondale/London, Southern Illinois UP/Feffer & Simons, pp. 6–25.
161. Rahv, P. 'Dostoevsky: two short novels', in his *Literature and the Sixth Sense*. Faber & Faber, pp. 271–9.
162. Rhode, E. 'Dostoevsky and Bresson', *Sight and Sound*, XXXIX, Spring, 82–3.
163. Serrano-Plaja, A. *'Magic' Realism in Cervantes: 'Don Quixote' as Seen Through 'Tom Sawyer' and 'The Idiot'*. Trans. by R. S. Rudder. Berkeley/Los Angeles/London, California UP, 216 pp.
164. Stern, J. P. 'The testing of the Prince: on the realism of Dostoyevsky's *The Idiot*', in R. Auty, L. R. Lewitter and A. P. Vlasto, eds, *Gorski Vijenac: A Garland of Essays Offered to Professor Elizabeth Hill*. Cambridge, MHRA, pp. 252–67.
165. Woodhouse, C. M. 'Dostoevsky', *L*, 22 October, pp. 543–4.

1971

166. Belyy, A. *Tragediya tvorchestva: Dostoyevsky i Tolstoy*. (Russian Titles for the Specialist, 15). Letchworth, Prideaux Press, 46 pp.
167. Davison, R. R. 'Camus' interest in Dostoevsky: the impact of Dostoevsky's novels on the Camus of *Le Mythe de Sisyphe*'. M.Phil. thesis, Leeds University.
168. Dostoyevsky, F. M. *Netochka Nezvanova*. Trans. by A. A. Dunnigan. Englewood Cliffs/Hemel Hempstead, Prentice-Hall, 201 pp.
169. — *The Notebooks for 'The Brothers Karamazov'*. Ed. and trans. by E. Wasiolek. Chicago/London, Chicago UP, 275 pp. Reissued in 1976. Review in *TLS*, 3 December, p. 1,505 ('Birth of a novel'). See also no. 186.
170. Field, A. *The Complection of Russian Literature*. Allen Lane, 324 pp.
Contains the following two articles on Dostoyevsky: 'Yury Tynyanov on Fyodor Dostoyevsky and Gogol' (pp. 66–83); 'Innokenty Annensky on Fyodor Dostoyevsky' (pp. 108–13).
171. Gray, S. *The Idiot*. Adapted from the novel by F. Dostoyevsky. Methuen, 112 pp.
172. Jones, M. V. 'Some echoes of Hegel in Dostoyevsky', *SEER*, XLIX.117, 500–20.

173. McMillin, A. B. Review of R. K. Schulz, *The Portrayal of the German in Russian Novels: Gončarov, Turgenev, Dostoevskij, Tolstoj* (Slavistische Beiträge, 42), Munich, Sagner, 1969, in *SEER*, XLIX.116, 469–70.
174. Okai, J. D. A. 'Dostoyevsky: his artistic rearrangement of reality as manifested in the development of his literary style, with particular reference to his earlier works'. M.Phil. thesis, School of Slavonic and East European Studies, London University.
175. Peace, R. *Dostoyevsky: An Examination of the Major Novels.* CUP, 347 pp.
 Review by R. M. Davison in *JRS*, XXII, 49–51; by J. D. Elsworth in *JES*, I, 395; by R. H. Freeborn in *SEER*, L.118, 120–1; in *TLS*, 9 April, p. 418 ('Holy sinners').
176. Strelsky, K. 'Lacenaire and Raskolnikov', *TLS*, 8 January, p. 47.
177. Thody, P. 'Jeeves, Dostoievski and the double paradox', *University of Leeds Review*, XIV.2, 319–31.
178. Williams, H. A. 'We are all responsible for all', *T*, 17 July, p. 14. (On religion in Dostoyevsky's work.)

1972

179. Chapman, M. C. Review of K. Mochulsky, *Dostoyevsky: His Life and Works*, trans. by M. A. Minihan, Princeton, Princeton UP, 1971, in *JRS*, XXIV, 59–61.
180. Clive, G. 'Dostoevsky and the intellectuals', in his *The Broken Icon: Intuitive Existentialism in Classical Russian Fiction.* Collier-Macmillan, pp. 30–62.
181. Crome, L. 'Recollections of Dostoevsky', *Anglo-Soviet Journal*, XXXII.3, 5–11.
182. Daglish, R. 'Moscow Diary', *Anglo-Soviet Journal*, XXXII.3, 11–17. (Critical judgements on current interest in Dostoyevsky by English and American writers.)
183. Dostoyevsky, F. M. *The Gambler, with Polina Suslova's Diary.* Ed. by E. Wasiolek. Trans. by V. Terras. Chicago/London, Chicago UP, 366 pp.
 Contains *The Gambler* and selected letters by Dostoyevsky; the diary and 'The Stranger and Her Lover' by Suslova. Review in *TLS*, 2 March 1973, p. 235 ('Legend of the Inquisitor').
184. — *Notes from Underground. The Double.* Trans. with introd.

by J. Coulson. (Penguin Classics). Harmondsworth, Penguin, 287 pp.

185. Grossman, L. P. *Seminariy po Dostoyevskomu. Seminar on Dostoevsky*. (Russian Titles for the Specialist, 32). Letchworth, Prideaux Press, 119 pp.
Text in Russian.
186. Jones, M. V. 'Dostoevskii's Notebooks', *JES*, II, 277–84.
Review article of the notebooks for the five major novels, ed. by E. Wasiolek, Chicago/London, Chicago UP, 1967–71.
187. — 'Dostoyevsky, Tolstoy, Leskov and *redstokizm*', *JRS*, XXIII, 3–20.
188. Keller, H. H. 'Prince Myshkin: success or failure?', *JRS*, XXIV, 17–23.
189. Kristeva, J. 'The ruin of a poetics', *Twentieth Century Studies*, December, 102–19.
Discusses the work by M. Bakhtin, *Problemy tvorchestva Dostoyevskogo*, 1929. This article also appears in S. Bann and J. E. Bowlt, eds, *Russian Formalism*. Edinburgh, Scottish Academic Press, 1973, pp. 102–21.
190. Kuznetsov, B. *Einstein and Dostoyevsky*. Trans. by V. Talmy. Hutchinson, 112 pp.
Review in *TLS*, 27 October, p. 1,288.
191. Neuhäuser, R. 'Recent Dostoevskii studies and trends in Dostoevskii research', *JES*, II, 355–73.
192. Nikol'sky, Yu. *Turgenev i Dostoyevsky. Turgenev and Dostoevsky*. (Russian Titles for the Specialist, 44). Letchworth, Prideaux Press, 108 pp.
193. Rozanov, V. V. *Dostoevsky and the Legend of the Grand Inquisitor*. Trans. by S. E. Roberts. Ithaca/London, Cornell UP, 235 pp.
Review in *TLS*, 21 July, p. 838.
194. Siefken, H. 'Man's inhumanity to man – crime and punishment: Kafka's novel *Der Prozess* and novels by Tolstoy, Dostoevsky and Solzhenitsyn', *Trivium*, VII, 28–40.
195. Trilling, O. 'Devils galore – a report from Warsaw [Polish stage adaptation of *The Devils*]', *Drama*, CIV, Spring, 60–3.
196. Wardle, I. '[on A. Wajda's theatre production of Dostoyevsky's *The Possessed*]', *T*, 30 May, p. 30.
197. Zellar, L. 'Conrad and Dostoyevsky', in G. Goodin, ed., *The English Novel in the Nineteenth Century: Essays in the Literary Mediation of Human Values*. Urbana/London, Illinois UP, pp. 214–23.

1973

198. Craig, D. and Egan, M. 'Dostoevsky's realism?', *Encounter*, XLI.3, 85–7.
Reply by J. Frank, XLI.3, p. 87.
199. Dewey, J. C. 'Dostoevsky and Hesse'. M.Phil. thesis, Nottingham University.
200. Frank, J. 'Dostoevsky's realism', *Encounter*, XL.3, 31–8. See also no. 198.
201. Freeborn, R. '*Crime and Punishment*', in his *The Rise of the Russian Novel: Studies in the Russian Novel from 'Eugene Onegin' to 'War and Peace'*. Cambridge, CUP, pp. 157–207.
202. Gibson, A. B. *The Religion of Dostoevsky*. S.C.M. Press, 216 pp.
Review by K. Bazarov in *Books and Bookmen*, XXI, October 1974, 28–30; by C. Pike in *JRS*, XXX, 1975, 47–8; in *TLS*, 12 October, p. 1,239.
203. Gregg, R. A. 'Two Adams and Eve in the Crystal Palace: Dostoevsky, the Bible, and *We*', in E. J. Brown, ed., *Major Soviet Writers: Essays in Criticism*. Oxford, OUP, pp. 202–8.
204. Jones, M. V. 'An aspect of Romanticism in Dostoyevsky's *Netochka Nezvanova* and Eugène Sue's *Mathilde*', *RMS*, XVII, 38–61.
205. Lampert, E. 'Dostoevsky', in J. F. I. Fennell, ed., *Nineteenth Century Russian Literature*. Faber, pp. 225–60.
206. Lary, N. M. *Dostoevsky and Dickens: A Study of Literary Influence*. Routledge & Kegan Paul, 172 pp.
Review by M. Greene in *SEER*, LII.127, 1974, 315; by M. V. Jones in *JES*, IV.I, 1974, 98; by S. Knight in *New Statesman*, 1 June, p. 816; by R. A. Peace in *MLR*, LXIX.2, 1974, 478–9; in *TLS*, 10 August, p. 923 ('Was Myshkin Pickwick?').
207. Lavrin, J. 'Dostoevsky and Tolstoy', in his *A Panorama of Russian Literature*. London UP, pp. 130–46.
208. Leatherbarrow, W. J. 'The rag with ambition: the problem of self-will in Dostoevsky's *Bednyye Lyudi* and *Dvoynik*', *MLR*, LXVIII.3, 607–18.
209. — 'Raskolnikov and the "enigma of his personality"', *FMLS*, IX.2, 153–65.
210. 'Was Myshkin Pickwick?'. Review of C. R. Proffer, ed., *The Unpublished Dostoevsky: Diaries and Notebooks, 1860–81*, Vol. 1, Ann Arbor, Ardis, 1973, in *TLS*, 10 August, p. 923.

1974

211. Carroll, J. *Break-Out for the Crystal Palace: The Anarcho-Psychological Critique – Stirner, Nietzsche, Dostoevsky*. Routledge & Kegan Paul, 188 pp.
Review by N. Walter in *THES*, 14 June, p. vi; in *TLS*, 5 July, p. 703.
212. Dostoyevsky, F. M. *Notes from Underground*. Trans. by M. Ginsburg. Introd. by D. Fanger. Toronto/London, Bantam, 158 pp.
213. Grossman, L. P. *Dostoevsky: A Biography*. Trans. by M. Mackler. Allen Lane, 647 pp.
Review by K. Bazarov in *Books and Bookmen*, August 1975, 16–17; by M. V. Jones in *TLS*, 21 February 1975, p. 198; by R. Luckett in *Spectator*, 28 December, p. 828; by M. Ratcliffe in *T*, 16 January 1975, p. 10.
214. Guest, J. Review of J. B. Dunlop, *Staretz Amvrosy: Model for Dostoevsky's Staretz Zossima*, Belmont, Nordland, 1972, in *Eastern Churches Review*, VI.1, 119–21.
215. Jackson, R. L. *Twentieth Century Interpretations of 'Crime and Punishment': A Collection of Critical Essays*. Englewood Cliffs/London, Prentice-Hall, 122 pp.
216. Jones, M. V. 'Dostoyevsky and an aspect of Schiller's psychology', *SEER*, LII.128, 337–54.
217. Kirilloff, A. 'The *outsider* figure in Dostoievsky's works', *RMS*, XVIII, 126–40.
218. Knight, S. 'The function of quotation in Dostoevsky: with special reference to *The Adolescent*', *University of Essex Language Centre Occasional Papers*, XIV, 69–89.
219. Leatherbarrow, W. J. 'Dostoevsky's treatment of the theme of Romantic dreaming in *Khozyayka* and *Belyye Nochi*', *MLR*, LXIX.3, 584–95.
220. Paris, B. J. *A Psychological Approach to Fiction: Studies in Thackeray, Stendhal, George Eliot, Dostoevsky and Conrad*. Bloomington/London, Indiana UP, 304 pp.
221. Peace, R. A. Review of E. Sandoz, *Political Apocalypse: A Study of Dostoevsky's Grand Inquisitor*, Baton Rouge, Louisiana State UP, 1971, in *SEER*, LII.126, 133.

1975

222. Batchelor, R. E. 'Dostoevskii and Camus: similarities and contrasts', *JES*, V, 111–52.

223. Bradbury, D. L. 'Formal structural analysis of Dostoevsky's *Besy*'. M.Litt. thesis, Edinburgh University.
224. Brody, E. C. 'Dostoevsky's Kirilov in Camus' *Le Mythe de Sisyphe*', *MLR*, LXX.2, 291–305.
225. Davison, R. M. 'The translation of surnames in Dostoevsky', *JRS*, XXX, 28–31.
226. Dostoevsky, A. *Dostoevsky: Reminiscences.* Trans. and ed. by B. Stillman. Wildwood House, 448 pp.
Review by J. Jones in *New Statesman*, 23 January 1976, pp. 102–3 ('Happy pebble'); by A. de Jonge in *TLS*, 23 January 1976, pp. 78–9.
227. Frank, J. 'Freud's case-history of Dostoevsky', *TLS*, 18 July, pp. 807–8.
228. Grossman, L. P. *Bal'zak i Dostoyevsky. Balzac and Dostoevsky.* (Russian Titles for the Specialist, 63). Letchworth, Prideaux Press, 67 pp.
Reprint of 1925 edn. Text in Russian.
229. Jones, P. *Philosophy and the Novel: Philosophical Aspects of 'Middlemarch', 'Anna Karenina', 'The Brothers Karamazov', 'A la Recherche du Temps Perdu' and of the Methods of Criticism.* Oxford, Clarendon Press, 216 pp.
The chapter on Dostoyevsky is on pp. 112–46. Review by R. Freeborn in *SEER*, LIV.2, 1976, 278–80; by R. Kuhns in *MLR*, LXXI.4, 1976, 876–7; by D. J. Richards in *JRS*, XXX, 44–5.
230. Jonge, A. de. *Dostoevsky and the Age of Intensity.* Secker & Warburg, 244 pp.
Review by J. Frank in *TLS*, 20 February 1976, p. 200; by C. A. Johnson in *Troika* [Leeds University], October, 8–11; by J. Jones in *New Statesman*, 2 May, pp. 589–90.
231. Mitchell, J. 'Dostoevsky's image of Christ', *Expository Times*, LXXXVI.4, 210–14.
232. Tynyanov, Yu. *Dostoyevsky i Gogol'. Dostoevsky and Gogol.* (Russian Titles for the Specialist, 65). Letchworth, Prideaux Press, 48 pp.
Reprint of 1921 edn. Text in Russian. A trans. of this appears in V. Erlich, ed., *Twentieth-Century Russian Literary Criticism.* New Haven/London, Yale UP, pp. 102–16.

1976

233. Batchelor, R. E. 'Malraux's debt to Dostoevskii', *JES*, VI, 153–71.

234. Calder, A. *Russia Discovered: Nineteenth-Century Fiction from Pushkin to Chekhov*. Heinemann, 302 pp.
Contains two chapters on Dostoyevsky: 'Underground Man: Dostoevsky to *Crime and Punishment*' (pp. 110–35); 'Revolt and the Golden Age: Dostoevsky's later fiction' (pp. 173–208).

235. Dolan, P. J. 'Dostoyevsky: the political gospel', in his *Of War and War's Alarms: Fiction and Politics in the Modern World*. New York/London, Free Press/Collier-Macmillan, pp. 36–69.

236. Dostoyevsky, F. M. *Dvoynik. The Double*. (Russian Titles for the Specialist, 92). Letchworth, Prideaux Press, 123 pp.
Text in Russian.

237. Frank, J. *Dostoevsky*. Vol. 1. Princeton/Guildford, Princeton UP, 401 pp. Vol. 1 is entitled 'The Seeds of Revolt, 1821–1849'. Also pub. in 1977 by Robson. Review by M. V. Jones in *SEER*, LVI.1, 1978, 121–2; by M. V. Jones in *THES*, 21 July 1978, p. 14; by B. Levin in *T*, 9 June 1978, p. 14 ('Glowing again with Dostoevsky's truth').

238. Freeborn, R. 'Dostoevsky', in R. Freeborn, G. Donchin, N. J. Anning, *Russian Literary Attitudes from Pushkin to Solzhenitsyn*. Macmillan, pp. 39–59.
Review by D. J. Richards in *MLR*, LXXII.4, 1977, 765–6.

239. — Review of V. Seduro, *Dostoevski's Image in Russia Today*, Belmont, Nordland, 1975, in *SEER*, LIV.4, 628–9.

240. Jones, M. V. *Dostoyevsky: The Novel of Discord*. (Novelists and Their World). Elek, 236 pp.
Review by R. M. Davison in *JRS*, XXXIII, 1977, 55–6; by J. D. Elsworth in *JES*, VI, 302–3; by R. Neuhäuser in *SEER*, LVII.3, 1979, 429–31; by A. D. Stokes in *MLR*, LXXII.3, 1977, 766–8.

241. — Review of S. Linnér, *Starets Zosima in 'The Brothers Karamazov': A Study in the Mimesis of Virtue*, (Stockholm Studies in Russian Literature, 4), Stockholm, Almqvist & Wiksell, 1975, in *JRS*, XXXII, 49–50.

242. — Review of W. Schmid, *Der Textaufbau in den Erzählungen Dostoevskijs*, München, Fink, 1973, in *SEER*, LIV.2, 280–1.

243. Knight, S. C. 'The function of quotation in Dostoevsky'. Ph.D. thesis, Essex University.

244. Krag, E. *Dostoevsky: The Literary Artist*. Trans. from the Norwegian by S. Larr. Oslo/Henley on Thames, Universitetsforlag/Global Book Resources, 317 pp.
Review by R. A. Peace in *SEER* LV.4, 1977, 535–6.

245. Leatherbarrow, W. J. 'The aesthetic louse: ethics and aesthetics

in Dostoevsky's *Prestuplenie i nakazanie*', *MLR*, LXXI.4, 857–66.

246. Pachmuss, T. 'Dostoievsky and T. S. Eliot: a point of view', *FMLS*, XII, 82–9.
247. Peace, R. Review of V. Seduro, *Dostoevski's Image in Russia Today*, Belmont, Nordland, 1975, in *Soviet Studies*, XXVIII.4, 632–4.

1977

248. Dostoyevsky, F. M. *Krotkaya. A Gentle Spirit.* Ed. with introd., notes and vocabulary by D. R. Hitchcock. (The Library of Russian Classics). Letchworth, Bradda, 97 pp.
Text in Russian; introd. in English.
249. — *Polzunkov*. (Russian Titles for the Specialist, 109). Letchworth, Prideaux Press, 61 pp.
Text in Russian.
250. Holquist, M. *Dostoevsky and the Novel.* Princeton / Guildford, Princeton UP, 202 pp.
Review by R. Freeborn in *SEER*, LVII.1, 1979, 110–11; by M. Jones in *JES*, X, 1980, 220–1.
251. Jones, M. V. Review of A. H. Lyngstad, *Dostoevskij and Schiller*, The Hague, Mouton, 1975, in *SEER*, LV.2, 240–1.
252. King, M. Review of *F. M. Dostoyevsky, A. G. Dostoyevskaya: perepiska*, ed. by D. S. Likhachev, Leningrad, Nauka, 1976, in *JRS*, XXXIV, 41–2.
253. Mihajlov, M. 'Dostoyevsky on the Catholic *Left*', in his *Underground Notes.* Trans. by M. M. and C. W. Ivusic. Routledge & Kegan Paul, pp. 51–9.
254. Orr, John. 'Tolstoy and Dostoevsky: passion and Russian society' and 'Dostoevsky: the demonic *Tendenz*', in his *Tragic Realism and Modern Society: Studies in the Sociology of the Modern Novel.* Macmillan, pp. 53–72 and 73–86.
255. Sutherland, S. R. *Atheism and the Rejection of God: Contemporary Philosophy and 'The Brothers Karamazov'*. Oxford, Blackwell, 152 pp.
Review by R. Freeborn in *SEER*, LVI.3, 1978, 440–1; by R. W. Hepburn in *Mind*, LXXXVIII, 1979, 312–14.

1978

256. Berry, T. E. *Plots and Characters in Major Russian Fiction.* Vol. 2. Hamden / Folkstone, Archon Books / Dawson, 265 pp.

Gives the plots and characters to selected works by Gogol′, Goncharov and Dostoyevsky.

257. Dostoyevsky, F. M. *The Idiot.* Trans. by H. and O. Carlisle. Introd. by H. Rosenburg. New York/London, New American Library/New English Library, 638 pp.
This trans. originally pub. in 1969.

258. — *Muzhik Marey. Stoletnyaya. The Peasant Marey. The Centenarian.* (Russian Titles for the Specialist, 126.) Letchworth, Prideaux Press, 32 pp.
Text in Russian.

259. Freeborn, R. Review of E. H. Lehrman, *A 'Handbook' to the Russian Text of 'Crime and Punishment'*, The Hague, Mouton, 1977, in *SEER*, LVI.3, 440–1.

260. Harries, R. 'Ivan Karamazov's argument', *Theology*, LXXXI. 679, 104–11.

261. Hingley, R. *Dostoyevsky: His Life and Work.* Elek, 222 pp.
Review by R. M. Davison in *MLR*, LXXIV.3, 1979, 765–6; by R. Freeborn in *SEER*, LVII.4, 1979, 587–8.

262. Kabat, G. C. *Ideology and Imagination: The Image of Society in Dostoevsky.* New York/Guildford, Columbia UP, 201 pp.

263. McCurry, R. M. 'Dostoyevsky: the image of virtue in his work after 1864'. M.Phil. thesis, School of Slavonic and East European Studies, London University.

264. Markovic, B. 'The application of theories of psychology by English and American critics to the novels of Dostoevsky from 1937 to the present'. M.Phil. thesis, Westfield College, University of London.

265. Nuttall, A. D. *'Crime and Punishment': Murder as Philosophic Experiment.* Edinburgh, Scottish Academic Press for Sussex UP, 126 pp.

266. Orr, J. 'The demonic tendency, politics and society in Dostoevsky's *The Devils*', in D. Laurenson, ed., *The Sociology of Literature: Applied Studies.* (Sociological Review Monograph, 26). Keele, University of Keele, pp. 271–83.

267. Peace, R. 'Dostoevsky's *The Eternal Husband* and literary polemics', *Essays in Poetics*, III.2, 22–40.

268. Snow, C. P. 'Dostoevsky', in his *The Realists: Portraits of Eight Novelists.* Macmillan, pp. 84–138.

1979

269. Beerman, R. Review of V. D. Dneprov, *Idei strasti postupki. Iz khudozhestvennogo opyta Dostoyevskogo*, Leningrad, Sovetskiy Pisatel′, 1978, in *Co-existence*, XVI, 122–5.
270. Dalton, E. *Unconscious Structure in 'The Idiot': A Study in Literature and Psychoanalysis*. Princeton / Guildford, Princeton UP, 236 pp.
271. Futrell, M. 'Dostoyevsky and Islam (and Chokam Valikhanov)', *SEER* LVII.1, 16–31.
272. Grossvogel, D. I. 'Dostoevsky: divine mystery and literary salvation', in his *Mystery and Its Fictions: From Oedipus to Agatha Christie*. Baltimore / London, Johns Hopkins UP, 53–73.
273. Ingham, D. 'Psychological criticism of Dostoyevsky in the English language, with special reference to the period since 1952'. M.Phil. thesis, Nottingham University.
274. Jones, M. V. 'Winter notes on autumn reading: five recent books on Dostoevsky', *JRS*, XXXVII, 32–9.
Reviews of J. Catteau (*La Création littéraire chez Dostoievski*), J. Frank (*Dostoevsky: The Seeds of Revolt*), R. Hingley (*Dostoyevsky: His Life and Work*), M. Holquist (*Dostoevsky and the Novel*), E. Vetlovskaya (*Poetika romana 'Brat′ya Karamazovy'*).
275. Leatherbarrow, W. J. 'Pushkin and the early Dostoyevsky', *MLR*, LXXIV.2, 368–85.
276. Offord, D. 'Dostoyevsky and Chernyshevsky', *SEER*, LVII.4, 509–30.
277. Peace, R. A. Review of M. Kravchenko, *Dostoevsky and the Psychologists*, Amsterdam, Verlag A. M. Hakkert, 1978, in *SEER*, LVII.4, 585–7.
278. Pritchett, V. S. 'The early Dostoevsky', in his *The Myth Makers: Essays on European, Russian and South American Novelists*. Chatto & Windus, 63–76.

1980

279. Davison, R. M. 'Dostoevsky's *The Devils*: the role of Stepan Trofimovich Verkhovensky', *FMLS*, XVI, 109–19.
280. Dryzhakova, E. 'Dostoevsky, Chernyshevsky, and the rejection of nihilism', *OSP*, XIII, 58–79.
281. Freeborn, R. Review of G. Rosenshield, *Crime and Punishment: The Techniques of the Omniscient Author*, Lisse, Peter de Ridder Press, 1978, in *SEER*, LVIII.3, 435–6.

282. Harries, R. 'Dostoevsky's vision of Christ's Resurrection', *T*, 5 April, p. 16.
283. Jones, M. V. 'Dostoyevsky and Europe: travels in the mind', *RMS*, XXIV, 38–57.
284. Jones, M. V. Review of J. Catteau, *La Création littéraire chez Dostoievski*, Paris, Institut d'Études Slaves, 1978, in *SEER* LVIII.1, 115–17.
285. Krasnov, V. *Solzhenitsyn and Dostoevsky: A Study in the Polyphonic Novel.* George Prior, 226 pp.
286. Leatherbarrow, W. J. 'Idealism and utopian socialism in Dostoyevsky's *Gospodin Prokharchin* and *Slaboye serdtse*', *SEER*, LVIII.4, 524–40.
287. Stokes, J. 'Wilde on Dostoevsky', *Notes and Queries*, XXVII.3, June, 215–16.
288. Williams, F. Review of V. Seduro, *Dostoyevsky in Russian and World Theatre*, North Quincy, Christopher Publishing House, 1977, in *SEER*, LVIII.1, 117–18.

1981

289. Burnett, L., ed. *F. M. Dostoevsky (1821–1881): A Centenary Collection.* Colchester, Department of Literature, University of Essex, 134 pp.
Contains the following articles on Dostoyevsky: L. M. O'Toole, 'Structure and style in the short story: Dostoevsky's *A Gentle Spirit*' (pp. 1–36); F. Spencer, 'Form and disorder in Dostoevsky's *A Raw Youth*' (pp. 37–57); L. Burnett, 'Dostoevsky, Poe and the discovery of fantastic realism' (pp. 58–86); G. M. Hyde, 'T. S. Eliot's Crime and Punishment' (pp. 87–96); P. Simpson, 'The rejection of the world: Dostoevsky, Ivanov, Camus' (pp. 97–108); A. Johae, 'Idealism and the dialectic in *The Brothers Karamazov*' (pp. 109–18); C. Panteli, 'Dostoevsky's aesthetic: dichotomy between reality and transcendence in Ivan Karamazov's nightmare' (pp. 119–26); G. Thurley, 'Dostoevsky – between psyche and psychology' (pp. 127–34).
290. Dostoyevsky, F. M. 'A strange man's dream: a fantastic story', trans. by M. Jones, in Richards, D., ed., *The Penguin Book of Russian Short Stories*, Harmondsworth, Penguin Books, pp. 98–121.
291. Goldstein, D. I. *Dostoyevsky and the Jews.* Trans. from the French. Austin/London, Texas UP, 256 pp.
Review by R. Alter in *TLS*, 3 July, pp. 751–2 ('The antisemitic Apocalypse').

292. MacPike, L. *Dostoevsky's Dickens: A Study of Literary Influence*. George Prior, 223 pp.
293. Miller, R. F. *Dostoevsky and 'The Idiot': Author, Narrator, and Reader*. Cambridge, Mass./London, Harvard UP, 296 pp.
294. Osborne, R. 'Music from Underground', *TLS*, 20 February, p. 195. (On BBC Radio 3's Dostoyevsky celebrations.)
295. Smith, T. G. 'Duality and dualism in Dostoevsky and Camus'. M.Phil. thesis, University of Nottingham.

Index to names

Index to Dostoyevsky's works published in Great Britain, 1945–81

Index

In principle this index includes all personal names mentioned in the text of this book. Exceptions are Dostoyevsky himself, fictional characters and historical figures in fictional contexts. Where the title of a well known work of fiction appears without specific mention of the author's name, a page reference is given under the author's entry. The bibliography, which has its own index, is not included – though the introductory survey is – and names mentioned in the footnotes to each chapter appear only where they are the objects of special comment.